INTRODU... ...Y

K LOAN

MANCHESTER
UNIVERSITY PRESS

FOR DAVID BEVINGTON

ALEXANDER LEGGATT

INTRODUCTION TO ENGLISH RENAISSANCE COMEDY

Manchester University Press
Manchester and New York

distributed exclusively in the USA by St. Martin's Press

The right of Alexander Leggatt to be identified as the author of this work has been
asserted by him in accordance with the Copyright, Designs and Patents Act 1988

Published by Manchester University Press
Oxford Road, Manchester M13 9NR, UK
and Room 400, 175 Fifth Avenue, New York, NY 10010, USA
http://www.man.ac.uk/mup

Distributed exclusively in the USA
by St. Martin's Press, Inc., 175 Fifth Avenue, New York, NY 10010, USA

Distributed exclusively in Canada
by UBC Press, University of British Columbia, 6344 Memorial Road,
Vancouver, BC, Canada V6T 1Z2

British Library Cataloguing-in-Publication Data
A catalogue record for this book is available from the British Library

Library of Congress Cataloging-in-Publication Data applied for

ISBN 0 7190 4964 4 *hardback*
    0 7190 4965 2 *paperback*

First published 1999

05   04   03   02   01   00   99   10   9   8   7   6   5   4   3   2   1

Typeset in Bulmer
by Koinonia, Manchester

Printed in Great Britain
by Bell & Bain Ltd, Glasgow

CONTENTS

Acknowledgements   *page* vi

A note on quotations   vi

1   Introduction   1

2   Lyly, *Endymion*   12

3   Greene, *Friar Bacon and Friar Bungay*   30

4   Shakespeare, *A Midsummer Night's Dream*   46

5   Marston, *The Malcontent*   70

6   Middleton, *Michaelmas Term*   89

7   Shakespeare, *The Tempest*   109

8   Jonson, *Bartholomew Fair*   135

9   Caroline comedy: Shirley, *The Lady of Pleasure*
    and Brome, *A Jovial Crew*   156

10 Conclusion   179

Further reading   183

Index   184

ACKNOWLEDGEMENTS

I am grateful to David Bevington for getting me started on this project, and to Anita Roy, Matthew Frost, Peter Corbin and the anonymous reader for Manchester University Press, for their advice and encouragement along the way. The imperfections that remain are my own responsibility.

A NOTE ON QUOTATIONS

Conventions for speech headings and stage directions have been regularized to conform to the current practice of the Revels plays. Quotations have been regularized to modern British spelling.

Introduction

THOUGH anyone else is welcome to eavesdrop, this book is primarily for students. Its aim is to introduce the comedy of the English Renaissance, not through the sort of broad survey that gives a bird's-eye view of the subject (with important writers getting a chapter, less important writers sharing a chapter, and major plays getting two or three paragraphs) but through a close study of nine selected plays that represent different periods, styles and authors, suggesting the range and variety of the genre at this period and examining some of its recurring preoccupations.

The broad survey has its uses, and some good discussions of this kind exist;[1] but it sacrifices, inevitably, the local life of the drama, the particularity of the individual play. And the generalizations in which it deals always carry the risk of falsification. The method of this book is rather to start with the local and work outwards to the larger picture. Its function as an introduction is not to say to the reader, now you have a broad view of Greene, or Jonson, but to say, now we have looked closely at one play by this writer, you can carry the questions and ideas this discussion generates into your reading of his other work and the work of his contemporaries. It follows that readers with an interest in one particular writer or play can read individual chapters in isolation; but the book as a whole aims at giving, through the accumulation of individual discussions, a sense of the whole field. That field is an eclectic one, and the plays have been picked for their variety. It may even appear (in the words of a reader who commented on this work in manuscript) that there is no such thing as Renaissance comedy, only Renaissance comedies. There is some truth in that; but, as we look at the comedies together, we can see that they are like members of the same family: they register initially as individuals, but when we look more closely we see detailed, sometimes surprising resemblances.

We shall return to the individual plays, and the reasons for their selection; but something should be said now of the curious mix of continuity and eclecticism that distinguishes comedy in general and English Renaissance comedy in particular. Comedy (and I am thinking primarily but not exclusively of stage comedy) has a paradoxical relation to the criticism that tries to understand it: it at once encourages and resists generalization. The tradition known as New Comedy, taking its earliest extant form in the Roman authors Plautus and Terence, revived in the Renaissance, and surviving with variations through both English and Continental drama virtually to the present day, has set what must be a record for sheer stubborn longevity. It is distinguished by recurring plot features: two lovers get together, overcoming opposition both internal and external. The solution is produced after a period of confusion, including an intrigue managed in Roman comedy by a clever slave, and managed more often in later comedy by the lovers themselves.[2] A generational conflict, young folks outwitting old folks, is frequently involved, and the solution often hinges on the discovery of a lost child, the recognition, generally by physical tokens, of a true identity. Though not exactly a staple of English stage comedy,[3] the clever slave, now a servant, survives in Figaro and Jeeves; and the recognition-token ending, perhaps the most shopworn device of New Comedy, still has enough life in it to be worth parodying. In Wilde's *The Importance of Being Earnest*, Jack finds his identity when Miss Prism finds her handbag, and in Orton's *What the Butler Saw*, lost children are reunited with their parents through the rejoining of a broken elephant brooch. (Orton's parody is more savage: the reunion leads not to a marriage but to the revelation of multiple incest.)

The characteristic Roman comedy setting is a space between houses; a seaport may be just down the road, but the play never leaves its neighbourhood. Later settings are more varied, but the local, domestic scale of the action – Jane Austen's three or four families in a country village – remains typical. From Plautus to Alan Ayckbourn, comedy deals not with the affairs of the great but with ordinary domestic life. The laughter it es comes from the intrigue and confusion through which its rs pass on their way to the happy ending, from the follies of the d their opponents, and from the observation of recognizable es, including the fools and curmudgeons who do not know how to live in society. The audience may be laughing at characters who suffer pain and bewilderment, but the scale, and the stakes, are low.

Laughter itself depends on an element of the predictable: the stock character, the running gag.[4] And New Comedy as I have described it sounds as though it has a built-in predictability. There are indeed some local traditions whose stock characters and stock plots allow one to generalize with relative confidence: *Commedia dell'arte*, Gilbert and Sullivan, television sitcoms. But as soon as we start thinking locally, particularly in the English tradition, the exceptions mount, the generalizations break down. There are comedies in which the happy ending is not a marriage but a divorce: Ben Jonson's *Epicoene*, George Farquhar's *The Beaux' Stratagem*. There are endings that leave us not satisfied but deeply uneasy, with the action either unresolved (as in the subplot of *Twelfth Night*) or resolved in such a way as to raise protest (the formally comic, deeply problematic ending of *Measure for Measure*). There are comedies in which the intrigue plot that brings lovers together is a vestigial remnant, or missing altogether, and the focus instead is on free-wheeling satire, a crazy extravagant scheme or a game of ideas. Those terms belong not so much to the New Comedy of Plautus and Terence as to the Old Comedy of Aristophanes, a tradition that keeps breaking into English drama from a variety of angles, shoving the domestic plot aside to make room for satire and burlesque. The result can be seen in some of Jonson (*Volpone*, *The Staple of News*) and in the tradition of the burlesque play that toys with theatre itself (Beaumont's *The Knight of the Burning Pestle*, Sheridan's *The Critic*). Tom Stoppard's *Jumpers*, with its philosophy professors doubling as acrobats, and its debates over religion, society and the possibility of knowledge, not to mention a murder mystery and two naked ladies, has strong affinities with Aristophanes but leaves New Comedy in the dust.

A predictable form, then, whose sheer predictability leaves it ripe for subversion, whose rules provoke constant challenge, whose exceptions are as characteristic as its conventions.[5] It is in the English Renaissance, in that remarkably creative period of drama that stretches from the 1580s to the closing of the theatres in 1642, that the eclecticism and unpredictability of comedy become particularly striking. This is in part because English Renaissance comedy is of very mixed parentage, with no single recognition token to give it a fixed identity in the New Comedy manner, and often, as we shall see, no fixed address. Plautus and Terence certainly feed into it, but by a variety of routes. Those playwrights were taught in schools and taken as models in academic discussions of comedy; in the latter they were frequently tamed by being moralized. The New Comedy conventions they exemplify passed into the English intellectual bloodstream both directly, through a study of the plays themselves, and through the mediation of academic interpretation. They also entered England through the *Commedia erudita* of Renaissance Italy (learned comedy, as opposed to the popular, professional *Commedia dell'arte*) which revived the old domestic intrigues in modernized form. A key example is Ariosto's play of disguise, deception and rival wooers, *I Suppositi*, Englished by George Gascoigne as *Supposes* (1566) and used by Shakespeare for the subplot of *The Taming of the Shrew*. The academic tendency to moralize Roman comedy created the 'Christian Terence' tradition, centred on the Low Countries, in which the cheerful debauchery of the original was transformed into a series of awful warnings about the dangers of prodigality. Renaissance literary critics, even the best of them, tended to parrot the notion that comedy is good for you, teaching lessons: in the words of Sir Philip Sidney, 'Comedy is an imitation of the common errors of our life, which he representeth in the most ridiculous and scornful sort that may be, so as it is impossible that any beholder can be content to be such a one.'[6] The randy young men, courtesans and parasites of Roman comedy might have been surprised to learn that that was their mission in life; but the educational function touches the practice of actual plays when we sense that the playwright's business is not just to tell a story and raise some laughs but to say something (not necessarily moral and uplifting) about life and society.

The Renaissance comedy that has something to say draws on the tradition of the Tudor interlude. In many of these plays what might look like a comic situation becomes the occasion for a debate, creating a play not of intrigue but of ideas, almost a precursor of the Shavian discussion play (though Shaw got there by his own route, and his English predecessors are much more formal and patterned).[7] Thus the heroine of Henry Medwall's *Fulgens and Lucrece* (c.1497), who has to decide between two rival suitors for her hand, one high-born but of dubious character, the other low-born but virtuous, makes them argue their different claims; the result is a debate not just between rival wooers but between different modes of social life. The play's claim to be either the first extant English comedy or an important precursor rests most obviously on the disruptive antics of the clowns A and B, whose comic routines parody both the main action and the whole notion of performance; but the patterned opposition of character types, and the clash of values inherent in that opposition, will also serve later comic writers. In John Heywood's *The Play of the Weather* (c.1533), type-characters representing a cross-section of society demand of Jupiter the weather that suits their needs; since they all demand something different, he decides to leave the weather as it is, mixed. The same author's *A Play of Love* (c.1529) introduces four characters: Lover not loved, Loved not loving, Lover loved, No lover nor loved. Which of the first two suffers the greater pain, which of the last two enjoys the greater pleasure? Each group debates, and submits its case for judgement by the other group; the conclusion is that there is nothing to choose. Shakespeare in particular will pick up the idea of love not just as the mainspring for an intrigue plot but as a problematic experience whose pains and pleasures are worth exploring.

If the tradition of the interlude gives English Renaissance comedy an intellectual structure to expand the implications of the plot, the tradition of romance (dramatic and non-dramatic) brings in a sense of plotting quite alien to New Comedy.[8] Instead of a tightly worked-out action on a domestic scale, completed in a single place on a single day, romance ranges freely over space and time, with loose and extravagant plots featuring wandering knights, princes and princesses, battles, monsters and large doses of magic. Surviving examples include the anonymous *Clyomon and Clamydes* (c.1570) and *Mucedorus* (c.1590); Beaumont's *The Knight of the Burning Pestle* (c.1607) burlesques the form, while Peele in *The Old Wives Tale* (c.1592), Greene in *Friar Bacon and Friar Bungay* (c.1589) and Shakespeare in his final romances make sophisticated use of it. It appears to have been a staple of early Elizabethan theatre, and, though most of the plays are lost, Sidney's complaint gives us something of their flavour. Romance's free sense of place, and the other freedoms this entailed, offended his neoclassical sensibilities:

you shall have Asia of the one side, and Afric of the other, and so many under-kingdoms, that the player, when he cometh in, must ever begin with telling where he is, or else the tale will not be conceived[.] Now ye shall have three ladies walk to gather flowers, and then we must believe the stage to be a garden. By and by, we hear news of shipwreck in the same place, and then we are to blame if we accept it not for a rock. Upon the back of that comes out a hideous monster, with fire and smoke, and then the miserable beholders are bound to take it for a cave. While in the meantime two armies fly in, represented with four swords and bucklers, and then what hard heart will not receive it for a pitched field?[9]

In the course of two hours, he goes on to complain, a prince and princess fall in love and get a child, who grows up and by the end of the play is himself in love and ready for a child of his own. The comedies we shall discuss in later chapters do not show this tradition in its purest (Sidney would say, impurest) form, any more than they show pure New Comedy; but they are the product of a volatile mix of ingredients of which this is perhaps the most explosive, and the one that sets English comedy farthest apart from the neoclassical control and largely domestic scale of its European rivals. It helps us understand the gulf that separates Shakespeare from Molière, Goldoni and Beaumarchais.

The eclecticism of the plays we shall examine follows naturally from such a mixed ancestry. They belong not so much to a tradition as to a series of interlinked mini-traditions. They also represent different types of theatrical occasion: our discussion will move back and forth between plays written for small private playhouses with all-boy companies and an exclusive clientele, and plays written for adult companies in large public playhouses with a mixed audience. If we tried to map out the field, so many plays are lost that the best map would have to include many blank spaces and broken lines. A few broad outlines may, however, be sketched in. It appears that in the 1580s and early 1590s romance was the dominant mode, though far from the only one. Writing for the popular, professional theatre, Peele and Greene use extravagant plots, ranging over time and space, making free use of magic. Writing for a children's company in a more courtly setting (to be examined in Chapter 2) John Lyly is equally extravagant, using fantastic settings and allegorical characters and actions; but his use of multiple plots that comment on each other gives a formal tightness to his work, and the pressure of ideas in the allegory owes something to the debates of the interlude. Shakespeare, whose comedy comes to fruition in the 1590s, draws on all the traditions. He creates in *The Comedy of Errors* a story of confusion based on Plautus's *Menaechmi* and set in a typical seaport town; but he fleshes out the lost-child convention with a fantastic tale, drawn from romance, of how the family was broken apart, and adds a touch of magic, though no literal magic, in the characters' persistent belief that supernatural forces are at work. He reverses this technique in *A Midsummer Night's Dream*, where the magic is quite literal but this time the characters seek natural explanations, and in the process construct a Heywood-like pattern of different modes of love.

Romance faded in the late 1590s as Chapman and Jonson went for more tightly plotted actions in closely defined courtly and urban settings.

These have their own stylization, so that the word 'realistic' is problematic if applied to them; but they dispense with magic and the supernatural. Around the same time, the open spaces of romance became the English countryside of comedies like Henry Porter's *The Two Angry Women of Abingdon* (c.1598) and the anonymous *The Merry Devil of Edmonton* (c.1602), where comic confusion that recalls Plautus occurs in a quite un-Plautine setting. Meanwhile the first extant London comedies appear, beginning in 1598 with William Haughton's *Englishmen for my Money*, in which witty English girls and their lovers play practical jokes on foreign suitors. Around the turn of the century the children's companies, newly revived, mined a vein of satiric comedy in courtly and urban settings, setting a fashion that quickly spread to the public theatres, whose comedies became more inclined to show, with a mix of satire and romance, the life of London. As the century advances, Beaumont and Fletcher begin the gentrification of comedy, with tales of love-intrigues among the propertied classes that begin a long development towards Restoration comedy. From the 1620s onward, Caroline comedy follows their lead in its focus on the gentry, but it preserves some of the eclecticism of its forerunners: its settings embrace city, court and country, and its manner ranges from the romantic to the satiric, both tamed a little for the sake of a new smoothness of surface.

As settings shift, the characters in individual plays seem to be always on the move: from the court to the country, the country to the city, the city to the suburbs. (We can hear Sidney protesting from his grave.) And the plays themselves are similarly on the move, in both the settings they show and the theatres they played in. This is reflected in the nine plays picked for discussion in this book, whose movements I would now like to track in general terms in order to suggest why each seems to me representative. Lyly's *Endymion* is centred on a court, albeit a fantastic one that allows no conventional sense of place. It is also centred, as strongly as any play under discussion, on a single authority figure, Cynthia – queen, goddess, moon and representative of Queen Elizabeth. Its action embraces magic, and interlude-like debates on the different claims of love and friendship. It represents the work of a courtly dramatist writing for a private theatre. Written for a public, professional company, Greene's *Friar Bacon and Friar Bungay* moves out to the countryside, celebrating not the sovereign but England itself. (The political implications of such decentring have been explored by Richard Helgerson, who shows that in the English imagination at this time the land was becoming more important than the ruler.)[10] Greene replaces the magic of the ruler with the magic of a subject, Friar Bacon, and instead of centring on one kind of authority shows different modes of authority in competition. Shakespeare in *A Midsummer Night's Dream*, also written for a public theatre, exploits the extravagance of romance and the tight plotting of New Comedy, mixing courtly, urban and country settings and characters in an interlude-style display of different modes of living and different ways of experiencing love. Like Greene he puts rival powers, social authority and magic, into conflict.

As the century turns and the reign of James begins, Marston in *The Malcontent* pulls back to a tightly defined setting, this time a court, reviving Lyly in one sense (his play too was initially written for children, and is extravagantly stylized) but depicting the court in a new satiric mode and making the central ruler-figure, Malevole–Altofront, more unstable and problematic. Middleton's *Michaelmas Term*, another satiric private-theatre play written for children, is also strongly centred: this time the centre is the city, a force that draws in and destroys dupes from the country. Its transformations, though they continue to use the language of magic, are part of an elaborate con-game. Shakespeare's *The Tempest*, following these two plays, may look like a throwback to the devices of romance; but Prospero's island is a setting as tight and magnetic as Marston's court and Middleton's London, and Shakespeare uses its magic as they use satiric intrigue, for an exploration of the emptiness of power. Once again, as in Lyly and Marston, there is a central authority figure; he looks as wise and all-powerful as Lyly's Cynthia but turns out to be as problematic as Marston's Altofront.

As Shakespeare's characters move from the court to the wood, or the court to the island, the characters of Ben Jonson's *Bartholomew Fair* move from the city to the Fair of the play's title, their adventures embodying both satiric insights into society and a parody of romance as the magic of the Fair, a somewhat earthier force than Puck's flower, works on them. And we should pause to note the movement of the plays themselves: *The Malcontent*, written for the children's company at the private Blackfriars, was picked up by the adult company at the public Globe; *The Tempest* would have played at both the Globe and the Blackfriars, which Shakespeare's company had taken over (around this time the children's companies either died or were absorbed into the adult companies); and *Bartholomew Fair*, having had its first performance at a down-market public playhouse, the Hope, was played next day at court. Jonson, we shall see, adjusts the text accordingly. The Caroline comedies that follow,

Shirley's *The Lady of Pleasure* and Brome's *A Jovial Crew*, were performed at the same private playhouse, the Cockpit in Drury Lane; but the comic setting goes on shifting. Shirley's London, like Middleton's, is a magnet for country folk and leads them into trouble; but the issues are fashion and behaviour where Middleton's are money, land and identity. Brome returns to the country, populated this time not by magician-friars or fairies but by beggars whose private commonwealth has its own quality of fantasy, and its own interlude-like usefulness in getting us to think about ways of living in society. While Lyly has celebrated authority and Marston has questioned it, Jonson in *Bartholomew Fair* shatters it; and in the Caroline plays that follow the authority figures, though not so overtly questioned, seem enervated.

These nine plays trace not a straight-line development in English Renaissance comedy (no such development exists) but rather a zig-zag course through different settings and styles, and different types of theatre. All this will be fleshed out in greater detail in the chapters that follow; but we should pause to notice some recurring features. There is, first of all, an overt political interest in many of these plays that is foreign to the New Comedy mainstream. While some settings are domestic and some actions are private, we also encounter rulers and their courts, and we are made to think about how power functions and how societies operate. In this respect English comedy touches on material that is more traditionally the province of tragedy; in fact *The Malcontent* has figured in discussions of tragedy with no great sense of incongruity. The recurring figure of the magician lets the playwright examine the strengths and vulnerability of a power which, though not of this world, helps us think about power in general. By the same token, sexual relations are not just the trigger for a plot mechanism; the power of sexuality itself – which can be, like other kinds of power, both creative and destructive – is held up for scrutiny. In the confusion of the comic intrigue, and in the risks the characters take in pursuing their desires, identity can become fragile; what may begin as donning a false nose to fool one's opponents can end by raising questions about the integrity of one's nature. The stakes of comedy are traditionally low; but here we do not always feel safe.

Not all these themes appear in every play, but I hope as the discussions accumulate the reader will get a sense that these plays, for all their variety, are talking to each other. Some of the dialogues on points of detail (to anticipate briefly) are surprising. The romance of *A Midsummer Night's Dream* may seem poles apart from the satire of *The Malcontent*; but both plays convey the sense that life is a dream. Middleton's grubby, cynical London and Prospero's enchanted island could hardly be more different as settings; but in both the same practical point is made about the role of clothing in constructing social identity. Links like these accompany the larger similarities, the variations on rulers, lovers and magicians, the family resemblances and family differences of court, country and city.

Anyone familiar with Shakespearian comedy will be aware of one notable omission. Where, in this selection of plays, are the strong, witty heroines who control the action? Where are Portia, Beatrice, Rosalind? We think of the strong heroine as an important recurring feature of the English comic tradition: Etherege's Harriet Woodvil, Congreve's Angelica and Millimant, Goldsmith's Kate Hardcastle, Austen's Elizabeth Bennet and Emma Woodhouse. Looking at the tradition as a whole, this may be a fair point. But to read that expectation back into Renaissance comedy is to find that Shakespeare in this respect is exceptional for his time, and not all of his own plays fall into line. The women of the comedies discussed here are, by comparison, secondary and passive, and in that way they are more typical of the field than Beatrice or Rosalind. Moreover, it could be said that the convention of the strong heroine only masks the reality we glimpse at the end of the play when we note that the heroine shows her strength by winning a man, and having done so she will dwindle into a wife. For much of its history English comedy, having let its women out to play, ends by calling them home.[11] In the plays under discussion, the comfort offered to modern sensibilities by the strong-heroine convention is largely unavailable. (Lyly's Cynthia is too special a case to qualify that statement; the same can be said of the title character of Middleton and Dekker's *The Roaring Girl*.) These women tend to be sexual and political trophies. But what we might call women's issues (the anachronism is more in the phrasing than the idea) are not altogether neglected. *A Midsummer Night's Dream* is particularly interesting, in that Shakespeare manages (I hope to show) a sensitive exploration of the women's experience without the use of the strong-heroine convention. And Shirley, towards the end of the period, does some surprisingly open thinking about his heroine's sexuality.

Open thinking is characteristic of all these plays: in their different ways they question, challenge and experiment. They take what can be the stultifyingly tight conventions of comedy, unlock them, and let in some air. In the process they expand, in various directions, our sense of what comedy can do. Watching them do this is the business of the chapters that follow.

Notes

1 Two brief surveys may be particularly recommended. Madeleine Doran, *Endeavors of Art: A Study of Form in Elizabethan Drama*, Madison, Wis., 1954, repr. 1964, pp. 148–85, surveys the mix of ingredients that went into the creation of English Renaissance comedy, with special emphasis on the New Comedy tradition of Plautus, Terence and their Renaissance successors. Jill Levenson, 'Comedy', *The Cambridge Companion to English Renaissance Drama*, ed. A.R. Braunmuller and Michael Hattaway, Cambridge, 1990, pp. 263–300, gives a good sense of the eclecticism of the genre. Two book-length surveys worth consulting are M.C. Bradbrook, *The Growth and Structure of Elizabethan Comedy*, new edn, London, 1973; and Leo Salingar, *Shakespeare and the Traditions of Comedy*, Cambridge, 1974.

2 Doran, *Endeavors*, p. 155.

3 There are examples in Ben Jonson's *Every Man in his Humour* and John Dryden's *Sir Martin Mar-All*. In the latter play the hero is so stupid that the heroine takes the logical step of marrying the servant instead.

4 Predictability can make even violence and death funny. The principle is illustrated in two classic British film comedies, *Kind Hearts and Coronets* (in which every murder victim is played by Alec Guinness) and *The Ladykillers* (in which corpses are dumped over a railway bridge into passing trains, accompanied by recurring sound effects: hiss as the screen fills with steam, bong as the body lands in the freight car). In the American television series *South Park*, I am informed by those who stay up late enough to watch it, a character called Kenny is killed in every episode.

5 I have explored the larger tradition of English comedy from this viewpoint in *English Stage Comedy 1490–1990: Five Centuries of a Genre*, forthcoming.

6 *Sidney's Apologie for Poetrie*, ed. J. Churton Collins, Oxford, 1907, repr. 1955, p. 30 (spelling and punctuation modernized).

7 On this tradition see Joel B. Altman, *The Tudor Play of Mind*, Berkeley and Los Angeles, 1978.

8 On this tradition see Salingar, *Shakespeare*, pp. 28–75 and Brian Gibbons, 'Romance and the Heroic Play', *Cambridge Companion*, pp. 207–36.

9 *Apologie*, p. 52.

10 *Forms of Nationhood: The Elizabethan Writing of England*, Chicago and London, 1992, esp. pp. 5, 10, 107–47.

11 For a discussion of this issue, including the change that overtakes comedy in the late twentieth century, see Susan Carlson, *Women and Comedy: Rewriting the British Theatrical Tradition*, Ann Arbor, 1991.

2

Lyly, *Endymion*

J OHN Lyly's *Endymion* was performed at court on 2 February (Candlemas) 1588, by the Children of Paul's. This boys' company had a playhouse of its own, possibly in the precincts of St Paul's Cathedral, an intimate space seating perhaps fifty to a hundred spectators.[1] When Lyly wrote for them, their principal business was performing plays at court, but the growing custom of charging admission to their playhouse for what were nominally rehearsals of their court appearances made them increasingly a commercial enterprise and gave their plays a double function: they were court entertainments for the Queen and public entertainments for an audience that wanted a vicarious taste of court life.[2] Little is known about the staging at either location, but G.K. Hunter has suggested that the court performances used what would now be called arena staging, with the audience surrounding the playing area rather than facing one way at a stage; this would give them a view not just of the play but of the principal spectator, the Queen. They did not just watch the play; they watched the Queen watching the play, and this is significant for *Endymion* in particular.[3]

Lyly, assuming he was present, would have been watching the Queen with particular care. He had achieved literary fame with his novel *Euphues* (1578), whose highly mannered prose created a brief but intense vogue and was still being parodied near the end of the century. Falstaff pokes fun at it in the tavern play in *1 Henry IV*: 'for though the camomile, the more it is trodden on the faster it grows, yet youth, the more it is wasted the sooner it wears' (1.4.396–9).[4] This mannered prose, called Euphuism, helps to create the deliberate artifice of Lyly's plays. But for Lyly literary fame was not enough. As a playwright working for the boys' companies, he aimed his work at court performance. He himself was angling for court preferment and for him, as for so many, it became an exercise in frustration. Around the time of *Endymion*, Elizabeth seems to have encouraged him to 'aim all [his] courses at the Revels, (I dare not say with a promise, but with a hopeful item of the reversion)'. He was appointed Esquire of the Body, but there is no record of his receiving payment.[5] His last years are a story of frustration and neglect, his court ambitions unfulfilled and his literary vogue a thing of the past.

The doubleness of *Endymion* goes beyond its dual nature as a play for the court and a play for the public. Through the central figure of Cynthia, moon-goddess and avatar of Queen Elizabeth, it participates in the quasi-religious cult of adoration that surrounded the ageing Virgin Queen, a cult that in Protestant England seems to have replaced devotion to the Virgin Mary and used some of the same language. At the same time it dramatizes the frustration entailed in pinning one's hopes on a parsimonious, evasive ruler who is more interested in inspiring devotion than in rewarding it. Lyly does not write the harsh anti-court satire we shall see in Marston; instead he offers a teasing interplay of overt adoration and half-concealed resentment, flattery and impudence, showing the Queen an image of herself as gracious and merciful, while hinting at ways she is actually falling short of the ideal. There is a certain impudence in his choice of story: in its most familiar form the myth of Endymion shows Diana, moon-goddess of chastity, departing from her own nature by falling in love with a mortal. Lyly, having by the title raised the expectation of something daring, then plays it safe by using a less familiar tradition in which it is the mortal who falls in love with the goddess; but some of the impudence remains.[6]

He also builds a sense of frustration into the dramatic form. In the New Comedy tradition of Plautus and Terence, the action is all bustle and intrigue as the clever servant works with the lovers to bring them together. Here, however, the whole point is that Endymion can never possess the moon, and the play offers not movement but stasis. The principal character's chief action is to sleep for forty years. The result is that we watch not an unfolding story but an unfolding vision (as in Heywood's *Play of Love*) of different types of relationship, in love and power, with the varied natures and values of the characters held up for our inspection, turning before us, as Peter Saccio puts it, 'like a display case in a gold museum'.[7] It may seem strange at first glance to compare Lyly to Samuel Beckett; but both write plays in a consciously artificial idiom, in which awareness of style is an important part of the effect, and in *Endymion* in particular Lyly anticipates Beckett by writing a play the point of which is that nothing happens. That stasis is part of the double effect, putting us in a timeless world where fixed adoration of the Queen is all the life one needs, while letting us sense the frustration of such a world.

The doubleness of theatre itself, the dual awareness of character and actor, must have been more acute than usual when the actors were all boys. Yet we need not imagine that the effect was consistent minaturization as small boys with piping voices absurdly mimed adult passions. Boys come in different shapes and sizes, and Lyly suggests the physical variety of his company when the braggart Sir Tophas accepts the pages Dares and Samias as his half-friends because they are half his size, reaching only to his waist (1.3.34–6).[8] Tophas later notes that, like Flute in *A Midsummer Night's Dream*, he has a beard coming (5.2.17–22). To the interplay of character and actor we may add the mixture of small boys and young adolescents.[9] The story of Endymion's love for the moon, which is also a courtier's devotion to the Queen, calls for a mix of seriousness and absurdity, and this mix may well have been reflected in the company itself, with the smaller boys as wisecracking pages, unconcerned with the central love affairs which were acted out by the principal, most experienced actors, poised on the brink of adulthood.

Even the allegorical idiom of the play is deliberately, playfully inconsistent. While Endymion loves the moon, he professes love for Tellus, the earth. Tellus's chief role in the play is to show the fury of a woman scorned: it is through her machinations that the witch Dipsas punishes Endymion by putting him into an enchanted sleep. Yet she is also the earth, and describes herself accordingly: 'Is not my beauty divine, whose body is decked with fair flowers, and veins are vines, yielding sweet liquor to the dullest spirits, whose ears are corn to bring strength, and whose hairs are grass to bring abundance?' (1.2.20–4). And she is a boy actor. This play of identities – woman, earth, actor – frees *Endymion* from the rigidity of one-on-one allegory and gives it a teasing, speculative quality that is vital to Lyly's purpose.

Other entertainments for the Queen left her in the audience, making her the recipient of flattery. When she became involved in the action, as she did in Sir Philip Sidney's *The Lady of May* (1578) and George Peele's *The Arraignment of Paris* (c.1584), it was in her own person, breaking the boundary that separates stage and spectator. In *The Lady of May*, strolling through the grounds of the Earl of Leicester at Wanstead, she was encountered by a pageant in which the title character was unable to choose between rival suitors, a forester and a shepherd, and asked the Queen to choose for her. (According to Marion Jones, she made the wrong choice and threw the performance into confusion.)[10] In *The Arraignment of Paris* the myth of the Trojan war is revised for her benefit. Diana, with the enthusiastic agreement of Venus, Juno and Pallas, awards the Apple of Discord to the nymph Eliza, who rules over a restored Troy, redeemed from its tragic history. Diana places the apple, represented by a golden ball, in Elizabeth's hands as she sits in the audience. Lyly, on the other hand, takes the risk of putting Elizabeth into the play as a character, Cynthia. As the real Queen watches the play, and the audience watches her, a boy actor presents her on stage. But as the boy is and is not Cynthia, Cynthia is and is not Elizabeth; the constant presence of the Queen in full view of the rest of the audience reminds us that Cynthia is a secondary creation, not the real thing.

Within the character herself the play of shifting identity continues. She is the moon, she is a goddess, she is a woman. In the opening scene Endymion's friend Eumenides berates him for the folly of loving the moon. He puts it quite literally; the moon is not a woman: 'There was never any so peevish to imagine the moon either capable of affection or shape of a mistress; for as impossible it is to make love fit to her humour, which no man knoweth, as a coat to her form, which continueth not in one bigness' (1.1.23–7). But as he speaks the moon becomes 'she' and acquires a temperament ('humour'). When Endymion declares, 'Such is my sweet Cynthia, whom time cannot touch because she is divine, nor will offend because she is delicate' (1.1.66–7), she seems both an invulnerable deity and a fragile mortal. Tellus and Endymion dispute Cynthia's nature, Tellus insisting that her rival is 'but a woman' whose beauty is 'subject to time' while Endymion compares her to the contradictory goddesses Venus and Vesta (love and domesticity). To Tellus's challenge, 'Wilt thou make her immortal?' he replies, 'No, but incomparable' (2.2.89–98). Is she mortal or immortal, subject to comparison or not? The dialogue dances around these possibilities. Corsites, who falls in love with Tellus when she is a prisoner in his charge, senses the danger he is in: 'Cynthia beginneth to rise, and if she discover our love we both perish, for nothing pleaseth her but the fairness of virginity' (4.1.72–4). Cynthia is here the literal moon rising in the sky, and a very particular Queen Elizabeth, notoriously jealous of love affairs and marriages between her male courtiers and her attendant ladies. The Epilogue finally detaches Elizabeth from Cynthia. It tells the fable of the wind and sun competing to make a traveller remove his cloak, and as it applies the fable Elizabeth is the sun. The moon we saw in the play was a mere reflector of the true light and power at the centre of the courtly cosmos.

Within the play the adoration the characters direct at Cynthia is shadowed by constant reminders that she is also subject to detraction. Endymion's complaint, 'O fair Cynthia, why do others term thee unconstant whom I have ever found unmovable?' (1.1.35–6), suggests that she can be accused of both fickleness and stubbornness. In his sleep he has a vision of Cynthia menaced by barking wolves, by allegorical figures of Ingratitude, Treachery and Envy, and by parasitic drones and beetles sucking the blood of a princely eagle (5.1.131–48). Within the play itself, critical voices are sometimes heard. Corsites's love for Tellus makes him attribute her imprisonment on Cynthia's orders to 'the malice of envy' (3.2.9–10); he calls her fortune 'too hard' (5.1.40). The courtier Zontes, on the other hand, seems to regret Cynthia's tendency to mercy; asked how she will decide the cause of Tellus and Dipsas, on trial for imposing an enchanted sleep on Endymion, he replies, 'I fear as in all causes: hear of it in justice and then judge of it in mercy' (5.3.10–11). (The same suggestion that Elizabeth's mercy is unwise touches the Mercilla episode in Book V of *The Faerie Queene*.) There is even a hint of self-criticism as Cynthia contemplates the sleeping Endymion: 'I favoured thee, Endymion, for thy honour, thy virtues, thy affections; but to bring thy thoughts within the compass of thy fortunes, I have seemed strange, that I might have thee stayed. And now are thy days ended before my favour begin' (4.3.83–7). She has played Elizabeth's delaying game, and now asks herself, did I miscalculate?

At the story level, Cynthia's benign power is contrasted with the black magic of the witch Dipsas, who on Tellus's orders puts Endymion into an enchanted sleep in which he ages forty years. Yet there is a revealing ambiguity in Tellus's self-accusation: 'Accursed girl, what hope hast thou to see Endymion, on whose head already are grown grey hairs, and whose life must yield to nature before Cynthia end her displeasure?' (4.1.15–17). Is Cynthia's displeasure directed at Tellus, or Endymion? Logically it should be the former, but the grammar of the speech more naturally suggests the latter, connecting Endymion's sleep with Cynthia's displeasure and suggesting that one can grow old and die waiting for her favour. The fairies who torment Corsites when he comes to move the sleeping Endymion into hiding declare, 'Saucy mortals must not view / What the Queen of Stars is doing' (4.3.34–5); as they leave they kiss

Endymion, anticipating the gesture with which Cynthia will wake him. The surface meaning, that Cynthia is protecting Endymion, is shadowed by suggestions that his sleep is somehow her responsibility.[11] This makes an unexpected link between Cynthia and the witch Dipsas. Tellus originally wanted Dipsas to make Endymion fall in love with her, but the witch declares that though she can darken the sun and change the course of the moon 'I am not able to rule hearts' (1.4.27). Cynthia, trying in the last scene to bring Eumenides and Semele together, sees a similar limitation in her own power: 'I will not command love, for it cannot be enforced. Let me entreat it' (5.4.239–40). The parallel between Cynthia and the witch on this point suggests that they are light and dark aspects of the same power. Philippa Berry recalls that 'Hecate, Roman goddess of witchcraft, ... was identified with the third, waning face of the moon: that is, of the triple or "triformis" Diana', and suggests of Tellus and Dipsas, 'perhaps these misogynistic representations ... contaminate by their proximity the icon of Elizabeth'.[12]

If her supernatural power has a malign aspect, that at least keeps her on the level of myth. But as a figure in a play she can also be very human. Her first appearance hardly suggests a serene, all-powerful majesty; she presides, with some effort, over a group of squabbling courtiers, and she is as snappish with them as they are with each other. They cannot even keep to the subject, which is Endymion's enchanted sleep:

Tellus. As good sleep and do no harm as wake and do no good.
Cynthia. What maketh you, Tellus, to be so short? The time was, Endymion only was.
Eumenides. It is an old saying, madam, that a waking dog doth afar off bark at a sleeping lion.
Semele. It were good, Eumedines, that you took a nap with your friend, for your speech beginneth to be heavy.
Eumenides. Contrary to your nature, Semele, which hath been always accounted light.
Cynthia. What, have we here before my face these unseemly and malapert overthwarts? I will tame your tongues and your thoughts, and make your speeches answerable to your duties and your conceits fit for my dignity; else will I banish you both my person and the world.   (3.1.6–20)

This moon-goddess seems to be presiding over an unruly playground. The sharp-tongued Semele is a particular source of irritation; when in a later scene Cynthia actually invites her to speak she replies as one who has had too many royal rebukes, 'Madam, I dare say nothing for fear I offend'

(4.3.68). Cynthia punishes this sarcasm by sentencing her to a year's silence on penalty of losing her tongue. In the last scene Semele breaks her silence, and Cynthia threatens to enforce the penalty. The misogynist joke about over-talkative women is coupled with an image of the Elizabethan state's power to silence its critics; but we also see that this particular critic is hard to silence.

Cynthia does not always seem secure in her power; nor does she always seem fully aware of it. She has to learn from Eumenides, who has got the message from a magic fountain, that she can cure Endymion's sleep with a kiss. This is news to her; she has been sending around the world for advice, and when she hears that she herself has the power, she declares, 'it cannot sink into my head that I should be signified by that sacred fountain' (5.1.11–12). She is, as the page Dares puts it, 'desirous to know the experiment of her own virtue' (5.1.4–5) and in that spirit of experiment she kisses Endymion. In the same spirit she undoes the spell by which Dipsas turned her assistant Bagoa (whom Sir Tophas now wants to marry) into a tree: 'it may be there are more virtues in me than myself knoweth of … I will try whether I can turn this tree again to thy true love' (5.4.289–92). She is clear enough about her power to punish; what she needs to learn is her power to restore.

She also needs to be warned about her capacity for cruelty. Endymion reports the vision he had in his sleep, which was acted in dumb-show before the audience: 'Methought I saw a lady passing fair but very mischievous, who in the one hand carried a knife with which she offered to cut my throat, and in the other a looking glass, wherein, seeing how ill anger became ladies, she refrained from intended violence' (5.1.88–92). She is accompanied by two other ladies, one with an expression of 'settled malice' (94), the other registering pity. They suggest the opposing forces in a morality-play psychomachia, a struggle for the soul of the central figure. The struggle is resolved: 'After long debating with herself, mercy overcame anger, and there appeared in her heavenly face … a divine majesty, mingled with a sweet mildness' (5.1.105–7). The message for Cynthia and for Elizabeth is, you will gain majesty by choosing mercy.[13] But as the three figures leave, the malign and pitying ones retain their aspects, suggesting that despite this one decision the ongoing conflict is unresolved, the lesson will have to be learned again.

If there is something risky in presuming to advise the Queen that she has something to learn about mercy, there is a further risk in the possibility that play embodies topical political meanings. On many occasions

Elizabeth's anger was roused by plays and sermons that presumed to comment on affairs of state. She interrupted preachers and ordered them to return to their texts; she berated Leicester for an anti-Spanish comedy at a time when relations with Spain were delicate; the possibility of her marriage was a forbidden subject. The degree to which critics have seen *Endymion* as a topical play about particular people has ebbed and flowed with critical fashion. In the nineteenth and early twentieth centuries elaborate lists were drawn up finding real-life counterparts for even minor characters;[14] by the middle of the twentieth century, with New Criticism insisting on the self-sufficiency of the text, topicality was out of favour; there are recent signs that it is coming back.[15] If Cynthia is Elizabeth, then is Endymion Leicester? Or Oxford? Is the imprisoned Tellus Mary Queen of Scots? The Prologue explicitly discourages such speculations: 'We hope in our times none will apply pastimes, because they are fancies; for there liveth none under the sun that knows what to make of the Man in the Moon' (7–9). By discouraging topical application, the Prologue admits it is possible. Yet if Elizabeth had been presented with a play overtly dramatizing contemporary political events – including, of all things, the crisis over Mary, executed the previous year – she would have been livid. It is the play's overt stance that no such meanings are intended. It is part of the play's mischief, the undercurrent of impudence beneath the flattery, that to deny topicality is to remind the audience of its possibility. Like high-wire artists capturing attention by putting themselves in danger, Lyly is at once courting the Queen and courting trouble, combining flattery and warning, fantasy and political comment.

Cynthia is a mortal ruler, admirable but not quite perfect, dealing somewhat tensely with the intrigues of a fractious court and the problems of politics. That is one side of the play's double game. The other, more prominent side is that she is a cosmic power, a principle beyond time and mortality, an idea. Nothing so petty as contemporary politics can touch her. Her power does not depend on dynastic inheritance or political ability; it simply is. As a circle is 'of all figures the perfectest', she is 'of all circles the most absolute' (3.4.177–9). Powers are attributed to her that go beyond the powers of the moon. Tellus, as earth, celebrates the fertility of her own body, but her attendant Floscula insists,

Your grapes would be but dry husks, your corn but chaff, and all your virtues vain, were it not Cynthia that preserveth the one in the bud and nourisheth the other in the blade, and by her influence both comforteth all things and by her authority commandeth all creatures. (1.2.30–4)

Making her submission in the last scene, Tellus addresses 'Divine Cynthia, by whom I receive my life and am content to end it' (5.4.59–60).

The paradox of the moon, always changing and always the same, is the paradox of Cynthia. (Elizabeth's motto was *semper eadem*, always the same.) It is the principle of Mutabilitie explored by Spenser in the last fragment of *The Faerie Queene*. When Endymion declares that 'Cynthia, being in her fullness, decayeth, as not delighting in her greatest beauty, or withering when she should be most honoured' (1.1.53–5), Lyly takes the risk of reminding the Queen of her real age, then quickly recovers: when Cynthia declines, that means she is young again (57–9). In her presence the free handling of time and place characteristic of Elizabethan drama has a symbolic function. There is 'a curious placelessness' about the play.[16] Are we in a court? There is no sense of interior space. Are we in the heavens? Then what is Sir Tophas doing there? The answer is that we are in an acting area, and a place of the mind, where (given the staging with different 'houses' Hunter and others have proposed)[17] all the play's locations, such as they are, are simultaneously present all the time. Time is equally free. History is telescoped: Pythagoras comes to Cynthia's court to give advice and stays to receive correction when she confutes the errors in his philosophy. Endymion sleeps for forty years and wakes an old man; no one else ages.[18] It is as though his sleep is a fall into mortality; in Cynthia's presence time stands still. It was a recurring motif in entertainments for Elizabeth that she could change the rules of time. 'At Kenilworth in 1575 the castle clock was stopped while she was there; at Bedington in 1599, Sir Francis Carew artificially delayed the ripening of his cherry trees so that her arrival seemed to produce spring out of season'.[19] Such is the power of Cynthia that in her presence the rules of time and space mean nothing. The Prologue warns us that even genre has broken down, into nonsense, or into something *sui generis*: 'We present neither comedy, nor tragedy, nor story, nor anything, but that whosoever heareth may say this: "Why, here is a tale of the Man in the Moon"' (9–12).[20] Like a power surge that blows all the circuits, Cynthia's presence breaks down time, space and meaning.

This sense of a unique power, beyond comprehension, makes it all the more extraordinary when Cynthia kisses Endymion. Dipsas has insisted the charmed sleep is unbreakable; the international experts Cynthia calls on are of the same opinion (2.3.32–4, 4.3.153–7). But the message Eumenides reads in the magic fountain is, 'When she, whose figure of all is the perfectest and never to be measured, always one yet never the same, still inconstant yet never wavering, shall come and kiss Endymion in his sleep, he shall then rise; else, never' (3.4.165-9). It is the uniqueness of Cynthia, which (as we have seen) she herself has some trouble grasping, that makes this unique action possible. She stresses, as she prepares to kiss him, that what she is about to do is extraordinary: 'although my mouth hath been heretofore as untouched as my thoughts ... I will do that to Endymion which yet never mortal man could boast of heretofore, nor shall ever hope for hereafter' (5.1.24-9). The moon kisses a mortal; an onstage representative of the Virgin Queen, in the presence of the court, bestows a kiss, the first and last of her life, on a man. It may have been, in performance, an electric moment.

In Endymion's devotion to Cynthia there is the same dance of meanings as we have seen in Cynthia herself. Loving the moon is an absurd folly. At the same time it has an edge of potential tragedy: Endymion tells Eumenides, 'Follow thou thine own fortunes, which creep on the earth, and suffer me to fly to mine, whose fall, though it be desperate, yet shall it come by daring' (1.2.84-7). The tragic overreacher is also a frustrated courtier,[21] resenting the compromises he has to make to curry favour in a less than perfect court: 'Have I not crept to those on whom I might have trodden, only because thou didst shine upon them?' (2.1.20-1). For all his adoration he allows some of this resentment to touch Cynthia herself: 'Have not injuries been sweet to me if thou vouchsafedst I should bear them?' (2.1.21-3). (It is the word 'injuries' that makes the difference.) When he describes himself as 'waxing old with wishing' (2.1.24) he prepares the audience to see his ageing while he sleeps as a sardonic image of what it means to wait for the Queen's favour.

As the Prologue proclaims the play to be neither tragedy nor comedy, its end is neither the fall Endymion expects nor the consummation he hopes for; though he vows 'either to die or possess the moon herself' (1.1.18-19) he does neither. He promises the feats of the romance hero – 'There is no mountain so steep that I will not climb, no monster so cruel that I will not tame, no action so desperate that I will not attempt' (2.1.7-9) – but 'all he really does is fall asleep'.[22] That sleep bears different interpretations: it suggests the frustration of waiting for Cynthia's favour, the penalty of being outside her power and therefore mortal, and the deadness of Endymion's relationship with Tellus, who is literally responsible for his enchantment. Corsites describes him (with bawdy overtones?) as 'Turned, I think to earth, with lying so long on the earth' (4.3.14). This is what the lower love does to you. At the same time it is a fortunate fall. When Eumenides rebukes Endymion with the words, 'Sleep would do thee more good than speech' (1.1.78–9) he speaks more truly than he knows: it is by sleeping that Endymion wins Cynthia's kiss. Sleep can also bring visions,[23] and Endymion has two: one teaching Cynthia the choice of mercy, the other warning her against her enemies.

While the Endymion of the myth sleeps in eternal youth,[24] Lyly's Endymion undergoes an ageing that in stage terms looks unnaturally fast. In Celtic stories of the fairy world time passes differently there and people emerge from what they thought was a night with the fairies to find themselves suddenly aged.[25] So it is with Endymion. His life is a year without a spring: in the words of Dipsas, 'Thou shalt sleep out thy youth and flowering time and become dry hay before thou knewest thyself green grass' (2.3.37–9). When he wakes he feels a terrible dislocation; not only has his youth gone, his sense of identity has gone with it: 'Endymion? I call to mind such a name' (5.1.42) Like Lear waking in Cordelia's tent – 'I will not swear these are my hands' (4.7.56) – he finds himself in a strange body: 'that this should be my body I doubt' (5.1.73–4). There is a sense of waste and loss: 'Am I that Endymion who was wont in court to lead my life, and in jousts, tourneys, and arms to exercise my youth? Am I that Endymion?' (5.1.67–9). He has touched on the mortality that Cynthia's timeless world holds in suspension.

The kiss has left him restored to life, but not to himself. The next stage, which comes three scenes later, is Cynthia's acceptance of his devotion. This involves an act of naming that shows her power over language. Endymion describes his feeling for her as eternal and unchanging, but dares not name it: 'The time was, madam, and is, and ever shall be, that I honoured Your Highness above all the world; but to stretch it so far as to call it love, I never durst' (5.4.157–9). But, like the Prologue that declares there are no topical references, this raises a possibility by denying it, and Endymion begins to nudge Cynthia in the direction he wants – 'nothing, without it vouchsafe Your Highness, be termed love' (5.5.165–6). At the same time he declares his own secret thought, and by declaring it breaks the secret: he will 'to myself, that no creature may hear, softly call it love' (5.4.171–2). Cynthia takes the hint: 'Endymion, this honourable respect of thine shall be christened "love" in thee, and my reward for it "favour"' (5.4.177–8).

Her phrasing is very careful. She is not, literally, accepting his love; she is allowing his respect to be called love. Her use of the passive voice implies that she is not so much naming this feeling herself as giving general permission to use the word. The reservation 'in thee' shows that like the kiss this is a special favour, not to be presumed upon by other courtiers. At the same time the favour is extraordinary. She seems to be using the word 'love' for the first time, inventing it for the occasion to do justice to a unique relationship. 'Favour' has the same new-minted quality. Like Adam in Eden, she is finding new sounds for new experiences. 'Christened' makes this new feeling a child, the only child they will have. The sense of dislocation Endymion felt on waking conveyed the loss of an old life; this feels like the start of a new one.

Yet the new words are also old, familiar words, and Cynthia (always changing, always the same) gives him permission to go on doing what he has been doing all along: 'Persevere, Endymion, in loving me' (5.4.179). With the permission goes a promise: 'Endymion, continue as thou hast begun, and thou shalt find that Cynthia shineth not on thee in vain' (5.4.185-7). It is just a promise, and with Cynthia one is not to look for more. Godot is always *going* to come, Clov is always *going* to leave, Cynthia is always *going* to show favour. *Semper eadem.* Yet the scene continues to play with the paradox of stasis and change, new and old. As Cynthia utters her promise Endymion's youth is magically restored. She is, characteristically, a bit surprised at her own power: 'What, young again?' (5.4.193); but Eumenides has told her earlier in the play, 'Your Majesty's words have been always deeds, and your deeds virtues' (3.3.64-5). With Cynthia, as so often, categories break down: she has a God-like power to act by speaking, and her acts do not have moral qualities, they *are* moral qualities. The power of her language restores Endymion's youth, without her conscious intention. One side of the play's double vision is that all she gives is a promise; the other side is that a promise is all Endymion needs. For a moment he has even participated in her nature; he declines, only to be young again. They have already been linked in the scene of Endymion's waking. Finding his own name unfamiliar when it is spoken by his friend Eumenides, he recognizes Cynthia before he recognizes himself, and she gives him his name back: 'I am Cynthia, and thou Endymion' (5.1.52). His identity depends on hers. By linking their names she proclaims a unique relationship; and, as the names distinguish them, they establish the permanent distance on which that relationship depends. As the Prologue declares that all one can say about the play is that it is a tale of the man in the moon, Cynthia in turn summarizes everything that can be said of the central relationship by declaring that she is Cynthia and he is Endymion.

Around the central, unique relationship are grouped other, more ordinary ones. As the story of Cynthia and Endymion presents idealism tinged with reservations, the stylization of allegory and hints of human reality, so these other relationships show an interplay of formula and human drama. Eumenides is caught in a formulaic contrast between male friendship and mere heterosexual love. Seeking a cure for Endymion, he comes to a sacred fountain that according to its keeper Geron offers 'remedy for anything' (3.4.23–4) so long as its waters are cleared by the tears of a faithful lover. Eumenides qualifies, by virtue of his love for Semele; he clears the water (Geron tells him he is the first to do so) and then hesitates between requesting a cure for Endymion and requesting Semele for himself. It is a choice between love and friendship, and as he himself puts it, 'The love of men to women is a thing common, and of course; the friendship of man to man infinite, and immortal' (3.4.121–3). He still hesitates, but Geron pushes him towards friendship, lecturing him on the fickleness of love and the transience of beauty. As Eumenides describes it, friendship has something of the uniqueness of Cynthia: 'Mistresses are in every place, and as common as hares in Athos, bees in Hybla, fowls in the air; but friends to be found are like the phoenix in Arabia, but one, or the philadelphi in Arays, never above two. I will have Endymion' (3.4.153–7). As he wakes from his enchanted sleep, Endymion recognizes Cynthia before he recognizes Eumenides, but while she gives Endymion his name his final acceptance of it depends on his friend: 'Ah, sweet Eumenides, I now perceive thou art he, and that myself have the name of Endymion' (5.1.72–3). Cynthia's power is greater, but she and Eumenides work together to restore Endymion.

Geron's warnings against the love of women seem to be borne out by Tellus, whose way of cursing Endymion is to imagine him in the grip of such love: 'The prime of his youth and pride of his time shall be spent in melancholy passions, careless behaviour, untamed thoughts, and unbridled affections' (1.2.65–7). While friendship is fixed and eternal, love is loose. When Eumenides describes his relations with Semele – 'She of all women the most froward, and I of all creatures the most fond' – Geron retorts, 'You doted, then, not loved' (3.4.62–4). Yet in the last scene the Eumenides–Semele relationship comes into its own. She turns him down, resenting his choice at the fountain. But when Cynthia sentences her to lose her tongue, and Eumenides offers to take the penalty on himself, she accepts him. Though it is shadowed by the joke about the value Semele puts on her tongue, there is an assertion here that breaks through the formulae of Geron's lecture. Eumenides has shown that love is not just a matter of transient, ungoverned passion; it is capable of sacrifice. In its own way it is as self-denying as Endymion's devotion to Cynthia.

Tellus's destructive passion for Endymion shows the dark side of love: 'He shall know the malice of a woman to have neither mean nor end, and of a woman deluded in love to have neither rule nor reason' (1.2.57–9). When her jailor Corsites falls in love with her, she rewards his devotion with treachery, setting him the impossible task of moving the sleeping Endymion into hiding; the fairies punish Corsites by pinching him and covering him with spots. Yet Tellus is not just a formula character embodying the play's misogyny. She is allowed a stoic dignity in her imprisonment: 'Cynthia may restrain the liberty of my body; of my thoughts she cannot' (3.2.6–7). As she approaches her final trial, the courtier Panelion sees her not as inherently evil but as fallen: 'Who would have thought that Tellus, being so fair by nature, so honourable by birth, so wise by education, would have entered into a mischief to the gods so odious, to men so detestable, and to her friend so malicious?' (5.3.1–4). She is allowed some pathos. For all her anger against Endymion she passes her time in prison making a picture of him; in a sense it is their child. At the end of the play she is allowed to keep it, suggesting that though she is married to Corsites a part of her will always want Endymion. Above all, the play gives her a genuine case against him. By his own admission, he is dissembling with her, falsely professing love to her as a cover for his love for Cynthia (2.1.25–9). We see him do it; and when to her challenge, 'Is it not possible for you, Endymion, to dissemble?' he replies, 'Not, Tellus, unless I could make me a woman' (2.1.67–8) the misogynist joke backfires: through the whole scene, without benefit of a sex change, he is lying to her. When in the last scene he denies, under questioning from Cynthia, that he loved Tellus and swore to honour her (5.4.152–3), he is still being economical with the truth.

All this leads Michael Pincombe to call Endymion a bounder and a cad.[26] Peter Saccio lets him off more gently: 'His only moral failure is a mild violation of Truth'.[27] Within the play, however, Tellus's servant Floscula, whose goodwill to Endymion is an insistent minor motif in the play's depiction of varied relationships, takes an utterly different view. Having heard her mistress denounce Endymion and vow revenge, she laments, 'what plots are cast to make thee unfortunate that studiest of all men to be the faithfullest!' (1.2.93–4). Given his record with Tellus, one might say he has not studied very hard; but Floscula's point seems to be that fidelity to Cynthia is the only fidelity that counts. As Cynthia's power breaks down time, space and meaning, it transforms values, defining virtues by their relationship to her. Given the ground rules of the allegory, this makes sense; all power, meaning and worth rest in Cynthia. But if Lyly had meant to leave it at that he would not have dramatized Endymion's perfidy so clearly or allowed so much space for Tellus's point of view. In so far as the play works as allegory, it is under the control of a vision centred absolutely on Cynthia; but it also works as drama, and that control is not total.

The witch Dipsas presents a simpler case. She embodies, as the more complex figure of Tellus does not quite do, the misogyny that is the reverse side of the play's adoration of Cynthia. We see this in the crone-comedy of Sir Tophas's tribute to her beauty: 'In how sweet a proportion her cheeks hang down to her breasts like dugs, and her paps to her waist like bags!' (3.3.59–61). Tellus celebrates the fertility of her body (1.2.20–8); Cynthia is above being praised in such terms; in Dipsas the female body is a sagging, exhausted mass. Her black magic is the converse of Cynthia's power, and works on Elizabethan fears of witchcraft directed against the crown. (In 1578 'three wax images transfixed by hog's bristles had been found, the central figure having "Elizabeth" inscribed on it'.)[28] Cynthia rises effortlessly above her: 'But know thou, Dipsas, and let all enchanters know, that Cynthia, being placed for light on earth, is also protected by the powers of heaven' (5.4.8–11). Cynthia breaks the witch's spell on Endymion, and in the end Dipsas repents and renounces her magic.

Cynthia's power shows not only in her defeat of Dipsas but also in the way Dipsas seems a mere parody and inversion of her. Though, as we have seen, the links between the characters may cast a shadow on Cynthia, the primary effect is that Dipsas is not a figure with claims of her own, as Tellus sometimes is; she is under the control of the play's overt purpose, the adoration of Cynthia. Sir Tophas is similarly under control when he functions as a parody of Endymion. He tries to emulate the hero's sleep, but manages only a short nap. Like Endymion he is in the grip of an irrational love, venturing against all advice on 'her whom none durst undertake' (3.3.75): in this case, Dipsas. As Jill Levenson suggests, our sense of Endymion's absurdity is deflected on to him.[29] Up to a point he is dependent on Endymion, as Dipsas is on Cynthia. But he has also a curiously pragmatic streak that gives him independent comic value, and keeps breaking the play's sealed world of courtly fantasy. If the play mystifies love, Tophas demystifies it: 'I think it but some device of the poet to get money' (1.3.12–13). He offends the pages who serve Endymion and Eumenides by asking 'Of what occupation are your masters?' (1.3.47). (Gentlemen don't have occupations.) Once he falls in love he introduces an element of bawdry: 'I cannot stand without another' (3.3.19). When Dipsas is reunited with her husband Geron, he switches his affections to Bagoa, whom Dipsas transformed into a tree. When Cynthia changes her back, Tophas becomes the one character to break the harmony of the multiple-couple ending. Seeing what he is getting, he exclaims, 'Bagoa? A bots upon thee!' (5.4.298). For much of the play he functions as a stock braggart, uttering mock-heroic threats to trout and sheep. But like later Elizabethan clowns he can be genuinely disruptive.

More subtly disruptive, and equally parodic, are Dares and Samias, pages to Endymion and Eumenides. The opening of their first scene sounds like the start of a comic subplot, as Dares asks, 'Now our masters are in love up to the ears, what have we to do but to be in knavery up to the crowns?' (1.3.1–2). In fact, like Endymion they do virtually nothing. They keep pointing this out, complaining of being at a loose end: Dares, finding his master is not providing him with a plot to parody, declares, 'I think he sleeps for a wager. But how shall we spend the time?' (4.2.2–3). When Sir Tophas takes to his bed, Samias asks the braggart's page Epiton the same question, 'how wilt thou spend thy time?' (4.2.50–1). This sense of having nothing to do parodies the frustration of the inactive courtier who can only wait for favour; but it also reflects the generally functionless quality of the pages in the play proper. The central characters have controlled, allegorical functions in the drama. The pages wander in and out, and the play finds no obvious use for them.

This counters the general impression of a world where everything is meaningful. Symptomatic of this world is Endymion's description of 'that fish – thy fish, Cynthia, in the flood Araris – which at thy waxing is as white as the driven snow and at thy waning as black as deepest darkness' (2.1.35–7). As in Lyly's mannered prose everything is organized, so in the natural world even a fish in a far-off river reflects the power of Cynthia. Lyly's vision is for the most part controlled, stylized and centralized. But not altogether: he allows more than one view of Cynthia and her power; he disrupts the fantasy of adoration with human feeling that makes it problematic and with incidental comedy that takes off on its own. Lyly rations Cynthia's appearances, holding back her first entrance till the opening of Act 3. While this increases our feeling of her latent power, it also allows us to listen to the play of many other voices, and to sense how much of the comedy's world lies beyond her. What could have been a clear, controlled allegory, harnessing the extravagance of romance to a central idea, the compliment to the Queen, becomes exploratory and eclectic. The play adds to the overt debates between high and low love and between love and friendship an implicit debate between the claims of the stylized, authoritarian perspective of allegory and a more open, natural vision.

Notes

1 Reavley Gair, *The Children of Paul's: The Story of a Theatre Company, 1553–1608*, Cambridge, 1982, pp. 44–55, 67.

2 Michael Shapiro, *Children of the Revels*, New York, 1977, pp. 13–14.

3 *John Lyly: The Humanist as Courtier*, London, 1962, p. 106.

4 Unless otherwise specified, all references to Shakespeare are to *The Complete Works of Shakespeare*, ed. David Bevington, New York, 1992.

5 Hunter, *Lyly*, p. 77.

6 Michael Pincombe, *The Plays of John Lyly: Eros and Eliza*, Manchester and New York, 1996, pp. 87–8.

7 'The Oddity of Lyly's *Endimion*', *The Elizabethan Theatre V*, ed. G.R. Hibbard, Toronto, 1975, p. 94.

8 All references to *Endymion* are to the Revels edition, ed. David Bevington, Manchester and New York, 1996.

9 Bevington speculates that Tophas and the Watch, who refer to other characters as 'children' and 'boys', were played by adults (Revels, pp. 57–8). But the effect might have been more comic if they too were boys, albeit older ones.

10 'The Court and the Dramatists', *Elizabethan Theatre*, ed. John Russell Brown and Bernard Harris, London, 1966, p. 180.

11 Bevington suggests the sleep reflects Endymion's sense of Cynthia's distance and indifference (Revels, p. 22). There is some question as to whether the song, which appears not in the first edition (1591) but in Edward Blount's 1632 collection of Lyly's comedies, is authentic. Bevington judges it is (Revels, pp. 2–3); Michael Pincombe considers it 'a later addition by another hand' (*Plays*, p. 100).

12 *Of Chastity and Power: Elizabethan Literature and the Unmarried Queen*, London and New York, 1989, pp. 129, 131.

13 David Bevington offers a complementary psychological reading, seeing the vision as reflecting Endymion's 'mingled fear and love toward his queen': *Tudor Drama and Politics: A Critical Approach to Topical Meaning*, Cambridge, Mass., 1968, p. 182.

14 See *The Complete Works of John Lyly*, III, ed. R. Warwick Bond, Oxford, 1902, pp. 10, 81–103.

15 Hunter notes Elizabeth's dislike of topical comment, and casts doubt on theories that Endymion represents Leicester or Oxford (*John Lyly*, pp. 148–9, 186–9). Bevington was equally sceptical in 1968 (*Tudor*, pp. 178–84) but in his recent Revels edition identifies Endymion with Oxford, Tellus with Mary Queen of Scots, Dipsas with the Whore of Babylon and (more tentatively) Sir Tophas with Philip of Spain (pp. 27–35, 43).

16 Saccio, 'Oddity', pp. 95–8.

17 *John Lyly*, pp. 107–10.

18 In 'John Lyly's *Endimion*', *Studies in English Literature*, XIV, 1974, Sallie Bond suggests that the rest of the court (Cynthia excepted) should age along with Endymion, and makes elaborate suggestions about changing wigs and beards (pp. 196–7). Carolyn Ruth Swift Lenz, 'The Allegory of Wisdom in Lyly's *Endimion*', *Comparative Drama*, X, 1976, disagrees (pp. 248–9); so does Bevington (Revels, p. 55). In fact the text is against it: there are references late in the play to Tellus's youth (5.4.41–2) and Sir Tophas's just-appearing beard (5.2.17–22).

19 Martin Butler, 'Private and Occasional Drama', *The Cambridge Companion to English Renaissance Drama*, ed. A.R. Braunmuller and Michael Hattaway, Cambridge, 1990, p. 131. See also Frances A. Yates, *Astraea: The Imperial Theme in the Sixteenth Century*, London, 1975, repr. 1985, pp. 104–5.

20 Introducing the proverbial expression as mere nonsense helps Lyly to control its dangerously bawdy possibilities.

21 Butler, 'Private', p. 131. Pincombe identifies the frustration as Lyly's own (*Plays*, p. 86).

22 Pincombe, *Plays*, p. 94.

23 Robert S. Knapp, 'The Monarchy of Love in Lyly's *Endimion*', *Modern Philology*, LXXIII, 1976, 357. Lenz equates Endymion's forty years' sleep with the periods of ordeal in the Bible ('Allegory', pp. 252–3).

24 Saccio, 'Oddity', p. 107.

25 Pincombe, *Plays*, p. 98.

26 *Plays*, p. 106.

27 *The Court Comedies of John Lyly*, Princeton, 1969, p. 180. Saccio capitalizes Truth because at this point he is reading the play as an allegory of the Four Daughters of God.

28 Anthony Harris, *Night's Black Agents: Witchcraft and Magic in Seventeenth-century English Drama*, Manchester, 1980, p. 28. See also K.M. Briggs, *Pale Hecate's Team*, London, 1962, p. 64.

29 'Comedy', *Cambridge Companion*, p. 272.

3

Greene, *Friar Bacon and Friar Bungay*

TO move from Lyly's *Endymion* to Robert Greene's *Friar Bacon and Friar Bungay* is to move into the open air. The play was produced at the Rose, somewhere between 1589 and Greene's death in 1592. The Rose, whose foundations, excavated in 1989, gave us our first direct look at the ground-plan of an Elizabethan public playhouse, was a fourteen-sided polygon with a stage at the north end of its yard, and the typical public-playhouse arrangement by which the groundlings in the yard crowded around the stage while more high-paying spectators watched from the surrounding galleries. The yard was open to the sky, and to the elements. The audience was a mixture of social classes. The playhouse was located in Southwark, south of the Thames; as with other public playhouses, its suburban setting put it in a somewhat disreputable area, outside the jurisdiction of the London authories with their persistent hostility to the theatre.

If Lyly offered entertainment for the court, and for a small public that wanted a taste of court fare, Greene's art was in every sense popular. The source for his play was a prose romance, *The Famous History of Friar Bacon*, whose first surviving edition dates from 1627[1] (well after Greene's death) suggesting that earlier editions had been read to pieces. Several performances at the Rose are recorded between 1592 and 1594; Thomas Middleton was commissioned to write a prologue and epilogue (not extant) for a court performance in 1602; and the title page of the 1630 reprint indicates that even at that late date the play was still in repertoire. Greene's own literary career was eclectic: in the course of a dissolute, impecunious and generally untidy life he wrote plays, prose romances, and journalistic pamphlets purporting to expose the underworld. If Lyly's play is directed in the first instance at the Queen, Greene's is directed at anyone who will pay the price of admission.

We have seen that Cynthia's power over her world is not total; but unquestionably she is the centre of authority. In *Friar Bacon and Friar Bungay* there is no single centre. Power, authority and dramatic interest are dispersed over a wide field. The magic of Friar Bacon, the attractions of Margaret (heroine of the romantic plot), the social power of Edward, Prince of Wales and the political authority of his father King Henry all compete for attention. As in the medieval religous drama that was still a recent memory and a living influence, Heaven and Hell (particularly Hell) are also sources of power to reckon with. But in Greene's play, as we shall see, there is no one controlling power, no place – not even Heaven – that matters more than any other. The monarch in particular is sidelined. King Henry has none of Cynthia's dramatic prominence, and his role is largely confined to presiding over festivities and showing off the achievments of his subjects to a group of visiting European dignitaries.[2]

In *Endymion* there is little sense of *where* we are. Loyalty is directed towards a person, not a land. In *Friar Bacon* the focus is reversed: an important part of the play's business is the celebration of England – its rich pastures, famous schools, powerful wizards and beautiful women. The visiting German Emperor's tribute to Oxford is characteristic:

> Trust me, Plantaganet, these Oxford schools
> Are richly seated near the river side;
> The mountains full of fat and fallow deer,
> The battling pastures laid with kine and flocks,
> The town gorgeous with high-built colleges,
> And scholars seemly in their grave attire,
> Learned in searching principles of art.   (9.1–7)[3]

The wealth and learning of Oxford seem an emanation of the richness of the land itself.

Greene's equivalent of the glamour Marlowe found in exotic place names and displays of wealth in *Tamburlaine the Great* is the sensual pleasure of English country life. This is not realistic reporting: from the beginning there is literary heightening that establishes a style and a mood. In the opening speech (anticipating the emotionally troubled openings of Shakespearian comedies like *The Merchant of Venice* and *As You Like It*) Lacy, Earl of Lincoln, contrasts the black mood he sees in Prince Edward with the country pleasure they have just enjoyed:

> Why looks my lord like to a troubled sky
> When heaven's bright shine is shadowed with a fog?
> Alate we ran the deer, and through the lawns
> Stripped with our nags the lofty frolic bucks
> That scudded 'fore the teasers like the wind.
> Ne'er was the deer of merry Fressingfield
> So lustily pulled down by jolly mates,
> Nor shared the farmers such fat venison,
> So frankly dealt, this hundred years before;
> Nor have I seen my lord more frolic in the chase,
> And now changed to a melancholy dump.   (1.1–11)

The thick spray of adjectives is typical: all through the play the words 'jolly', 'merry' and 'frolic' recur like Homeric epithets. A sense of speed, life and open-air action runs throughout, making a sharp contrast with the courtly stasis of *Endymion*.

Edward's troubled mood is the first sign of the disruptive role he will play in the love-plot. He is in love with Margaret, daughter of the keeper of Fressingfield (a village in Suffolk), and his intentions are strictly dishonourable. When the fool Rafe suggests that he switch identities with the prince to beguile love (since love does not strike fools), the carnivalesque inversion – 'thou shalt put on my cap and my coat and my dagger, and I will put on thy clothes and thy sword, and so thou shalt be my fool' (1.31–3) – embodies not just the suggestion that Edward is a fool for love, but a mocking challenge to all authority. Falstaff's impersonation of the King in the tavern play in *1 Henry IV*, and the ironic role-switches Lear's fool proposes to his master, are in the same tradition.

In the long run Greene restrains the effect: to let Edward pursue his love in secret, Rafe impersonates the prince (unconvincingly) but Edward does not impersonate Rafe. In his new role Rafe is disruptive, but within limits. He and the other courtiers are involved in a tavern brawl in which, according to the Constable, they nearly kill a vintner (7.39). But the upshot of the incident is to demonstrate that the gentry can get away with anything: the Oxford authorities are mollified as soon as they learn the identity of the brawlers: 'courtiers may make greater scapes than these. / Will't please your honour dine with me today?' (7.115–16). Rafe, brawling in the prince's person, suggests a displaced version of the wild Prince Hal tradition, and the scene touches on the disreputable underworld that counters authority in many contemporary history plays – genuinely rough and violent in the anonymous *The Famous Victories of Henry the Fifth* (c.1588), tamed but still recognizable in Shakespeare's *Henry IV* plays. But these (apart from Rafe and Bacon's servant Miles) are high-class louts, the Oxford dons defer to the court, and one of the courtiers promises to 'satisfy the vinter for his hurt' (7.117–18). (You can do anything you like to the lower orders so long as you tip them properly.) Class authority is confirmed, and the incident concludes amicably. Rafe's most acutely disruptive comedy touches not the prince but the university, his threat to 'make a ship that shall hold all your colleges, and so carry away the Niniversity with a fair wind to the Bankside in Southwark' (7.73–6). He is not just drawing on the Ship of Fools tradition; he is evoking the Bankside playhouse where the Oxford characters are currently being impersonated, taking a fool's privilege of disrupting the play with metatheatrical jokes.

Edward's authority is challenged not so much by Rafe as by the superior power of love. He sets Lacy to woo for him, and Lacy falls in love with Margaret himself – more honourably than Edward, for he intends to marry her. Lacy has a brief internal struggle in which (reversing the priorities of the fountain scene in *Endymion*) he chooses love over friendship, and counters the charge of treachery by noting that he is honourably restraining Edward's lust. Love, he declares, 'makes no exception of a friend, / Nor deems it of a prince but as a man' (6.58–9). Edward at first is angry, and demands Margaret for himself: 'Edward or none shall conquer Margaret' (8.52). But then he realizes that in such a conquest he would lose:

> Edward, art thou that famous Prince of Wales
> Who at Damasco beat the Saracens,
> And brought'st home triumph on thy lance's point,
> And shall thy plumes be pulled by Venus down?   (8.112–15)

He thinks of what is fitting for an English prince, and wins the victory not just over Venus but over himself: 'Conquering thyself, thou get'st the richest spoil' (8.121). This is one of a number of moments of choice and renunciation in the play, as characters weigh the claims of conflicting powers and conflicting loyalties. Edward sees himself as more truly a prince in surrendering his power than he was in exercising it.

Edward's desire for Margaret, and Rafe's ironic role as the prince's adviser, provide the first occasion for the magic of Friar Bacon. For all its entertainment value – and much of the play's energy derives from this – Bacon's magic, like Edward's authority, is problematic from the start. It is Rafe who first proposes that Edward enlist Bacon in his campaign to win

Margaret. Rafe sees something improper and disruptive in Bacon's magic: 'he can make women of devils, and juggle cats into costermongers … he shall turn me into thee' (1.96–101). Edward immediately sees a connection between this carnivalesque inversion and his own illicit desires:

> For why our country Margaret is so coy[,]
> And stands so much upon her honest points,
> That marriage or no market with the maid,
> Ermsby, it must be nigromantic spells
> And charms of art that must enchain her love …   (1.121–5)

In the source, Bacon helps a pair of young lovers against the girl's father, acting the role of the clever servant in a New Comedy plot; his role here, acting on Edward's behalf, is to disrupt Lacy's marriage to Margaret. His first major use of his magic works against the sympathies of the play, and, given his evident status as the play's hero, the audience will find its own sympathies pulled in different directions.

Initially, Bacon seems all-powerful. When Edward reacts badly to an impudent joke from Bacon's servant Miles – 'Gog's wounds! Warren, kill him' (5.55) – Bacon makes Edward and his friends unable to draw their weapons. There are no magic passes, no fireworks; Bacon's mere presence is enough: 'Could you not judge when all your swords grew fast / That Friar Bacon was not far from hence?' (5.76–7). He goes on to penetrate their disguises and read their minds. He takes a showman's pride in his power; Andrew V. Ettin has noted his habit of speaking of himself in the third person, a sign that he is 'always "on"'.[4] While the Oxford authorities are daunted when they learn the brawlers are gentlemen, Bacon will not defer even to royalty. He denies that the Prince of Wales has any right to strike his servant: 'What means the English prince to wrong my man?' (5.71–2). Yet, like Lyly's Dipsas, he has no power over love. When Edward asks him to win Margaret for him, Bacon goes silent and thoughtful (5.107–9). He can let Edward watch Lacy and Margaret through his magic glass, and he can block their wedding by reducing Friar Bungay, who tries to conduct it, to inarticulate stammering: *'Bungay is mute, crying, "Hud, hud"'* (6.151.1). Like Cynthia he can command silence; but he cannot win Margaret for Edward, or make Margaret and Lacy out of love with each other.[5]

His clearest triumph comes when he is playing for England. At this point there is no conflict in the audience's sympathies. The visiting Emperor has brought his own magician from Germany; his full name, Don Jacques Vandermast (7.16), is a sinister combination of Spanish, French and German; he boasts of victories over scholars in the major European universities.[6] National pride is at stake. In the first round Vandermast defeats Friar Bungay. Bungay conjures up a tree with a dragon shooting fire; Vandermast conjures up a spirit representing Hercules, who breaks the branches of the tree; Bungay is unable to stop him. But as Vandermast glories in his victory, Bacon enters, naming himself with a quiet authority that cuts across the German's voluble boasting: 'Men call me Bacon' (9.121). (For a moment, the ideal casting would seem to be Clint Eastwood.) Bacon defeats Vandermast, again without stage effects: in his presence the spirit of Hercules is unable to act. He then commands the spirit to transport Vandermast back to Germany, and King Henry congratulates him: 'Bacon, thou hast honoured England with thy skill, / And made fair Oxford famous by thine art' (9.165–6).[7]

Yet there may be a small shadow over the triumph. Vandermast, a sulky loser, mutters that 'Bacon doth more than art' (9.147), implying something suspect in his power. In fact it is clear throughout the play that Bacon's magic is diabolical; the spirits he commands come from Hell. The sequence that leads to Bacon's repentance begins with the failure of his next major project, the brazen head that by speaking 'strange and uncouth aphorisms' (2.172) will help him compass his grand design, surrounding England with a wall of brass. Whether England *needs* a wall of brass is a question: when King Henry welcomes his foreign visitors 'To England's shore, whose promontory cleeves / Shows Albion is another little world' (4.6–7) he claims that England has its own natural defences. Bacon's pride, however, is invested in the project. In his first scene he humiliates his fellow scholar Burden for doubting the brazen head, demonstrating what Burden is up to in his frequent visits to Henley by conjuring up '*a Woman with a shoulder of mutton on a spit, and a Devil*' (2.118.1–2). ('Mutton' being a slang term for prostitute, there is more to the revelation than Burden's eating habits.) Yet Bacon's easy victory over Burden is ironic in retrospect: the brazen head proves his own undoing.

There is a recurring motif in magic tales in which one symbolic object holds the key to a magician's power. In George Peele's *The Old Wives Tale* (c.1592) the magic of the evil conjurer Sacrapant depends on a light inside a glass buried under the earth; when the glass is broken and the light put out, his power dies. Bacon has so much credit invested in the brazen head that it becomes such an object. On the night the head is due to speak, Bacon and Bungay, who have watched by turns for sixty days, are unable to stay awake; Bacon tells his servant Miles to watch, and to wake him if the head speaks. Everything depends on the most vulnerable point, Bacon's clownish servant. Bacon warns him, 'If that a wink but shut thy watchful eye, / Then farewell Bacon's glory and his fame' (11.36-7). The head speaks, Miles fails to wake his master, and the experiment ends in ruin. Kerstin Assarsson-Rizzi sees Bacon's trust of Miles as an Aristotelean *hamartia*, a tragic error;[8] in an idiosyncratic and provocative reading, William Empson sees Miles's role as exemplifying the importance of involving the common people in magic, and declares he 'was right ... in letting the head spoil'.[9]

Miles, who has a clown's interest in matters like food and drink, lives at the level of physical reality. It is at that level that Bacon is defeated; dependent on his own body, he cannot stay awake. The head speaks three times, and its pronouncements are simple: 'Time is ... Time was ... Time is past' (11.55, 67, 77). Told to expect 'strange and uncouth aphorisms' (11.20), Miles refuses to wake his master until the head says something more interesting than this. In fact the head is declaring the basic condition of life: the inexorable passage of time, which Cynthia can control and Bacon cannot. Bacon is defeated by the power that defeats us all, and he laments, 'My life, my fame, my glory, all are past' (10.99).

He also sees his fate as one of the special defeats of tragedy, the fall of an overreacher. He has stressed throughout that while he calls up demonic forces he can control them. Now he sees he has presumed too far:

> But proud Astmeroth, ruler of the north,
> And Demogorgon, master of the fates,
> Grudge that a mortal man should work so much.
> Hell trembled at my deep, commanding spells;
> Fiends frowned to see a man their over-match.
> Bacon might boast more than a man might boast ...   (11.110-15)

It is also possible that the judgement has come not from below, but from above: '*a lightning flasheth forth, and a hand appears that breaketh down the Head with a hammer*' (11.76.1-3). According to Kurt Tetzeli von Rosador, 'Emblematic tradition ... images God as ... a hand'.[10]

One more incident, however, is required to bring Bacon from regret to repentance. Two students, sworn friends, ask to use Bacon's magic glass to see what their fathers, Lambert and Serlsby, also friends, are doing. They see their fathers kill each other in a fight over Margaret, and in rage the students repeat their fathers' action, leaving four corpses on the stage. Bacon, who earlier could prevent Edward and his followers from using their weapons and reach into the distant place shown in the glass to strike Bungay with dumbness, has no power to prevent the killings. Throughout the scene he seems flat and exhausted, depressed by the failure of the brazen head. When Bacon used the glass to let Edward watch Lacy and Margaret, he told him, 'Be still, my lord, and mark the comedy' (6.48). In the Lambert–Serlsby scene, as the fathers appear in the glass with rapiers and daggers, Bacon declares, 'Bungay, I smell there will be a tragedy' (13.36). Instead of preventing the sons from looking he tells them, echoing his instructions to Edward, 'Sit still, my friends, and see the event' (13.63). Each scene with the glass presents a play within the play. The first is a comedy, in which Bacon can intervene and which to some extent he can control. The second is a tragedy, and Bacon seems fatalistically determined to let the tragedy run its course. When the brazen head was smashed, Bacon lamented the loss of his own fame and power. Now he goes a stage further, seeing his magic as evil in its effects – 'This glass prospective worketh many woes' (13.76) – and using one of the students' weapons he breaks it himself.

Throughout the play the diabolical source of Bacon's power has been clear. It has also been treated as a non-problem. Bacon has not, like Faustus, sold his soul. He controls the fiends; he even claims to control Satan himself:

> The great arch-ruler, potentate of hell,
> Trembles, when Bacon bids him or his fiends
> Bow to the force of his pentageron. (2.49–51)

Bacon's audiences, for the most part, simply enjoy his achievements. His Oxford colleague Clement sets the general attitude:

> Bacon, we come not grieving at thy skill,
> But joying that our academy yields
> A man supposed the wonder of the world ... (2.36–8)

The theatre audience seems invited to take the same attitude. But the tragedy of the mirror, coming on top of the failure of the brazen head, leads Bacon himself to repent, accuse himself of blasphemy and renounce his magic in serious Christian terms:

> Bacon must be damned
> For using devils to countervail his God.
> Yet, Bacon, cheer thee, drown not in despair.
> Sins have their salves. Repentance can do much.

Think Mercy sits where Justice holds her seat, ·
And from those wounds those bloody Jews did pierce,
Which by thy magic oft did bleed afresh,
From thence for thee the dew of mercy drops
To wash the wrath of high Jehovah's ire,
And make thee as a new-born babe from sin.
Bungay, I'll spend the remnant of my life
In pure devotion, praying to my God
That he would save what Bacon vainly lost. (13.96–108)

The most startling information here is that Bacon has used his magic to toy with the Crucifixion; but because of that Crucifixion even this blasphemy can be forgiven. The higher power of Heaven, which has seemed irrelevant through most of the play, now seems the only power that matters, and Bacon submits to it, acknowledging that his own power was not just empty but dangerous.

The fun is over, but in a larger sense not the comedy. Bacon's fate is the reverse of Faustus's; in spiritual terms, he has a happy ending. (It is tempting to see Greene's comedy as a reply to Marlowe's tragedy, but the likelihood is that Greene's play was written first.)[11] The story of Bacon allows the audience both to enjoy the magic show and to register misgivings about the source of Bacon's power, his use of it, its limits and the pride he has invested in it.[12] In the end, having steered close to tragedy, Bacon avoids it, not by clinging to his power but, like Edward, by surrendering it.

In many ways his story runs parallel to that of Margaret. Her beauty, like his magic, is an enchanting, dangerous power.[13] The disaster of the second scene with the glass, in which Lambert and Serlsby kill each other in their rivalry over Margaret, links these powers together. Margaret brings fame to Fressingfield as Bacon brings fame to Oxford. Lambert calls her

Suffolk's fair Helen and rich England's star,
Whose beauty tempered with her huswifery
Makes England talk of merry Fressingfield! (10.35–7)

Edward's first sight of her associates her with the richness and sensual pleasures of the land as Oxford is linked to the lush pastures that surround it:

She turned her smock over her lily arms
And dived them into the milk to run her cheese;
But, whiter than the milk, her crystal skin,

> Checked with lines of azure, made her blush,
> That art or nature durst bring for compare.   (1.79–83)[14]

But in the same speech Edward compares her to Venus and Pallas, two of the three goddesses in the story of the judgement of Paris, linked with the start of the Trojan war. He goes on to compare her to Lucrece, and himself to Tarquin (86–8). Lambert's tribute to her beauty compares her to Helen, and Margaret herself sees the danger in the image:

> Should I be Helen in my froward fates,
> As I am Helen in my matchless hue,
> And set rich Suffolk with my face afire?   (10.93–5)

The classical references make Margaret a source of danger to the men she attracts. She is also in danger herself, as she is compared to women who suffered terrible fates: Lucrece, Semele, Danaë (1.86–8, 3.14–18, 10.117). The allusions evoke the Trojan war, and women destroyed by men or by the power of gods.[15]

When Edward finds his true destiny in betrothal to Eleanor of Castile, he compares himself to Paris being smitten with Helen, and Apollo with Daphne (12.6–11) and for once the suggestions of danger are switched off; but they operate strongly for Margaret. She causes the deaths of four men, and it looks for a while as though she herself has been betrayed by Lacy. As the diabolical nature of Bacon's magic is for most of the play a problem everyone agrees to ignore, the violation of class barriers involved in her affair with Lacy – when he offers marriage, she declares, 'I little think that earls will stoop so low' (6.121) – seems at first to be no bar to love. She promises to make class difference part of their marriage, being 'A wife in name, but servant in obedience' (6.124), and that seems to resolve the question. But there is something disingenuous in her refusal of Lambert and Serlsby on the grounds that she is too humble to wed a wealthy local squire (10.47–8), when in fact she has accepted the Earl of Lincoln. Moments later she receives a letter from Lacy breaking off the engagement, declaring her 'but mean dainties' (10.129–30), announcing his engagement to a Spanish lady, and (like Warren tipping the vintner he has beaten) paying her off with £100. Like Bacon harnessing the powers of Hell, like Semele and Danaë having affairs with gods, Margaret has aimed too high, and is paying the price.

Or so it seems; there are hints that the letter is not what it appears. But Margaret takes it seriously, and follows Bacon's lead in renouncing the fame and power her beauty gave her and dedicating herself to Heaven. In a

scene that follows directly after Bacon's repentance, she appears dressed
as a nun, ready to enter a convent. As Bacon has chosen the wrong power,
Margaret has chosen the wrong love, and now she turns her life around by
reversing her choice:

> I lovèd once; Lord Lacy was my love;
> And now I hate myself for that I loved,
> And doted more on him than on my God.   (14.12–14)

Her repentance, like Bacon's, is serious and specifically Christian:
'Farewell to friends and father; welcome, Christ' (14.30). Her father tries to
draw her back to the world, invoking her fame: 'Oh, bury not such beauty
in a cell, / That England hath held famous for the hue' (14.2–3). This is the
equivalent to the regret for lost glory Bacon feels at the failure of the brazen
head. It is not enough to deflect Margaret's repentance, but coming as it
does at the beginning of the scene it may allow the audience a divided
response to her choice of Heaven over earth.

What follows brings us back to earth with a crash. Lacy and his
friends enter, '*booted and spurred*' (14.38.1). The sheer sound of their
entrance will have a breezy macho quality, and Ermsby's comment on the
sight of Margaret and her father, 'The old lecher hath gotten holy mutton
to him. A nun, my lord' (14.44–5), is so crass in its comedy that its attempt
to bring us back to the pleasures of life may well backfire. Lacy's own
rebuke is not much better:

> A nun? What holy father taught you this,
> To task yourself to such a tedious life
> As die a maid? 'Twere injury to me
> To smother up such beauty in a cell.   (14.54–7)

As to the letter that has caused her such pain, and led to her repentance,
Lacy dismisses it with wave of his hand: ''Twas but to try sweet Peggy's
constancy' (14.73). He seems to be saying, don't you recognize a plot
convention when you see one?

At this point the modern reader may well feel that Margaret's
response to Lacy should be a swift uppercut to the jaw. She holds out for a
while – 'Margaret hath made a vow which may not be revoked' (14.78) –
but after a brief struggle she surrenders:

> The flesh is frail. My lord doth know it well,
> That when he comes with his enchanting face,
> Whatsoe'er betide, I cannot say him nay.

> Off goes the habit of a maiden's heart;
> And, seeing Fortune will, fair Fremingham,
> And all the show of holy nuns, farewell.
> Lacy for me, if he will be my lord. (14.86–92)

She eases her surrender by changing the terms of the problem: the commanding power is no longer God but Fortune, and convent life is a matter not of prayer but of show. Ermsby puts her choice starkly: 'God or Lord Lacy' (14.83). God loses.

For Greene's first audience the letter trick might have seemed acceptable as part of the Patient Griselda motif, in which Margaret's constancy is tested;[16] and their Protestant sympathies would endorse the brusque dismissal of the convent. When Lacy responds to Margaret's surrender by asking what she has for breakfast, and she replies, 'Butter and cheese and humbles of a deer' (14.107), his assumption that she belongs in the kitchen jars on modern sensibilities, but puts us firmly back in the world of sensual pleasure – food, drink and hunting – in which the play, as a comedy, has spent so much of its time. Yet Margaret's choice of Lacy divides modern critics. John Weld assumes the audience's response will be 'relief and laughter'.[17] But for Charles W. Hieatt, Margaret 'sinks from a noble heroine to a doting, weak-willed girl'; and Charles W. Crupi finds this a disturbing scene, to which varied reactions are possible.[18] Before writing off such reactions as anachronistic, we should note that a mixed response is called for within the scene itself. When Ermsby asks, 'I pray thee, my Lord of Sussex, why art thou in a brown study?' Warren replies, 'To see the nature of women, that be they never so near God, yet they love to die in a man's arms' (14.101–4). The standard pun on death as orgasm makes Warren's line a joke, and draws us back to comedy. But his mood, 'a brown study', makes it a slightly troubled comedy.

In three adjacent scenes Bacon chooses Heaven, Margaret chooses earth and Miles chooses Hell. As punishment for his part in the failure of the brazen head, Bacon has sent a devil to torment him (the play, as we shall see, is ambiguous about whether Bacon's magic has actually been destroyed). When we first saw a devil in the play, in Bacon's discomfiture of Burden, it came on with the hostess of the Bell Inn at Henley, who carried a shoulder of mutton on a spit. This links Hell with the sort of pleasure that matters to Miles, and in this spirit he questions the devil about Hell: 'Have you not good tippling houses there? May not a man have a lusty fire there, a pot of good ale, a pair of cards, a swinging piece of chalk, and a brown toast that will cap a white waistcoat on a cup of good drink?' The devil replies, 'All this you may have there' (15.35–40). This does not sound like damnation: the swinging piece of chalk suggests a reckoning that need never be paid. Miles says he would like to be a tapster; the devil replies, 'Thou shalt' (15.48). Thus encouraged, Miles rides to Hell on the devil's back.

The genial comedy of the scene links Hell with the pleasures of the earth, pleasures already associated in a different way with Margaret. Like Margaret's choice, Miles's decision for Hell works against the religious solemnity of Bacon's repentance. But we notice how clipped and taciturn the devil's replies are. It is as though there are things he is not saying about the price of this pleasure, because Miles has not asked. Climbing on the devil's back, Miles assumes he can control the pace: 'if I find your pace either a trot or else uneasy, I'll put you to a false gallop; I'll make you feel my spurs' (15.64–6). Greene ends the scene with the wonderful but I think ambiguous stage direction, '*Exeunt roaring*' (15.69.1). Assuming, as the wording implies, that Miles and the devil are roaring together, are they sharing a bit of demonic energy? Or does Miles realize as the devil takes off that the devil is controlling the pace, and he has made a mistake?

Bacon's choice of Heaven is presented quite seriously, and at the time nothing challenges it. The very different choices made by Margaret and Miles go in the other direction, and the audience's judgement of them is left open. Finally, the clear impression made by Bacon's renunciation is complicated in the last scene, celebrating the joining of Edward and Eleanor, when King Henry asks Bacon why he is so silent and he replies,

> Repentant for the follies of my youth,
> That magic's secret mysteries misled,
> And joyful that this royal marriage
> Portends such bliss unto this matchless realm. (16.36–9)

This grinding change of gear introduces the last use of Bacon's magic, his prophecy of England's future under the ultimate result of this marriage, Queen Elizabeth. Has Bacon surrendered his magic or not? The shift in tenses as he introduces the prophecy leaves us wondering if it is a new achievement of his magic or an old one recalled: 'I find by deep prescience of mine art, / Which once I tempered in my secret cell' (16.42–3).[19] It may be part of the tribute to Elizabeth that for this one occasion Bacon's renunciation is suspended and he is allowed to use his magic again.[20]

Elizabeth, embodied (with some reservations) as an onstage character in *Endymion*, is here projected into a remote, golden future. She offers not a solution to the play but a vision beyond the play. She is not named, but when Bacon declares, 'From forth the royal garden of a king / Shall flourish out so rich and fair a bud' (16.45-6) the audience will have no doubt who he means. Foretelling a reign of peace, and drawing on the legend that Britain like Rome was founded by refugees from Troy, Bacon's vision completes the play's references to Paris, Helen and the Trojan war by calling London 'Troynovant' (16.44). He imagines the goddesses, including Venus, Juno and Pallas (competitors in the judgement of Paris), deferring to the superior beauty of Elizabeth. As in Peele's *The Arraignment of Paris* (c.1584) Elizabeth solves the problem of the Apple of Discord and embodies the redemption of Troy.

All this, however, is in the future. Elizabeth seems far more remote than in *Endymion*, and the play, designed for a public theatre, does not depend on her presence. In the end King Henry brings us back to the pleasures of the world, and to a celebration of England, not its monarch: the tables are spread with 'viands such as England's wealth affords' (16.70). England's wealth has been seen in many ways: the richness of its land, the beauty of Margaret, the magic of Bacon. Even Hell seems a good English pub. The last note Henry strikes, however, is not just celebratory but competitive: 'Thus glories England over all the west' (16.76). The play, I have suggested, offers different centres of power, in contrast to the single-centred vision of *Endymion*. It also shows powers in competition, bringing the debating format of the Tudor interlude more fully into the action. In the lead-in to the magic contest Burden and Vandermast debate the opposing claims of pyromancy (fire-magic) and geomancy (earth-magic). Vandermast defeats Bungay, to be beaten in turn by Bacon. Bacon wins easy victories over Burden and Vandermast, but not over the love of Margaret and Lacy, or the demands of his own body when it requires sleep. Edward may beat the Saracens but he has to let Lacy claim Margaret. Margaret herself, whose beauty gives her power over men, surrenders first to Heaven, and then to Lacy as her lord. Even God is not invincible: he may have won Bacon's soul, but he loses a round to Lacy, and Bacon's repentance is put on hold for the sake of Elizabeth. Bacon, Margaret and Miles, all sympathetic characters, choose different destinations in the grand scheme of things. In its presentation of the pleasures of life, the play shifts back and forth between celebration and renunciation.[21] The uncertainties that touch *Endymion* are more pervasive here. There is no power that is not vulnerable, and Bacon's power, the most prominent in the play, is the most vulnerable of all.

Notes

1 J.A. Lavin, Introduction to the New Mermaid edition of *Friar Bacon and Friar Bungay*, London, 1969, p. xiv.

2 For a very different reading, giving Henry a commanding central role, see Charles W. Hieatt, 'Multiple Plotting in *Friar Bacon and Friar Bungay*', *Renaissance Drama*, n.s. XVI, 1985, 21–3. Kurt Tetzeli von Rosador reads the spectacle of the final scene as a celebration of royal authority, though he adds that the play ultimately subverts this authority: see 'The Sacralizing Sign: Religion and Magic in Bale, Greene, and the Early Shakespeare', *Yearbook of English Studies*, XXIII, 1993, 40.

3 All references to *Friar Bacon and Friar Bungay* are to the text in *Drama of the English Renaissance, I: The Tudor Period*, ed. Russell A. Fraser and Norman Rabkin, New York, 1976.

4 'Magic into Art: The Magician's Renunciation of Magic in English Renaissance Drama', *Texas Studies in Language and Literature*, XIX, 1977, 277.

5 Anthony Harris, *Night's Black Agents: Witchcraft and Magic in Seventeenth-century English Drama*, Manchester, 1980, p. 122.

6 In a production at the University of Guelph in 1966, Vandermast sported a Kaiser Wilhelm moustache.

7 The nationalist element in Bacon's victory suggests a popularized version of the actual ambitions of John Dee, who wanted to use occult arts to further what he saw as England's God-given mission to bring about a new Golden Age. See John S. Mebane, *Renaissance Magic and the Return of the Golden Age*, Lincoln and London, 1989, pp. 84–6.

8 *Friar Bacon and Friar Bungay: A Structural and Thematic Analysis of Robert Greene's Play*, Lund, 1972, p. 30.

9 *Some Versions of Pastoral*, London, 1935, repr. 1986, pp. 33–4. Empson calls Miles 'the fool who becomes the critic' (p. 34). John Weld compares his relation to Bacon with Rafe's relation to Edward; in both cases the servant takes the master's place, and exemplifies his folly. See *Meaning in Comedy: Studies in Elizabethan Romantic Comedy*, Albany, 1975, pp. 142–3.

10 'Sacralizing', p. 39.

11 Lavin, Introduction, p. xii. On the longstanding opposition of the church to the practice of magic, see Keith Thomas, *Religion and the Decline of Magic*, New York, 1971, pp. 253–63.

12 Harris notes that, while Bacon avoids Faustus's fate, 'like Faustus, he lacks the humility and discipline of the magus; he too is motivated largely by a desire for fame and honour' (*Agents*, p. 121).

13 Empson, *Versions*, p. 33.

14 According to Cecile Williamson Cary, milk is linked in the iconographic tradition with health and virtue: 'The Iconography of Food and the Motif of World Order in *Friar Bacon and Friar Bungay*', *Comparative Drama*, XIII, 1979, 154.

15 On the play's use of classical allusions, see Assarsson-Rizzi, *Friar*, pp. 116–21.

16 Assarsson-Rizzi, *Friar*, p. 72.

17 *Meaning*, p. 145.

18 Hieatt, 'Plotting', p. 33; Crupi, *Robert Greene*, Boston, 1986, pp. 126–9.

19 Foretelling the future was one of the uses of magic the church particularly condemned: see Thomas, *Religion*, p. 255.

20 Greene's public, celebratory ending is very different from the ending of the source, in which Bacon dies after two years as a penitent recluse, never leaving his cell.

21 Weld, *Meaning*, pp. 146–8.

4

Shakespeare, *A Midsummer Night's Dream*

A MIDSUMMER *Night's Dream*, like *Friar Bacon and Friar Bungay*, is a creation of the public theatre. It was performed by the Lord Chamberlain's Men, around 1595 or 1596, at the Theatre in the northern suburb of Shoreditch. Many scholars have speculated that it was also performed at, and perhaps commissioned for, an aristocratic wedding; for some the speculation amounts to a certainty, and the only problem is to determine which wedding. In fact there is not a shred of evidence, internal or external, to support this theory; it is a self-perpetuating tradition with no basis in fact.[1] When we think of the play's original performance it is best to think not of an elegant occasion with a courtly audience in a candle-lit hall but of a normal afternoon in an outdoor playhouse (possibly a bit run-down: the Theatre was twenty years old by this time) with rulers, aristocrats, clowns and fairies exposed in daylight to an audience almost as miscellaneous as the play's cast of characters. Shakespeare was not, in the first instance, an entertainer to the court or the gentry but a working professional playwright, an actor and a shareholder in his company, which had established itself as the leading company of its time. He wrote for the paying public.

His comedy, like Greene's, has a wide focus. Power and authority are dispersed over various centres, and no one centre dominates the others. The play opens with Theseus, its highest temporal authority, not in his public role as ruler but in his private role as a man impatient for his wedding night. Like Endymion depending on Cynthia's power, he is waiting for the moon to change:

> Now, fair Hippolyta, our nuptial hour
> Draws on apace. Four happy days bring in

> Another moon – but O, methinks, how slow
> This old moon wanes! She lingers my desires
> Like to a stepdame or a dowager
> Long withering out a young man's revenue.   (1.1.1–6)[2]

In the Renaissance Theseus had an unsavoury reputation, which the play will later touch on (2.1.77–80), as a man who habitually raped and abandoned women.[3] One hint of this in his opening speech may be the fact that he refers to his desires, not Hippolyta's. But if rape is an expression of uncontrolled male power, that power is now (like Edward's in *Friar Bacon*) reined in. Theseus has submitted to the conventional requirement of abstinence before marriage, on which Prospero will lay great stress in *The Tempest*, and he knows, despite his impatience, that he simply has to wait. He imagines himself not as a mighty ruler but as an ordinary man dependent on a relative for his estate. The moon, embodied in Cynthia in *Endymion*, will haunt the language of this play; it makes its first appearance as a malignant old woman, against whom Theseus feels powerless.

In reply, Hippolyta not only counsels patience but hints that he is making a neeedless fuss:

> Four days will quickly steep themselves in night;
> Four nights will quickly dream away the time;
> And then the moon, like to a silver bow
> New bent in heaven, shall behold the night
> Of our solemnities.   (1.1.7–11)

In this debate Hippolyta may be said to have the edge. The play's double-time scheme – by the end the four days have somehow collapsed into two – confirms her claim that the time will pass quickly. For the audience it will be more like two hours. The inconsistency may also suggest the belief that time spent among the fairies passes at a different rate from time in the normal world.[4] In any case, Hippolyta's sense of time – lightness and speed – is a better prediction of the play's action and manner than Theseus's fear that the days will drag. Her view of the moon is also more positive; the new-bent bow suggests an arrow about to be fired (like Cupid's dart, which turns an ordinary flower into a love-charm), an action about to begin. It also evokes the moon-goddess Diana, huntress, protectress of women and patroness of chastity; Theseus will indeed have to wait. The issue between Theseus and Hippolyta is not just impatience versus patience but male desire against female control. It is a debate that will be repeated in the woods when Lysander asks to sleep beside Hermia and she insists he keep his distance.

This is also Hippolyta's last speech in the scene, though far from her last speech in the play. The silence into which she lapses having made her point reminds us that she is not just a bride but a captive. Our first impression is of an urbane, good-humoured couple who address each other on equal terms; but Theseus reveals what lies behind that relationship when he recalls, 'Hippolyta, I wooed thee with my sword, / And won thy love doing thee injuries'. When he promises to wed her 'in another key – / With pomp, with triumph, and with revelling' (1.1.16–19) we may reflect that a triumph traditionally included a procession of captives.[5] As an Amazon she represents (like Radigund in Book V of *The Faerie Queene*) a female power threatening male authority; Theseus has subdued that power by force.[6] Yet he sees his coming marriage as an 'everlasting bond of fellowship' (1.1.85). This mixed view of their relationship raises questions about the relations between men and women – passing fancy or permanent commitment, dominance or fellowship? – that will run through the play, providing a deeper exploration of love than we have seen in *Endymion* or *Friar Bacon*.

The impression of Theseus's power is quickly deflated when his command for general merrymaking is countered as soon as it is uttered: Egeus enters 'Full of vexation ... with complaint / Against my child, my daughter Hermia' (1.1.22–3). Not only does Egeus cut across the mood Theseus has tried to establish; the ruler finds himself dealing with a domestic squabble in which his own hands are tied by the law. He is as far as he could be from the stage tyrant, the part to tear a cat in, that Bottom briefly impersonates. The issue shifts to Hermia, her control over her own life as opposed to her father's claim of absolute power over her; the next part of the scene centres on her. If Theseus tries to cover his power over Hippolyta by changing war to merrymaking and conquest to fellowship, Egeus's assertion of his power over his daughter is harshly naked. He wants her to marry Demetrius; she wants to marry Lysander; he invokes a law by which he can give her 'either to this gentleman, / Or to her death' (1.1.43–4). He virtually equates the two possibilities, since they both show his power. It is Theseus who recalls (prompted by Hermia, who seems to sense her father is not telling the whole truth) that there is a third possibility: she could enter a nunnery. Egeus wants her obedient, or dead.

Theseus claims to be bound by the law 'Which by no means we may extenuate' (1.1.120). The most he can do is drop hints that once he gets Egeus and Demetrius alone he will try to talk them around (1.1.114–16). He expounds the theory behind the law, a theory Louis Adrian Montrose has called 'a fantasy of male parthenogenesis':[7]

> What say you, Hermia? Be advised, fair maid.
> To you your father should be as a god,
> One that composed your beauties, yea, and one
> To whom you are but as a form in wax,
> By him imprinted, and within his power
> To leave the figure or disfigure it.
> Demetrius is a worthy gentleman. (1.1.46–52)

He tries to speak gently, and in the end he offers a reason for submission other than Egeus's power. But that power, as he describes it, is total, and he expounds it with an eloquence that conveys his belief in it. Egeus, and Egeus alone, gave her life. The image Theseus uses is not organic but mechanical, the printing of a form on inert matter. He seems to forget that there was at some stage of this process a pregnant woman. This plays into Egeus's demand for obedience or death; she is her father's daughter, or she is nothing.[8]

The abolition of monastic orders in England denied women one means of independent life and, for those who could have risen to be abbesses, a chance to exercise authority. When Theseus describes to Hermia her other possibility, a cloistered life, he tries to make it sound unattractive:

> For aye to be in shady cloister mewed,
> To live a barren sister all your life,
> Chanting faint hymns to the cold fruitless moon.
> Thrice blessèd they that master so their blood
> To undergo such maiden pilgrimage;
> But earthlier happy is the rose distilled
> Than that which, withering on the virgin thorn,
> Grows, lives, and dies, in single blessedness. (1.1.71–8)

He is asking, in effect, wouldn't you rather go to bed with a man, any man, than live like this? Her reply is not the one he is fishing for:

> So will I grow, so live, so die, my lord,
> Ere I will yield my virgin patent up
> Unto his lordship, whose unwishèd yoke
> My soul consents not to give sovereignty. (1.1.79–82)

She seems prepared to make the choice that Margaret made, and then rescinded, in *Friar Bacon*. The echoing of 'my lord' and 'his lordship' shows that in getting as much control over her own life as the law allows she is defying Demetrius and Theseus together, as well as Egeus. What is at stake for her in her desire for Lysander is not just her love for this one man but her freedom to make her own choice – Lysander, having listed his claims, makes it clear that her choice of him is the principal one (1.1.99– 104) – and she determines to assert that freedom one way or another.

Once they are left alone, Lysander and Hermia share a stylized passage of lament in which he lists the crosses of true love and she responds with appropriate complaints. The male–female conflicts of the first part of the scene are left behind as the two voices work together. Even when they are actually disagreeing they appear to agree. Like Hippolyta, she counsels patience (1.1.150–2); having said, 'A good persuasion. Therefore hear me, Hermia' (1.1.156), he goes on to counsel action. His plan is to flee the male-dominated community of Athens to a place ruled by a benevolent mother-figure:

> I have a widow aunt, a dowager
> Of great revenue, and she hath no child.
> From Athens is her house remote seven leagues –
> And she respects me as her only son –
> There, gentle Hermia, may I marry thee,
> And to that place the sharp Athenian law
> Cannot pursue us.   (1.1.157–63)

We glimpse, beyond the borders of the play, an alternative power. This time the dowager is not the sterile, oppressive figure of Theseus's opening description of the moon, and her childlessness is not mere barrenness but frees her for acts of charity. In every respect she offers a counter to the authority of Theseus. But her house lies beyond the borders of the play: the lovers never get there.

They find themselves trapped instead in the liminal space of the wood, which they thought of simply as the place they would journey through to find safety. And the wood is dominated by an extreme form of male–female conflict, the quarrel of Oberon and Titania. The lovers have no inkling of this, or even of the fairies' existence, but it spills over into their own relationships to produce comic chaos. The fairies operate in a natural world in which conflict is the norm. (Shakespeare, who came from the country, never sentimentalized nature.) Titania orders her attendants: 'Some to kill cankers [caterpillars] in the musk-rose buds, / Some war with reremice for their leathern wings' (2.2.3–4). The lullaby they sing to her is designed to ward off counterattack from snakes, spiders, beetles and other natural enemies. These conflicts are miniaturized and fantastic. But Titania also complains that her feud with Oberon has produced deepening chaos in the natural world, and this is presented more seriously. For an English audience in the 1590s, a period of bad weather, crop failures and famine,[9] the speech has local resonance:

> The ox hath therefore stretched his yoke in vain,
> The ploughman lost his sweat, and the green corn
> Hath rotted ere his youth attained a beard.
> The fold stands empty in the drownèd field,
> And crows are fatted with the murrain flock.
> The nine men's morris is filled up with mud,
> And the quaint mazes in the wanton green
> For lack of tread are undistinguishable.   (2.1.93–100)

The lush England of *Friar Bacon and Friar Bungay*, with its agricultural wealth and its country pastimes, is in ruins. The moon is, as for Theseus, malevolent:

> Therefore the moon, the governess of floods,
> Pale in her anger, washes all the air,
> That rheumatic diseases do abound ...   (2.1.103–5)

Under a waning moon – and according to Theseus's opening speech that is the time of the play – Diana takes the form of 'Hecate, goddess of witchcraft, death, and the underworld'.[10]

While the fairies are surrounded by a general sense of darkness and disorder, the terms of their own conflict are very specific, and very human. Oberon and Titania argue about authority, the issue in the debate over Hermia in Act 1, and fidelity, the problem of the lovers once they come to the forest. Oberon's 'Am not I thy lord?' draws Titania's retort, 'Then I must be thy lady' (2.1.63–4), which punningly combines an assertion of her authority with a claim that he should be faithful to her; and they go on to accuse each other of affairs with Hippolyta and Theseus. But the real issue between them is the Indian boy Oberon wants from her. Though he regularly appears in productions, he does not appear in the text. The question is not just who possesses him but how he is to be imagined,[11] and the conflict embodies the competing claims of men and women. Robin, speaking for Oberon's side of the question, calls him 'A lovely boy stol'n from an Indian king' (2.1.22) – no mention of a mother – and goes on to contrast his master's desire to involve the boy in manly action with Titania's treating him as a pet, and as a chance to do some flower arranging:

> And jealous Oberon would have the child
> Knight of his train, to trace the forests wild.
> But she perforce withholds the lovèd boy,
> Crowns him with flowers, and makes him all her joy.   (2.1.24-7)

As Theseus imagines a child created without a mother, Titania, closer to reality but not quite there, suppresses all reference to the boy's father:

> His mother was a vot'ress of my order,
> And in the spicèd Indian air by night
> Full often hath she gossiped by my side,
> And sat with me on Neptune's yellow sands,
> Marking th'embarkèd traders on the flood,
> When we have laughed to see the sails conceive
> And grow big-bellied with the wanton wind,
> Which she with pretty and with swimming gait
> Following, her womb then rich with my young squire,
> Would imitate, and sail upon the land
> To fetch me trifles, and return again
> As from a voyage, rich with merchandise.
> But she, being mortal, of that boy did die;
> And for her sake do I rear up her boy;
> And for her sake I will not part with him.   (2.1.123-37)

This bonding of two women, sharing private jokes and confidences, contemplating the mystery of life and death in a pregnant woman's body, is a richer and more poignant version of the schoolgirl friendship between Hermia and Helena that the latter will recall during their quarrel in the forest. It sets against the play's concentration on heterosexual love a glimpse of a life that only women can share. They joke about the votaress's parody of the male activity of trade; but the power and wealth her pregnancy embodies are also fatal to her. Women die giving life. Men (as in *The Merchant of Venice*) risk their merchandise; women risk everything. The bond this shared knowledge creates is the key to Titania's refusal to give up the boy to Oberon. Being a votaress her friend had taken vows, made a commitment to a female community, as Hermia would if she entered a nunnery; in return Titania is committed to her; the reiterated 'For her sake' locks the idea into place.

This is a challenge to Oberon, and his answer lies in the magic flower that creates, or rather enforces, heterosexual love.[12] The magic of *Endymion* and *Friar Bacon* had, as we saw, no power to compel love. The flower functions more like the magic of folk-belief, in which love-charms and aphrodisiacs played a major role.[13] In one sense, however, it does not create love at all, in that it does not create love-relationships. It produces only single-minded obsession: its function, in Oberon's words, is to 'make or man or woman madly dote / Upon the next live creature that it sees' (2.1.171–2). Seeing Helena in the grip of unrequited love for Demetrius, Oberon plans to use the drug on Demetrius not to produce harmony between them but simply to reverse the roles of pursuer and pursued: 'Ere he do leave this grove, / Thou shalt fly him, and he shall seek thy love' (2.1.245–6). He orders Robin, 'Effect it with some care, that he may prove / More fond on her than she upon her love' (2.1.265–6). Even without Robin's mistake in applying the flower to Lysander, its effect as Oberon imagines it will be not to solve the male–female conflict but perpetuate it in a new form. Its effect on Lysander is not just to make him love Helena but make him hate Hermia. Undrugged, he showed he could respect her wishes; now, like Egeus, he sees her as his to dispose of: 'And here with my good will, with all my heart, / In Hermia's love I yield you up my part' (3.2.164–5). Joan Stansbury has argued that in the early scenes Demetrius and Helena show an inferior kind of love, childish and lacking in judgement, and the effect of the flower is to drag Titania and Lysander down to their level.[14] It is rough magic, and the comedy it creates depends on its reductiveness.

When Oberon explains how the flower was hit by Cupid's dart he lets us glimpse, once again, a figure beyond the borders of the play, who embodies different values:

> A certain aim he took
> At a fair vestal thronèd by the west …
> But I might see young Cupid's fiery shaft
> Quenched in the chaste beams of the wat'ry moon,
> And the imperial vot'ress passèd on,
> In maiden meditation, fancy-free. (2.1.157–64)

Elizabeth again.[15] She is Lyly's Cynthia, beyond ordinary love; she is Greene's visionary figure, remote from the world of the play. She is a votaress, like Titania's friend, and a vestal, as Hermia would be to escape Demetrius. She represents a self-sufficiency that never needs to act, and (like Lysander's aunt) an authority that is never called on. No drama could be made out of her, certainly no comedy, and she emphasizes by contrast the fact that the drama and the comedy of this play stem from the conflicts of men and women, conflicts that the flower, which Cupid's dart hits instead of her, serves to inflame. If the play were performed for Elizabeth she would be made to feel not (as in Lyly) her centrality but her divine irrelevance.

Titania, who as fairy queen might be thought to suggest Elizabeth (Spenser's Faerie Queene) is not her representative but her opposite. Lyly's Cynthia is the unchanging, untouched recipient of adoration, bestowing one kiss as a unique concession. Titania is love's helpless victim, constantly kissing and embracing her strange lover (4.1.1–4, 39–44). Oberon aims to show his power over Titania by twisting her affections, making her bestow adoration, not receive it, and he is determined she will bestow it on 'lion, bear, or wolf, or bull, / On meddling monkey, or on busy ape' (2.1.180–1). He orders, as he anoints her eyes, 'Wake when some vile thing is near' (2.2.40). Oberon's plan is on the face of it bizarre: to make his own wife in love with someone (or something) else, getting power over her at the cost of making himself a cuckold. It is a price he seems willing to pay in order to humiliate and degrade her. The joke is on him, though he never quite realizes it: she gets not some vile thing but Bottom with the ass's head, and their relationship (as we shall see) is as decorous in manner as it is indecorous in appearance.

When Oberon sees Titania asleep with Bottom in her arms, the crudeness of his earlier fantasies of humiliation breaks up into a more shifting, contradictory reaction: 'Welcome, good Robin. Seest thou this sweet sight? / Her dotage now I do begin to pity' (4.1.45–6). He comes to gloat, but his feelings soften. In describing his ultimate victory, he reports dispassionately his own cruelty and her gentleness:

> When I had at my pleasure taunted her,
> And she in mild terms begged my patience,
> I then did ask of her her changeling child,
> Which straight she gave me … (4.1.56–9)

He had earlier predicted, 'I'll make her render up her page to me' (2.1.185). Now, less coercively, he 'asks', and she grants. But if he can allow himself a touch of regret at the way he has treated her it is because, in the end, he has had his way: 'And now I have the boy, I will undo / This hateful imperfection of her eyes' (4.1.61–2).

Titania's commitment to the votaress vanishes like a dream. When Oberon reports that she has treated Bottom as she treated the Indian boy, crowning him with flowers, the logic of his plot becomes clear. Bottom replaces the boy in her affections, and (as with Lysander, though less obtrusively) when a new love is created an old one dies.[16] It remains to kill the new love, and 'all things shall be peace' (3.2.377). Oberon has reasserted the claims of heterosexual love, and his own power as ruler and husband, through the crude magic of the flower. The result is a harmony celebrated in music and dance, designed to win us over; and thanks to the brilliant comedy of her scenes with Bottom, Titania's obsession has never seemed as degrading as Oberon imagined. But if as we watch Titania's placid submission to him we recall her speech about the votaress – and it is one of the play's most eloquent passages – we may feel that something has been lost: not just her own spirit and fire, which are dampened in the end, but a commitment the power of whose claims she made us feel and has now forgotten.

Titania's love for Bottom looks like an image of licence: in a free interval before order is restored, a fairy loves a mortal, a queen loves a commoner, and a man sports an ass's head like a carnival mask. To an outside view – that of Theseus – the mortal lovers' sojourn in the forest suggests a similar licence. Finding them lying together on the ground, he jokes about St Valentine's day, and the rite of May (4.1.131–2, 138–9). But Hermia has discouraged Lysander's attempt to lie too close to her, and when Demetrius threatens to rape Helena she simply does not believe him: 'Your virtue is my privilege' (2.1.220). Ironically, it is not licence but restraint that gets the lovers into trouble; finding Hermia and Lysander lying far apart, Robin assumes he has the right man, calling him 'this lack-love, this kill-courtesy' (2.2.83). He mistakes chastity for unkindness. Whatever suspicions Hermia or the audience may have of Lysander's real motives, he offers to lie close to her as a sign of commitment – 'One turf shall serve as pillow for us both: / One heart, one bed, two bosoms, and one troth' (2.2.47–8) – and in putting him off she inadvertently precipitates the breaking of that commitment.

If there is licence in the forest, it is the licence to break promises and betray loyalties, as Titania does. The lovers are caught up not so much in a game of cross-wooing as in angry arguments and recriminations. As the quarrel of Oberon and Titania affects the climate, it colours the relationships of those who enter their territory. Helena has already been betrayed by Demetrius, who loved her before he switched allegiance to Hermia. Perhaps thinking of her friend's experience, Hermia registers a persistent anxiety about Lysander's fidelity. Promising to meet him, she swears 'By all the vows that ever men have broke – / In number more than ever women spoke', invokes Aeneas's betrayal of Dido (1.1.173–6) and adds, 'Keep word, Lysander' (1.1.222). Her last words before they fall asleep in the forest are 'Thy love ne'er alter till thy sweet life end' (2.2.67). She later insists, 'The sun was not so true unto the day / As he to me' (3.2.50–1), but she is in a night world governed by the inconstant moon, and the real anxiety behind her continued references to fidelity comes out in her dream of a serpent eating her heart while Lysander 'sat smiling at his cruel prey' (2.2.156).[17]

Lysander's image of commitment as two bosoms with a single troth is echoed when Helena recalls her schoolgirl friendship with Hermia; this too, like Titania's commitment to the votaress, is damaged by the power of magic when Helena imagines Hermia is in a confederacy against her:

> We, Hermia, like two artificial gods
> Have with our needles created both one flower,
> Both on one sampler, sitting on one cushion,
> Both warbling of one song, both in one key,
> As if our hands, our sides, voices, and minds
> Had been incorporate. So we grew together,
> Like to a double cherry: seeming parted,
> But yet an union in partition,
> Two lovely berries moulded on one stem.   (3.2.203–11)

Helena goes on to accuse Hermia of betraying that friendship by joining with the men in mockery of her, and she makes it, like the conflict over the Indian boy, a matter of men against women: 'Our sex as well as I may chide you for it' (3.2.218).

But there is, to use Helena's own word, something artificial about the commitment she describes. What makes Titania's speech about the votaress moving is its sense of a relationship between two utterly unlike beings: a mortal, pregnant woman and an immortal fairy. For Titania the votaress is something rich and strange, not just a repetition of herself. (The Bottom–Titania relationship is a comic version of this love of something quite other.) What Helena describes is not so much affection or relationship as cloning. Titania's betrayal of her friendship is a matter of regret, muted by the way it happens in silence. Helena's claim of schoolgirl affection collapses in broad farce as the women start insulting each other in playground taunts about their relative heights, Hermia demanding, 'How low am I, thou painted maypole?' (3.2.296) and Helena declaring, 'She was a vixen when she went to school, / And though she be but little, she is fierce' (3.2.324–5). So much for schoolgirl friendship, and identical cherries. Beneath the farce, Shakespeare offers something more subtle than the love–friendship debate of *Endymion*: Helena has idealized friendship as a compensation for the pain of love as she has experienced it, and more immediately as a way of making Hermia feel guilty. Under pressure, the idealized vision cracks quickly. The play's depiction of heterosexual love seems at first to confirm the *Endymion* view that it leads to unhappiness; this unhappiness centres on Helena. Of the four lovers she is the one who is made the object of love by magic; she is also the touchiest, the quickest to take offence. She is in tension from the beginning: beneath her professions of friendship for Lysander and Hermia there is a strong undercurrent of jealousy and resentment, and a suspicion that Hermia has somehow stolen Demetrius from her by trickery: 'O, teach me how you look, and with what art / You sway the motion of Demetrius' heart' (1.1.192–3). The mutual accusations of the forest are already latent in Athens; and Helena herself is already guilty of betraying friendship for the sake of love, as she reveals her friends' plans to Demetrius. Her frustration with Demetrius has already been, to put it mildly, bad for her self-esteem: 'I am as ugly as a bear, / For beasts that meet me run away for fear' (3.2.100–1). Offered love by Lysander and Demetrius, she takes it as a bad joke and reacts with anger. She assumes that 'I love you' really means 'I hate you': 'Cannot you hate me – as I know you do – / But you must join in souls to mock me too?' (3.2.149–50). Hermia, when she finds Lysander and Demetrius both professing love for Helena, goes through a long period of simple bewilderment, pleading for explanations, before she explodes in anger; Helena explodes at once.[18]

Yet all this confusion, painful to the lovers and amusing to the audience, is part of a move towards final harmony. In breaking friendship for the sake of love the magic imitates a natural process we have already glimpsed in Athens. There are suggestions of a transitional stage between same-sex bonding and heterosexual love, a three-way friendship of Helena, Hermia and Lysander: the meeting place in the forest is where they once met together to observe the rite of May (1.1.166–7). The forest itself, the place of transition, marks the successive stages of the lovers' developing relationships. It is the setting for schoolgirl confidences – according to Hermia, in the forest rendezvous she and Helena 'Upon faint primrose-beds were wont to lie, / Emptying our bosoms of their counsel sweet' (1.1.214–15) – then for a three-way friendship of a man and two women; and finally for heterosexual love acted out, turned into conflict and ultimately restored.

Bacon's magic, for all its entertainment value, is a dangerous power that finally does more harm than good, and he himself turns against it. The double effect of the fairies' magic is more finely balanced. It is not just a matter of creating disruptive obsessions and then curing them. When the lovers wake and prepare to return to Athens, they are both free of magic and bound by it. Lysander has been restored to his original love not by the wearing off of one drug but by the application of another that acts as an antidote. Demetrius is still under the first spell; but it has restored his original affection for Helena. In both cases it takes the intervention of magic to restore the normal. And more has happened than simply a realignment of two love affairs. As they slowly return to daylight the lovers' voices work together with a new smoothness and harmony:

Demetrius. These things seem small and undistinguishable,
    Like far-off mountains turnèd into clouds.
Hermia. Methinks I see these things with parted eye,
    When everything seems double.
Helena.   So methinks,
    And I have found Demetrius like a jewel,
    Mine own and not mine own.   (4.1.186–91)

Something like the original group of three friends has been restored, with the addition of Demetrius as a fourth. Two quarrelling sets of couples now form a larger, more harmonious unit. As they compare impressions they recognize they have just seen Theseus, Hippolyta and Egeus, and they return to the community Lysander and Hermia thought they had to leave. The proper alignment of love allows the creation of a larger network of relationships. More important, Helena's 'Mine own and not mine own' suggests an improvement in the quality of the love. In place of the obsessive, exclusive demands we have seen the lovers make is an acknowledgement that the possession of love is never total. Helena imagined Hermia as a clone of herself; Bottom wants to play both Pyramus *and* Thisbe. But love, as Helena now experiences it, recognizes the otherness of the other person, who is possessed and not possessed, as the men are enchanted and not enchanted and their experience is a dream and not a dream. Helena, the most obsessed and unhappy of the lovers, is the one who has this insight: the worse the ordeal, the deeper the final understanding.

    The magic, apparently crude and disruptive, has been the agent in leading the lovers towards a deeper maturity and a richer experience of relationship. Robin's sense of the action as just a show of folly put on for his amusement – 'Shall we their fond pageant see? / Lord, what fools these mortals be!' (3.2.114–15) – is part of the truth, and embodies part of the audience's response. But it is not the whole truth. Nor is the play content with his view of the lovers' final relationship as simply a matter of men possessing women: 'The man shall have his mare again, / And all shall be well' (3.2.463–4). Helena has a finer sense than that of how far love means possession.

Robin is equally reductive in describing the Bottom–Titania affair: 'My mistress with a monster is in love' (3.2.6). While Oberon expects something crude and grotesque, Shakespeare knows a trick worth two of that. Helena, finding herself the recipient of unexpected love, is furious and counterattacks violently. Bottom is phegmatic and detached; above all, he is polite: 'Methinks, mistress, you should have little reason for that. And yet, to say the truth, reason and love keep little company together nowadays – the more the pity, that some honest neighbours will not make them friends' (3.1.135–9). He suggests, as tactfully as he can, that Titania is wrong to love him; the rebuke is softened by courtesy and tolerance. Titania picks up the spirit of Bottom's response, instructing her attendants, 'Be kind and courteous to this gentleman' (3.1.155). Instead of a lurid image of bestiality (we need to remember that Bottom's transformation is only from the neck up) we get a love affair couched in courtly politeness with, on Bottom's part, considerable restraint. Not quite sure what to make of Titania, he spends most of his time chatting amiably with her entourage. When she exerts her power over him, forbidding him to leave the wood and commanding his silence (3.1.143–4, 191), the potential harshness is softened by the promise of hospitality: 'Feed him with apricots and dewberries, / With purple grapes, green figs, and mulberries' (3.1.157–8). She thinks not just of what she wants from Bottom but of what Bottom might want.[19] As there is more to the operation of the flower that the simple confusion Robin sees, there is more to Titania's love of Bottom than the grotesque humiliation Oberon expects. The comedy of incongruity gains unexpected subtlety from the consideration they show each other. Titania's reaction when she comes out of the spell, 'O, how mine eyes do loathe his visage now!' (4.1.77), does not quite do justice to the experience she has had and suggests once again that in returning to Oberon she has lost something.

Robin's commentary invites the audience to simple, mocking laughter, in line with the practical jokes he enjoys playing (especially, we note, on women (2.1.47–57)); the play itself invites a larger response, including Robin's perspective but not confined to it. As the magic flower invites us to think about the actual working of love, the other principal use of magic, Bottom's transformation, invites us to think about the working of theatre. The ass's head is quite frankly a theatrical prop. It comes from the same trunk as the different beards Bottom offers to wear (1.2.80–6) and it satisfies his ambition to play in a mask: 'An I may hide my face, let me play Thisbe too' (1.2.45). In *Friar Bacon and Friar Bungay* a good deal of the magic is conveyed not by special effects but simply by actors acting: in the scenes with the glass, one set of characters spies on another set, supposedly miles away; distance is abolished simply by having them share the same stage. With equal simplicity, the effect of the magic flower is left entirely to the actors playing Titania, Lysander and Demetrius. Bottom, to don the ass's head, retires from the stage, puts it on in the tiring-house, and returns. No flash powder, no special effects. On Oberon's orders, Robin removes the head, on stage, as Bottom sleeps. Productions sometimes devise ways of hiding the moment from the audience to make it seem more like magic when Bottom appears as his old self again. But the open stage of an Elizabethan playhouse, lit by daylight, lacking in scenery and with a wrap-around audience, is no place to hide anything. I suspect Robin should remove the head in full view of the audience, so that we see Bottom emerge again as if we were in the tiring-house watching an actor shed his costume and his character, to emerge as himself. To watch the play's magic at work is, simply and frankly, to watch theatre at work.

Theatre is a power, and that power, like those of Theseus, Egeus and Oberon, is debated throughout the play, and its strengths and weaknesses are explored. *Pyramus and Thisbe* is the principal vehicle for this. Like other dramatic burlesques, from Beaumont's *The Knight of the Burning Pestle* through Buckingham's *The Rehearsal* to Stoppard's *The Real Inspector Hound*, it makes us think, as it entertains us, about how theatre operates, about the assumptions it makes and the tricks it uses.[20] It does so in part by reversing the usual procedures. When in the show of the Nine Worthies in *Love's Labour's Lost* (c.1594) Costard declares 'I Pompey am' and Berowne retorts, 'You lie; you are not he' (V.ii.543), we see the audience rejecting one of the ground rules without which theatre is impossible: impersonation. Quince and his colleagues insist on breaking the rules themselves, informing the audience that the lion is really Snug, Pyramus is really Bottom and the swords will do no harm. The audience of *A Midsummer Night's Dream* agrees to imagine that the stage is a wood, and the normal-sized actors playing the fairies can hide in acorn-cups. Quince, arriving in the forest for a rehearsal, uncreates illusion: 'This green plot shall be our stage, this hawthorn brake our tiring-house' (3.1.3–4). Pointing, presumably, to the real stage and tiring-house, he turns them back into what they really are.[21]

At the same time he and his colleagues have great faith in their power to *create* illusion. Considering the problem of bringing moonshine on to the stage, they decide at first to leave the casement open and let the real moon do the job. But they evidently think Starveling will do it better. Is Shakespeare recalling that Lyly in *Endymion* let an actor impersonate the moon? Of all the actors Starveling gets the roughest treatment from the audience: he is the only one who is interrupted to the extent that he cannot carry on. But in general the actors imagine they are wielding a powerful force that if anything will have to be restrained. Bottom is confident about the emotional impact of his acting: 'If I do it, let the audience look to their eyes. I will move storms' (1.2.22–3). The raw energy of his performance as a lion – no lines, just roaring – could, Quince fears, go even further: 'An you should do it too terribly you would fright the Duchess and the ladies that they would shriek, and that were enough to hang us all' (1.2.66–8). Quince and his colleagues imagine their art as powerful enough to be dangerous; if they are not circumspect they will offend the greater, more dangerous power of the state, and suffer accordingly.[22] It should be noted, in view of the scant respect for the feelings of women the play's more high-born men show, and of Robin's delight in teasing older women, that the actors are particularly concerned about the feelings of the ladies, who may be frightened by the lion and distressed by the killings.

Their solution to is restrain the power of theatrical illusion by constant reminders of reality. The lion, whose uncontrolled roaring may be terrifying, is given lines to speak that immediately humanize him, and bring the actor under control by restraining his freedom to improvise. The audience will be assured that the lion is really Snug, and that Pyramus is really Bottom. Shakespeare himself uses the same device to keep Bottom's transformation inoffensive: chatting with Titania and her attendants, he is thoroughly and unshakably himself, no more a monster than Snug is a lion.[23] In performance Quince's actors carry out this strategy with some success: Theseus pays tribute to the lion as 'A very gentle beast, and of a good conscience' (5.1.225). But Quince's nervousness shows in his mispunctuation of the Prologue. Not only does the sheer repetition of its claims of good will show anxiety in itself; he inadvertently turns some of them into insults, so that he is constantly treading a fine line between accommodation and the offence he is so anxious to avoid:

> If we offend, it is with our good will.
> That you should think, we come not to offend
> But with good will. To show our simple skill,
> That is the true beginning of our end.
> Consider then we come but in despite.
> We do not come as minding to content you,
> Our true intent is. All for your delight
> We are not here. That you should here repent you
> The actors are at hand ...   (5.1.108–18)

Later Bottom takes the risk of correcting Theseus, who has suggested that the wall, 'being sensible', should return Thisbe's curses: 'No, in truth, sir he should not. "Deceiving me" is Thisbe's cue. She is to enter now, and I am to spy her through the wall. You shall see, it will fall pat as I told you' (5.1.180–5). Polite as always, he has spotted an audience member in need of help, and accordingly helps him. Even in this extempore moment the general strategy of Quince and his company holds. They have potentially great power over their audience, as their audience has over them; they must treat that audience with tact and courtesy.

Whether their courtesy is returned is another matter. When King Henry presides over the magic contest in *Friar Bacon* he can take a simple satisfaction in the general display of skill and the English magician's victory. Theseus and his fellow audience members have a more delicate task. Hippolyta does not want to face it: 'I love not to see wretchedness o'ercharged, / And duty in his service perishing' (5.1.85–6); but Theseus determines to receive the show as the offering of 'simpleness and duty' (5.1.83), and he gives a lecture on the gracious acceptance of even the most incompetent expressions of loyalty (5.1.89–105). Yet his courtesy has a touch of condescension, and the actual reaction he and his fellow audience members give is a volatile combination of ironic praise – 'Well run, Thisbe.' 'Well shone, Moon' (5.1.260–1) – witty criticism – 'This passion, and the death of a dear friend, would go near to make a man look sad' (5.1.282–3) – and simple rudeness. Theseus offers a final gracious tribute only after allowing himself a last insult, and he does not bother to link the two with an apology: 'Marry, if he that writ it had played Pyramus and hanged himself in Thisbe's garter it would have been a fine tragedy; and so it is, truly, and very notably discharged' (5.1.349–52). It is possible, however, for the actor to show Theseus realizing he has made a slip and offering the last part of the speech as reassurance; and Hippolyta's reaction to Pyramus's lament, 'Beshrew my heart, but I pity the man' (5.1.285), can be played as embarrassment for the actor or a genuine response to the character. The relations of play and audience involve tricky negotiations between offence and courtesy, on both sides, and different productions can strike the balance differently.

The main effect, of course, is that the actors have nothing like the power they think they have and if their feeble performance is to have any impact it must be because the audience uses its own power to help them out:

Theseus. The best in this kind are but shadows, and the worst are no worse if imagination amend them.
Hippolyta. It must be your imagination, then, and not theirs.   (5.1.210–13)

But at the time Shakespeare wrote, 'the best in this kind' were the Lord Chamberlain's men, who are performing the play. As Quince's company rehearses outside the town, Shakespeare's company rehearsed, and performed, in the suburbs. They were a commercial enterprise, and Flute imagines that Bottom's reward for playing Pyramus will be not the appreciation of the intelligentsia but sixpence a day (4.2.18–22). Both companies draw their personnel from the ranks of artisans and tradesmen. These hints of identification between Quince's company and Shakespeare's work more than one way. There is self-deprecating humour, as when Chaucer the poet shows Chaucer the pilgrim telling the worst of the Canterbury Tales. But there may also be a warning not to be too quick to dismiss the actors' show as merely feeble, drawing only condescending laughter. We are watching not just Athens's worst actors, but England's best, and the latter group may well be up to something.

In some ways, though not in the way Quince and company fear, *Pyramus and Thisbe* is genuinely disruptive. It may not produce unbearable pity and terror, but it brings another world, another kind of life, into Theseus's court, and the result is a liberating challenge to decorum. Egeus, trying to prevent the performance, insists the actors are the wrong class, 'Hard-handed men that work in Athens here', and tells his ruler, 'It is not for you' (5.1.72, 77).[24] He is overruled. The bergomask that, by Theseus's own choice, ends the performance is 'Usually identified as a clownish, rustic dance'.[25] Peter Holland has pointed out that in choosing a classical story the mechanicals are trespassing on what was normally the territory of university students, learned amateurs and educated playwrights.[26] The love scene by the wall includes the scatological comedy associated with the subversive vice-characters of morality plays like

Mankind: 'My cherry lips have often kissed thy stones'; 'I kiss the wall's hole, not your lips at all' (5.1.189, 200).[27] Just by appearing at court, the actors are challenging a social barrier (unlike the professional companies of Shakespeare's time they are not under royal or aristocratic patronage); and one of the most striking incidents in their play is the disappearance of a wall.

They have a disruptive effect within *A Midsummer Night's Dream* itself, picking up and parodying motifs from the main play. Pyramus and Thisbe have parent trouble, they vow eternal fidelity, and they meet in the dark outside the town, where they become the victims of confusion. The bloodstained mantle, and Pyramus's lament that 'lion vile hath here deflowered my dear' (5.1.286), suggest both the staining of the flower by Cupid's dart and the experience the women will undergo on their wedding nights, not long after the play is over.[28] The obvious maleness of Flute, who resists playing Thisbe because he has a beard coming, reminds the audience of the maleness of the actors playing Titania, Hippolyta, Helena and Hermia.[29] I have suggested that the play raises serious issues about the relations between men and women; but all its females are really males, and we may wonder if this is one more example of male coercion or a warning not to take such questions too seriously. (The disruption, in other words, affects not just the play but my academic interpretation.)

There is, finally, something uncanny in theatre itself. There was a contemporary story of a performance of *Doctor Faustus* at Exeter at which, during the conjuring scene, one devil too many appeared on stage and there was a general rush for the doors.[30] Bottom is transformed while rehearsing *Pyramus and Thisbe*; he misses an entrance cue (which, perhaps significantly, is a vow of fidelity, 'As true as truest horse that yet would never tire' (3.1.97–8)), and in the interval created by that missed cue Robin transforms him. In theatre as in other kinds of magic, one misstep can be serious. When at the end of the play the fairies invade the palace of Theseus (who does not believe in fairies) the invasion begins with Robin's line, 'Now the hungry lion roars' (5.1.362), making a link back to *Pyramus and Thisbe*. An invasion by one kind of shadows, the actors, leads to an invasion by another kind, the fairies. It is as though the mechanicals, by their indecorous and disruptive presence at court, have broken a hole in a wall, and anything can get through. When the actors imagine they are dealing with a troublesome power that needs to be handled with care, they may be speaking more truly than they know.

The fairy invasion offers both a blessing on Theseus's wedding and a final challenge to his authority. In general, the power relations that have been debated through the play are still under negotiation in the last act. When he saw the lovers asleep in the right configuration, Theseus forgot about the law and overruled Egeus. In the Quarto version of the last act Egeus is simply dropped; he does not appear, and there is no reference to him. The Folio gives him Philostrate's role of objecting to *Pyramus and Thisbe*, and he is overruled again. But he is still making his presence felt. (The new arrangement also allows him an unexpected sense of humour: he confesses that the preview of the mechanicals' play made him weep with laughter.) The Folio also has Lysander read out the titles of the alternative entertainments Theseus rejects, letting him share Egeus's role as master of ceremonies, and raising the possibility that as he has taken his daughter he is about to take his job. Hermia and Helena are completely silent throughout the act, suggesting that the men-versus-women debates are resolved by the assertion of male authority in marriage, in which the women are reduced to silence. But Hippolyta redresses the balance: having had only one speech in the first scene, she debates with Theseus throughout the last act.

Their key debate occurs at the beginning of that act: Theseus's disbelief in the lovers' story, part of his general disbelief in imagination and the supernatural, is countered by her insistence that the story 'grows to something of great constancy' (5.1.26). But what story have the lovers told? In a way their experience is the converse of Bottom's. He wakes back in his rehearsal, still waiting for his cue, then gradually realizes he has had 'a most rare vision' – but a vision that is not to be spoken of: 'Man is but an ass if he go about to expound this dream' (4.1.202–4). His plan to get Peter Quince to write a ballad of his dream for him to sing before the Duke never materializes. On his return to his fellows, he is torn between a desire to tell all and a determination to tell nothing, and he tells nothing.[31] During their forest sojourn, the lovers have, unlike Bottom, no sight of the fairies, no inkling of their existence. They think they have been dreaming, and they go off to recount their dreams. We never see what follows. (Shakespeare, like Bottom, can be reticent.) But they will presumably discover they have all had the same dream, and whatever story they construct to tell Theseus it leads him to remark, 'I never may believe / These antique fables, nor these fairy toys' (5.1.2–3). The lovers (for our amusement) have been through mutual betrayal and humiliation; they have said terrible things to each other. Have they decided, as a way of coping with the discomfort, to blame it all on the fairies? If that is the case (and the play provokes the question without answering it) then Theseus's disbelief is, and is not, justified. The lovers have no evidence at all that fairy magic has been at work; they have devised the story for their own needs. They just happen to be right.

Theseus's scepticism is of course given the lie direct by the entrance of the fairies themselves into his own palace. His final couplet, 'A fortnight hold we this solemnity / In nightly revels and new jollity' (5.1.360–1), sounds like the ending of the play, and as the highest-ranking character he has the right, by a convention of Elizabethan playwriting, to the last word. But as his earlier call for merriment was disrupted by the entrance of Egeus, his final attempt at closure is broken by the entrance of Robin. The fairies' blessing of the bride-beds shows the limits of Theseus's thinking in another way. He has been looking forward with increasing impatience to that night's pleasure. They are thinking nine months ahead, and more:

> So shall all the couples three
> Ever true in loving be,
> And the blots of nature's hand
> Shall not in their issue stand.
> Never mole, harelip, nor scar,
> Nor mark prodigious such as are
> Despisèd in nativity
> Shall upon their children be.   (5.1.398–405)

With the words 'ever true in loving' Oberon banishes the fear of infidelity, and heals the harm his magic has done. But the chief harm associated with fairies in Shakespeare's time was their threat to newborn children. Just when they were most vulnerable, the fairies might steal them, leaving a weak, sickly fairy child, a changeling, in their place. It was a warning to guard one's children carefully.[32] Without explicitly recalling that belief, Oberon does what Quince and his actors do: reassures us that his power, much as we may fear it, will do no harm. Instead of threatening mortal children, they bless them. And to think of changelings is to raise another question the play provokes but does not answer: do these fairies, Shakespeare's fairies, have children? Robin calls the Indian boy a changeling, but there is no reference to a fairy child left in his place. He is simply stolen. There are no references to fairy children anywhere. Oberon and Titania's only offspring are figurative: Titania says of the evils their quarrel has produced in nature, 'We are their parents and original' (2.1.117). The fairies regularly call the other characters 'mortals'; are they themselves outside the cycle of birth and death, unable to die or to reproduce? Traditional fairies, of course, have children, and there are tales of fairy funerals.[33] But if any writer can re-think tradition, Shakespeare can. The fairies are the most powerful characters in the play; but there may be one power, natural to mortals, that they lack. If so there is an extra poignancy in Titania's fascination with her pregnant friend, and in the final blessing of the bride-beds. Yet it is a power that makes the mortals vulnerable: it was in childbirth that the votaress died.

Throughout the play power is debated, and no one power, neither the authority of Theseus nor the magic of Oberon, holds final sway. In place of the single central authority of Lyly's Cynthia, the play presents two rulers, Theseus and Hippolyta, who from the beginning are engaged in debate, qualifying our sense that Thesus is simply, indisputably, in charge. (There is a more piquant contrast with Lyly: the Bottom–Titania affair reads almost as a parodic inversion of Cynthia's relations with Endymion; this time a queen helplessly adores a mortal, who responds with wary courtesy.) Greene's interest in competing forces becomes a more intricate exploration of different forms of authority: the coercive worldly power of Thesus and Egeus, the magic of Oberon, the magic of theatre. Robin is an ironic version of the Plautine clever slave, producing a period of confusion through being confused himself. That confusion becomes the occasion for a fuller view than Lyly and Greene have attempted of the nature of love, the demands it makes, the way it develops and matures. In the play's conflict of forces, there is coercion, resentment and, directed against the mechanicals, a certain amount of snobbery. Yet Annabel Patterson sees in *A Midsummer Night's Dream* 'an idea of social play that could cross class boundaries without obscuring them, and by those crossings imagine the social body whole again'.[34] And there is a subtler sense of gender relations than we see in Margaret's surrender to Lacy. The ultimate benevolence of the play's vision lies in the possibilities it offers of courtesy, loyalty, self-deprecation; of the love embodied not in the magic flower but in Helena's 'Mine own, and not mine own'; of the relations between art and its audience embodied not in the heckling of the courtiers but in the final offer of Robin, so like the goodwill of Quince and his actors, 'Give me your hands, if we be friends, / And Robin shall restore amends' (5.1.428–9).

Notes

1 For the arguments against the aristocratic-wedding theory, see Stanley Wells, '*A Midsummer Night's Dream* Revisited', *Critical Survey*, III, 1991, 14–18.

2 All references to *A Midsummer Night's Dream* are to the Oxford Shakespeare edition, ed. Peter Holland, Oxford and New York, 1994.

3 Holland, Introduction, pp. 53–4.

4 K.M. Briggs, *The Anatomy of Puck*, London, 1959, p. 14; and see chapter 2, n. 24.

5 Productions have sometimes emphasized Hippolyta's captive state. In the 1935 film directed by Max Reinhardt and William Dieterle she first appears 'defeated and downcast, with a large snake coiled around her': Jay L. Halio, *Shakespeare in Performance: A Midsummer Night's Dream*, Manchester and New York, 1994, p. 86. In John Hancock's 1966 production in San Francisco she was dragged on in a cage and 'her lines snarled with biting sarcasm' (Holland, commentary, p. 131).

6 Louis Adrian Montrose, '"Shaping Fantasies": Figurations of Gender and Power in Elizabethan Culture', *Representing the English Renaissance*, ed. Stephen Greenblatt, Berkeley, Los Angeles and London, 1988, p. 36. John Weld sees the defeat of the Amazon as an allegory of passion subdued by reason: *Meaning in Comedy: Studies in Elizabethan Romantic Comedy*, Albany, 1975, p. 193.

7 'Shaping', p. 40.

8 Egeus's view would have seemed almost as extreme in Shakespeare's time as it does now. General opinion seems to have favoured a sensible give-and-take, with parents and children showing due regard for each other's feelings. See Keith Wrightson, *English Society 1580–1680*, London, 1982, repr. 1990, pp. 71–9, 115.

9 D.M. Palliser, *The Age of Elizabeth: England under the Later Tudors 1547–1603*, 2nd edn, London and New York, 1992, pp. 58–9.

10 Philippa Berry, *Of Chastity and Power: Elizabethan Literature and the Unmarried Queen*, London and New York, 1989, p. 144.

11 William W. E. Slights, 'The Changeling in *A Dream*', *Studies in English Literature*, XXVIII, 1988, 262.

12 Or at least that is how it functions in the play. What would happen if (for example) the first person Lysander saw on waking was Demetrius is a question the play does not address.

13 Keith Thomas, *Religion and the Decline of Magic*, New York, 1971, pp. 233–4.

14 'Characterization of the Four Young Lovers in "A Midsummer Night's Dream"', *Shakespeare Survey*, XXXV, 1982, 58. In *Endymion* Floscula compares love created by enchantment to artificial flowers and fish taken with poisoned bait (1.2.76–83).

15 For a full account of the imperial imagery compressed into this passage see Frances A. Yates, *Astraea: The Imperial Theme in the Sixteenth Century*, London, 1975, repr. 1985, pp. 29–120.

16 In a sentimental moment in the 1935 film the Indian boy, rejected, turns away in

tears (Halio, *Performance*, p. 90). Shakespeare gives him no presence, and therefore no feelings; the effect is of a custody battle in which the child is never heard from.

17 As Peter Holland points out, this is the only genuine dream in the play (Introduction, p. 4); he offers a Freudian reading of it (pp. 13–15).

18 Helena's role as the problem child among the lovers is suggested in Peter Hall's 1968 film: as the four lovers sleep, Helena (Diana Rigg) is sucking her thumb.

19 As Montrose sees it, she treats him as a child ('Shaping', p. 35).

20 It is sometimes the occasion for theatrical in-jokes. In Adrian Noble's 1994 Royal Shakespeare Company production, for example, Quince bore a suspicious resemblance to Laurence Olivier during his period as director of the National Theatre.

21 Michael Shapiro, 'The Casting of Flute: Planes of Illusion in *A Midsummer Night's Deam* and *Bartholomew Fair*', *The Elizabethan Theatre XIII*, ed. A.L. Magnusson and C.E. McGee, Toronto, 1994, p. 152.

22 Theodore B. Leinwand, '"I Believe We Must Leave the Killing Out": Deference and Accommodation in *A Midsummer Night's Dream*', *Renaissance Papers 1986*, n.p. , p. 13. Though there is no record of actors being hanged, the fear that the authorities would move against the theatre was sometimes borne out in the years following *A Midsummer Night's Dream* – notably in 1597, when a now-lost play called *The Isle of Dogs* gave such offence that some members of the company (including Ben Jonson) were imprisoned and the Privy Council threatened to ban all performances and demolish the playhouses.

23 As William C. Carroll puts it, 'his identity is never clearer than when it has been lost in another shape': *The Metamporphoses of Shakespearean Comedy*, Princeton, 1985, p. 150.

24 I follow the Oxford edition, which in turn follows the Folio in assigning to Egeus the role given to Philostrate in the Quarto. Most editions follow the Quarto.

25 Holland, commentary, p. 250.

26 Introduction, p. 92.

27 Thomas Clayton has suggested that Wall's chink might be not between his fingers but between his legs: '"Fie, What a Question's That If Thou Wert Near a Lewd Interpreter": The Wall Scene in *A Midsummer Night's Dream*', *Shakespeare Studies*, VII, 1974, 101.

28 Holland, commentary, p. 247.

29 Shapiro, 'Casting', pp. 149–50.

30 E.K. Chambers, *The Elizabethan Stage*, III, Oxford, repr. 1951, p. 424.

31 Fairies were 'jealous of their privacy', and it was thought unwise to speak of one's dealings with them: Thomas, *Religion*, p. 614.

32 Briggs, *Anatomy*, p. 15; Thomas, *Religion*, p. 612.

33 Briggs, *Anatomy*, pp. 218–19.

34 *Shakespeare and the Popular Voice*, Cambridge and Oxford, 1989, p. 69.

5

Marston, *The Malcontent*

W ITH Marston's *The Malcontent* we move indoors again. After lying dormant through most of the 1590s the boys' companies of the private playhouses at Paul's and Blackfriars revived around the turn of the century. Smaller than the public playhouses and charging higher prices, these indoor houses catered to a clientele that was, or liked to fancy itself, exclusive. Though their repertoire was varied, it offered a particular emphasis on satiric comedy. John Marston, one of their leading writers, had begun his career as a writer of non-dramatic satire. His works were among those ordered burned by the Archbishop of Canterbury in 1599, and when in the epistle to the reader that acts as preface to *The Malcontent* he makes the usual claim that his satire is not aimed at particular individuals, there is an embattled quality we do not find in Lyly's warnings against the topical application of *Endymion*: 'in despite of my endeavours, I understand some have been most unadvisedly over-cunning in misinterpreting me, and with subtlety (as deep as hell) have maliciously spread ill rumours, which, springing from themselves, might to themselves have heavily returned' (12–16).[1] This angry defensiveness may reflect his experience of having been (almost literally) burned once before. Marston is also working within a tradition of satiric performance established in the revels of the Inns of Court, the London law schools that functioned as England's third University. Marston had been associated with the Middle Temple, and many of the Blackfriars audience were Inns of Court men. Philip J. Finkelpearl's description of the revels as 'a mixture of disorderly conduct, mock solemnity, and a serious miming of dignified roles'[2] is not a bad description of *The Malcontent*.

In the Induction John Webster wrote when the play was appropriated by the adult players at the Globe, the leading actor Richard Burbage, who played the title role, is made to defend the rights of the satirist: 'such vices as stand not accountable to law should be cured as men heal tetters, by casting ink upon them' (68–70). A certain nervousness about how far those rights can go registers in the printing history: in different copies, references to the corruption of the church appear and disappear.[3] The play's daring was likely part of its appeal, and that appeal was considerable. Three editions were printed in one year, 1604, and, though the next edition was not until 1744, the play was still being performed in 1635. One evidence of its impact is that what looks like a mild passing joke, 'no fool but has his feather' (5.3.40) seems to have become a popular catch-phrase. In Webster's Induction for the Globe, Will Sly, playing an audience member, removes the feather from his hat and puts it in his pocket: 'Do you think I'll have jests broken upon me in the play, to be laughed at? This play hath beaten all your gallants out of the feathers; Blackfriars hath almost spoiled Blackfriars for feathers' (39–42). (Some years ago the publication of a book called *Real Men Don't Eat Quiche* caused a number of restaurants to serve something called 'cheese pie'.)

The fact that the adult company at the Globe adopted the play is another sign of its popularity. In doing so, however, they changed its character somewhat. Webster's Induction opens with a dispute in which the Tire-man discourages Sly from sitting on the stage, a private-playhouse custom the public playhouses had not accepted; from the beginning, the theatrical occasion feels different. Burbage refers to the additional scenes that have been added to pad out the performance and 'to abridge the not-received custom of music in our theatre' (83–4). (One of the additions is the Induction in which he speaks these lines.) The additions, which apart from the Induction may be partly or entirely by Marston, appear in the play's third printing. The music Burbage refers to would have been musical interludes played between the acts while the candles were being trimmed. But the crucial difference would have been in the age (and size) of the actors. Defending their appropriation of the play, Burbage calls it fair exchange for the boys' taking over *The Spanish Tragedy*: 'Why not Malevole in folio with us, as Jeronimo in decimo-sexto with them?' (78–9). At the Globe, *The Malcontent* would have benefited from the acting of 'the best in this kind'; but moving into a public playhouse lit by daylight, with its music reduced to the songs and flourishes the text requires and fully adult players for the male roles, it may also have lost something of the concentration and stylization of the Blackfriars performance.

At the same time it is fitting that its earliest stage history should have this shifting, unstable quality, since instability is essential to the play itself. Besides having a double life between two playhouses, *The Malcontent* was written sometime in the transition between two reigns. It can be dated as early as 1602 or as late as 1604;[4] Elizabeth died, and James succeeded her, in 1603. The play reflects a certain anxiety about governance. Its political action covers an unsettled year in the history of Marston's imaginary Genoa. The old Duke, Altofront, was banished but in the disguise of the malcontent Malevole he has returned to spy on his usurping successor Pietro; Pietro in his turn is (apparently) murdered by Mendoza, who succeeds him very briefly, only to be overthrown by Altofront. *Endymion* centred on a ruler who seemed fixed for eternity, beyond time and change; in *The Malcontent* the centre cannot hold. The legitimate ruler, banished to the margins, takes the opposition role of social critic and intriguer. Malevole–Altofront is a key figure in the disguised-ruler tradition that includes Middleton's *The Phoenix* (c.1603) and Shakespeare's *Measure for Measure* (c.1604). The question of who is really in charge, and the sense that the ruler is in hiding, may reflect the political anxieties of the period 1602–4: the uncertainty over who would succeed Elizabeth and the fact that even when James did so the curtailment of his public appearances by an outbreak of plague kept him largely hidden from his new subjects.[5] As *The Malcontent*'s satiric mode makes it sharply different from the celebratory comedy of *Endymion*, *Friar Bacon* and *A Midsummer Night's Dream*, so its view of authority as not just open to question but profoundly unstable means that, while it returns to the centred political vision of Lyly, it does so in a newly radical spirit. Once again we are focused tightly on a court and its ruler; the wide social range of Greene and Shakespeare is sharply contracted. But who is the ruler, and *what* is a ruler? Pietro, nominal Duke for most of the action, is clearly a transitional figure; Mendoza is no sooner established than he is deposed; and Altofront sardonically introduces himself as 'last year's Duke' (1.4.8).

While Cynthia answers to no one, Marston's Dukes seem dependent on two unseen, capricious forces: the fickle populace (non-existent in Lyly) and the offstage, unnamed but evidently formidable Duke of Florence. Altofront complains that while he ran a stable, equitable government – 'My throne stood like a point in the midst of a circle, / To all of equal nearness' – he not only 'wanted those old instruments of state, / Dissemblance and Suspect' but fell victim to the mob's itch for change:

the crowd
(Still lickerous of untried novelties),
Impatient with severer government,
Made strong with Florence, banished Altofront. (1.4.9–17)

One of the signs that the time is ripe for his return is the report of the loyal
courtier Celso: 'that beast with many heads, / The staggering multitude,
recoils apace' (3.3.5–6). Altofront's image of government as a point in the
centre of a circle recalls the stability and perfection of Cynthia; but the
reality is that his power ebbs and flows with popular favour. Another sign
of his imminent return is the message Bilioso brings back from the Duke of
Florence, who having originally matched his daughter Aurelia to Pietro
and banished Altofront now wants Aurelia executed, Pietro banished and
Altofront returned (4.5.81–3). As the Blackfriars actors would have
seemed imitation adults, the Dukes of Genoa seem at times to be imitation
dukes, absurdly preoccupied with their own power when in reality they
are puppets and Florence pulls the strings.

Yet at the end of the play, of Florence's three commands (kill Aurelia,
banish Pietro, restore Altofront) only the last is obeyed. The fact that his
message comes through Bilioso, a worthless old time-server, cheapens it;
and in the last analysis Florence's power, which could have been more
impressive for being unseen, seems as capricious, arbitrary and trivial as
that of the fickle populace. As Bacon's magic fades against the authority of
God, all worldly power in *The Malcontent* is finally distanced and unreal.
At the end of the play, in a speech added to the third printing, Altofront
surveys the 'strange accidents of state' (5.6.137) he has seen, warns against
the fickleness of the people, and concludes:

Yet thus much let the great ones still conceit
When they observe not Heaven's imposed conditions,
They are no kings, but forfeit their commissions. (5.6.147–9)

There is no such thing as an absolute right to rule; even the divine right of
kings has to be earned, and can be forfeited. That this was dangerous
doctrine as England entered the reign of King James (who was much
preoccupied with that right) is indicated by the fact that on some copies
'kings' has been changed to 'men'.

It is questionable whether any of the dukes of Genoa can claim
anything so dignified as divine right. Certainly not Pietro: he owes his
office to his marriage with Florence's daughter Aurelia. Mendoza, who
will overthrow him, calls him 'this weak-brained Duke, who only stands

on Florence' stilts' (3.3.85–6). Celso dismisses him as 'the too soft Duke' (3.3.11); we see that softness when, thinking to die of grief at Aurelia's adultery with the courtier Ferneze, he names Mendoza his heir, thus clearing the path for his own overthrow (2.3.65–75). While Ferneze has been caught in Aurelia's bed, Mendoza was there first. Given his role as usurper Pietro could have been a flamboyant tyrant; instead he is an amiable dupe and a cuckold. He is reluctant to engage even in the princely pastime of hunting, declaring it is 'unfit one beast [the horned cuckold] should hunt another' (3.4.4–5). Shakespeare uses hunting to create an air of princely glamour around Theseus and Hippolyta; Pietro has no glamour at all.

What he does have is a certain good nature that gives him a positive role in the long run. He shows one attribute of the good prince, licensing the plain speaking of Malevole: 'I like him, faith; he gives good intelligence to my spirit, makes me understand those weaknesses which others' flattery palliates' (1.2.28–30). He is less sanguine when Malevole's intelligence includes the news that Mendoza is cuckolding him. But even when he is about to catch her with Ferneze (on whom Mendoza has shifted the blame) he still exclaims, 'God knows I love her!' (2.3.65) and this love, though it may initially appear a sign of weakness, lays the groundwork for a reconciliation. In the end a repentant Pietro helps restore Altofront. T.F. Wharton has suggested that Pietro truly exemplifies the 'virtuous outsider', which is theoretically Altofront's role;[6] yet even in the final disposition of this character there is a certain confusion between pious withdrawal and political action:

> In true contrition I do dedicate
> My breath to solitary holiness,
> My lips to prayer; and my breast's care shall be,
> Restoring Altofront to regency.   (4.5.128–31)

He is playing not one virtuous role but two, and they don't quite add up. It is not the only such confusion in the play.

Mendoza seems to be the true villain. While Pietro is a uxorious cuckold, Mendoza, whom Malevole greets as 'you whoreson hot-reined he-marmoset' (1.5.7), is a sexual predator. The heat he generates is both sexual and political. In Malevole's words, 'Celso, the court's a-fire; the Duchess's sheets will smoke for't ere it be long; impure Mendoza, that sharp-nosed Lord that made the cursed match linked Genoa with Florence, now broad-horns the Duke, which he now knows' (i.4.33–7).

Cuckolding the Duke, he is betraying the match he himself made, and if (as we shall see) Aurelia is a political and sexual trophy, Mendoza is getting her by underhanded means. As the Duke's favourite he has a grand sense of his own power, dismissing a party of suitors with the words, 'I can and will' (1.5.1). He sees himself as the centre of attention in a grotesquely obsequious court, surrounded by 'petitionary vassals licking the pavement with their slavish knees' (1.5.28–9). The wonderful confusion in his imagery reflects something unstable in the character himself. His time as Duke is so brief that he never really establishes himself; and early in the play his gloating over his conquest of Aurelia turns into comic frenzy when she drops him for Ferneze.

We have seen how Lyly stylizes his female characters, with the grotesque witch Dipsas diametrically opposed to the perfect Cynthia. Mendoza's shifting relations with Aurelia lead him to pronounce contrary set-pieces on the perfection and corruption of women, which draw on contemporary stereotypes but are also linked, with comic obviousness, to the character's own interests. So long as he thinks he is in command of Aurelia, women are 'preservers of mankind, life-blood of society'. But Mendoza, being what he is, cannot pay tribute to their key virtue of chastity without betraying his own sexual interests: 'O Paradise! how majestical is your austerer presence! how imperiously chaste is your more modest face! but, O, how full of ravishing attraction is your pretty, petulant, languishing, lasciviously-composed countenance!' He concludes with a parody of *Hamlet*: 'in body how delicate, in soul how witty, in discourse how pregnant, in life how wary, in favours how judicious, in day how sociable, and in night how – O pleasure unutterable!' (1.5.37–48). Once Aurelia turns against him, of course, women are 'monsters in nature, models of hell, curse of the earth … slaves unto appetite, mistresses in dissembling, only constant in unconstancy' (1.6.85–91). (Pietro, reporting in disguise on his own 'suicide', attributes a similar diatribe to himself.)

The attack on female inconstancy is conventional, though Aurelia's own conduct justifies it to some degree. What the play emphasizes, however, is the way women are used as pawns in the sex-and-power games played by the men. For a while it seems that whoever gets Aurelia gets Genoa; it was her match with Pietro that gave Pietro the dukedom and led to Altofront's banishment (1.4.19–22). When she cuckolds Pietro she makes his rule unstable,[7] and she herself, reconciled with Mendoza, plans the next logical step: 'I'll make thee Duke. We are of Medicis' (2.5.79). As Aurelia goes, so goes the state. Confident of her own power, she does not realize that while Mendoza is temporarily dependent on her, in the long run he is simply using her. When Ferneze and the bawd Maquerelle warn her of his disloyalty – 'he loved you but for a spurt, or so' (1.6.19) – they are lying as part of Ferneze's seduction of her; but they are also predicting what Mendoza will really do. His first act on becoming Duke is to banish her.

Aurelia, unstable in herself, has power to make only illegitimate dukes, and once she has served her purpose she is discarded. By the end of the play she, like Pietro, has turned penitent. The political and sexual trophy who really matters is Altofront's wife Maria, whose salient feature is her constancy. Mendoza tries to consolidate his position by marrying her, and his failure to win her hand predicts his own loss of power. Mendoza is cynical about marriage, seeing it as a convenience of state, to be overturned if the public interest (that is, his own interest) requires it: 'A kingdom's safety should o'er-peise slight rites' (5.6.2). Maria, however, sees her marriage to Altofront as a commitment unto death: 'Do, urge all torments, all afflictions try; / I'll die my lord's as long as I can die' (5.6.30–1). As Aurelia's sexual inconstancy is a sign of the state's political instability Maria, withdrawn from court and imprisoned in a citadel, embodies through her chastity the political constancy Genoa has lost.

She also makes it hard for Altofront to sustain his role as the cynical, destructive Malevole. He makes a bawdy joke out of the initial failure of his request for an interview, claiming he 'must have a stiffer warrant, or no pass into the Castle of Comfort' (4.3.116–17). Her constancy, which delights him as Altofront, is a challenge to Malevole's cynical view of the world. For a while he tries to accommodate it while keeping the misogyny of the Malevole pose intact; then he simply gives up:

Maquerelle, tell thee, I have found an honest woman. Faith, I perceive, when all is done, there is of women, as of all other things, some good, most bad; some saints, some sinners. For as nowadays no courtier but has his mistress, no captain but has his cockatrice, no cuckold but has his horns, and no fool but has his feather; even so, no woman but has her weakness and feather too, no sex but has his – I can hunt the letter no further – [*Aside*] O God, how loathsome this toying is to me! That a duke should be forced to fool it!
(5.3.35–44)

Maria not only frustrates Mendoza; she breaks down Malevole. In the process she suggests how much her husband's adoption of this role has been a betrayal of himself, as opposed to her own single-minded constancy.

The instability of the state finds its equivalent in the instability of the central character. Through the discussion so far, I have called him sometimes Malevole and sometimes Altofront; it is a confusion the play itself encourages. Altofront is supposed to be his real identity, Malevole his disguise; but in practice the line between the characters is blurred. When he complains of insomnia, in what is virtually a soliloquy (Bilioso is on stage, but he appears not to notice him), he does so not in his own person but in his adopted role: 'Only the malcontent, that 'gainst his fate / Repines and quarrels – alas, he's goodman tell-clock!' (3.2.11–12).[8] Reporting to Celso, who knows his secret, he sees the disorder of the court as an opportunity for both his characters, sliding from one to the other: 'Discord to malcontents is very manna; / When the ranks are burst, then scuffle Altofront' (1.4.38–9). One way to see the Altofront–Malevole connection is as an early example of Stanislavskian acting: Altofront uses Malevole as a way of expressing his real bitterness and frustration as a deposed ruler.[9] Yet there is also a contradiction between the roles. Malevole promotes and relishes discord and disorder: the out-of-tune music that opens the play comes from his chamber. He attacks corruption with a salacious relish that suggests imaginative participation in it. That participation is symbolized by his links with Maquerelle, whom he describes as 'my mistress' (1.3.87). He shares a bawdy song with her, their voices working together with suspicious ease (5.2.1–4).[10] Philip J. Finkel-pearl describes the stock malcontent, frustrated, melancholic, overeducated and underemployed, as 'a prime source of danger to the kingdom since he was readily available for schemes against the established order. In these, he could be relied on to employ special skills acquired in Italy for plotting and murder.'[11] The figure of order is a figure of disorder; the prince is an enemy to the state. The paradox may be resolved by noting that, since the state itself is in disorder, opposition to it is the truest loyalty. This logic recalls the use of inversion in popular protest (men dressed as women, the parodic use of titles): to invert a world that is already upside-down is to put it right again.[12] Yet the sense of a contradictory nature, an uneasy combination of prince and satirist, Alexander and Diogenes in the same character, persists. As Pietro comments, listening to the discordant music from Malevole's chamber, 'The elements struggle within him; his own soul is at variance within herself' (1.2.26–7).

In soliloquy, Altofront reflects that though he has lost office the malcontent role gives him a new power:

> Well, this disguise doth yet afford me that
> Which kings do seldom hear or great men use –

> Free speech; and though my state's usurped,
> Yet this affected strain gives me a tongue
> As fetterless as is an emperor's.   (1.3.161–5)

But he evidently has this freedom only because he is licensed by the Duke. In the first scene Pietro invites him on to the stage: 'I give thy dogged sullenness free liberty; trot about and bespurtle whom thou pleasest' (1.2.10–12). He is let out of his kennel, but on a lead; the Duke's collar is around his neck. The contradiction between his claim of free speech and his role as licensed entertainer is repeated in his later role as hired killer, another stock use of the malcontent. When Mendoza orders him to murder the Duke he exclaims in glee, 'My heart's wish, my soul's desire, my fantasy's dream, my blood's longing, the only height of my hopes!' (3.3.75–6). But he is acting as Mendoza's creature, and Mendoza of course plans Malevole's own death as part of the deal. Moreover, his blood-thirstiness is only a pose: he spares Pietro, enlists him in his own cause and contrives a false report of his death. In this case it is clear that Altofront can distance himself from Malevole, and control the irony in the latter's role; it is less clear that he realizes the restriction on his free speech as a satirist.

Altofront, his 'real' identity, never comes into focus as sharply as Malevole does. Altofront seems to be not so much what he is when alone – we have seen how the Malevole personality invades his soliloquies – as what he is with his follower Celso. It is his greeting to the latter, which he delivers in the person of Malevole, that first lets us hear a different voice from him: 'Alas, poor Celso, thy star's oppressed; thou art an honest lord; 'tis pity' (1.3.66–7). In his first soliloquy he reveals that he is not what he appears; but he does not speak his true name until Celso has entered, and Michael Scott notes that his self-introduction – 'Behold forever-banished Altofront' (1.4.7) – makes Altofront sound like one more role for him to play.[13]

Perhaps the strongest argument for seeing Altofront as the character's essential nature, directing Malevole as opposed to sharing space with him, is the conservative basis of so much of the play's (and the character's) satire. Marston's epistle to the reader declares, 'I have not glanced at the disgrace of any but of those whose unquiet studies labour innovation, contempt of holy policy, reverend comely superiority, and established unity' (20–2). When Mendoza offers to make Malevole a great man and he replies, 'Nay, make me some rich knave, and I'll make myself some great man' (3.3.120–1), he is mocking a world in which reverend superiority and established unity have given way to material power. When he gloats over the way he has troubled Pietro's peace by stirring his jealousy, he adds a tag, '*Beneath God, naught's so dear as a calm heart*' (1.3.172), that seems to break free of its context (the mockery of Pietro) and express an underlying longing for peace, a longing that can be shared by jealous husbands, malcontents and deposed princes. Settled order is embodied not just in Maria but in the Captain whose duty it is to guard her in the citadel, and who declares, 'I received the guardianship of this citadel from the good Altofront, and for his use I'll keep't, till I am of no use' (5.2.77–9). Malevole–Altofront is delighted: 'Captain Conscience, I love thee Captain' (5.2.81–2). The citadel is not so much a prison as a place of retreat where old values are respected and preserved.

A similar place of retreat is the hermit's cell the disguised Pietro describes to the banished Aurelia:

> My cell 'tis, lady; where, instead of masks,
> Music, tilts, tourneys, and such courtlike shows,
> The hollow murmur of the checkless winds
> Shall groan again, whilst the unquiet sea
> Shakes the whole rock with foamy battery.
> There usherless the air comes in and out;
> The rheumy vault will force your eyes to weep,
> Whilst you behold true desolation.
> A rocky barenness shall pierce your eyes,
> Where all at once one reaches, where he stands,
> With brows the roof; both walls with both his hands. (4.5.12–22)

This is the equivalent of the cloistered retreats offered Margaret in *Friar Bacon* and Hermia in *A Midsummer Night's Dream*. But they are characters in romantic comedies, where such a life cannot finally compete with love and marriage. Aurelia is in a satiric comedy, in which the idea of withdrawal from the world's corruption is more compelling. The cell offers a retreat from and a contrast to the empty pride and luxury of the court; it also offers Aurelia what Hermia and Margaret do not need, chastisement and penitence for her sins. Her response to Pietro's description is 'It is too good' (4.5.23). Cleansed and penitent, she is reconciled with her husband. Malevole–Altofront offers Ferneze (who has been discovered with Aurelia and badly wounded) a similar retreat: 'Come, I'll convey thee to a private port, / Where thou shalt live (O happy man) from court' (2.5.156–7). There is throughout the play a strong imaginative pull away from the court, to places of austerity and retreat where a life of integrity can be lived. Altofront feels this pull himself, and this means that his determination to get his dukedom back, and his success in doing so, form one more contradiction in his character.

There is an essentially conservative stance behind the play's, and Malevole's, attack on the court itself. According to Malevole the palace has become a brothel: 'I would sooner leave my lady singled in a bordello than in the Genoa palace' (3.2.28–9). Early in the play he fixes on a minor character, Ferrardo, as symptomatic of the court's rampant sexuality. Ferrardo, according to Malevole, will try anything: he is the Duke's catamite (1.2.6–9), and he runs wild among the women: 'he goes sucking up and down the palace into every hen's nest, like a weasel' (1.3.23–4). The bawd Maquerelle conveys the general tone when, chatting with a page and finding he has turned fourteen, she immediately treats him as a client (4.1.4–8). This rampant sexuality threatens social breakdown, as Malevole implies in one of the additions when he warns Pietro that adultery, by confusing parentage, can lead to unwitting incest (1.3.131–8).

Malevole is also much concerned with the breakdown of the church. On his first entrance he claims he has just been at 'the public place of much dissimulation, the church', where he dealt with a usurer (1.3.4–7). Marston himself would later abandon writing and become a priest; already the state of the church seems a serious issue for him, judging by the frequency with which the play returns to it. Once again the centre cannot hold; there are too many faiths on offer: 'Sects, sects; I have seen seeming Piety change her robe so oft, that sure none but some arch-devil can shape her a petticoat' (1.3.11–13). Bilioso, in one of the additions, reflects the reduction of religion to time-serving: he is 'Of the Duke's religion, when I know what it is' (4.5.94). Throughout the sixteenth century, as England shuttled back and forth between Catholic and Protestant rulers, many English people must have taken the same shifty line. There is a general weakening of religious sensibility among the characters. Pietro speaks of Lucifer being 'thrust out of the presence' (1.2.20) as though Heaven were just one more court. When Pietro threatens to kill Mendoza and demands he say his prayers, Mendoza replies, 'I ha' forgot 'um' (1.7.2–3). One of Malevole's key images of the world's corruption is the desecrated church: 'I ha' seen a sumptuous steeple turned to a stinking privy; more beastly, the sacredest place made a dog's kennel; nay, most inhuman, the stoned coffins of long-dead Christians burst up, and made hogs' troughs: *Hic finis Priami*' (2.5.128–32).[14] We touch here on the conservatism of the play's satire, its sense of a good old order ruined.

Other moments hint at a pervasive smell of corruption: the stage has to be perfumed before Pietro's first entrance (1.1.6–9); Malevole refuses Mendoza's command to 'come hither', telling him, 'Thou hast a certain strong villainous stench about thee my nature cannot endure' (5.4.7–9). We may be tempted to take such moments as home truths about the world. Yet Malevole's most eloquent statement of *contemptus mundi* is not disinterested satire; it is part of Altofront's political agenda. He tells Pietro to renounce his political ambition:

> Come, be not confounded; th'art but in danger to lose a dukedom. Think this – this earth is the only grave and Golgotha wherein all things that live must rot; 'tis but the draught wherein the heavenly bodies discharge their corruption; the very muck-hill on which the sublunary orbs cast their excrements. Man is the slime of this dung-pit, and princes are the governors of these men …
>
> (4.5.108–15)

Once again the character is divided: Malevole pours contempt on worldly power so that Pietro will be willing to surrender it to Altofront.[15] 'Think this' turns the speech from an objective statement to an idea adopted for the nonce; it is what Altofront needs Pietro to think. As for himself, if the earth is a dung-heap, he plans to climb to the top of it.

In this case Malevole's detachment from the world serves Altofront's worldly purposes. We might expect, behind his satire on the deterioration of the church, a belief in a firm Providential order to set against human instability; but for Altofront the cosmos itself is unstable, and that instability is not just a source of fear but an opportunity. When Pietro repents, and Ferneze and Celso join him as allies, Altofront greets the upward turn in his fortunes:

> Who doubts of Providence that sees this change?
> A hearty faith to all!
> *He needs must rise who can no lower fall;*
> For still impetuous vicissitude
> Touseth the world. Then let no maze intrude
> Upon your spirits; wonder not I rise;
> *For who can sink that close can temporize?*
>
> (4.5.141–7)

The opening tribute to Providence is erased as Malevole goes on to credit what sounds like Fortune's wheel (what goes down must come up), then some more chaotic and unpredictable force, then his own devious political skill. Far from asserting a stable cosmic order, Altofront offers a grab-bag of possibilities. There is a shiftiness even in his view of his own skill; after the cynical aphorism about temporizing he ends the speech with a more dignified tag: '*Mature discretion is the life of state*' (4.5.151). The speech begins with Providence and ends with statesmanship; in between is chaos, a random world in which the winners are those who keep their wits about them. The instability of the court is an opportunity for Mendoza and Altofront alike. Mendoza's 'the multitude / Irresolutely reeling; we in force' (2.5.83–4) and Altofront's 'When the ranks are burst, then scuffle Altofront' (1.4.39) convey the same excitement at seizing the moment. As satire *The Malcontent* expresses the longing for a stable order; as political comedy it conveys the excitement of a game of skill and chance.

The ending seems to present an image of order. Mendoza, with unconscious irony, plans to celebrate his accession with a show of past dukes, exemplifying the continuity of the office he is usurping. His own attitude to the show is casual and flippant:

> What shape? Why, any quick-done fiction;
> As some brave spirits of the Genoan Dukes,
> To come out of Elysium, forsooth,
> Led in by Mercury, to gratulate
> Our happy fortune; some such anything;
> Some far-fet trick, good for ladies, some stale toy or other,
> No matter, so't be of our devising.   (5.4.65–71)

(Is it significant that Mercury was not only 'guide of the dead'[16] but a common treatment for venereal disease?) Mendoza utters this speech over what he thinks is the dead body of Malevole – who is really alive, and really Altofront, the once and future Duke who will replace Mendoza. Mendoza's show will be a more significant affirmation of the Genoan Dukedom than he realizes; the dukes he has summoned up will strip off their disguises and overpower him.

The ultimate effect, however, is mixed. The masquers are Altofront and his allies Pietro, Celso and Ferneze. Two of these really are former Dukes, the third a figure of loyalty, the fourth a more dubious character. The stage direction for their entrance suggests their power is not just the natural authority of the office but something more practical: they enter, to music, '*in white robes, with duke's crowns upon laurel wreaths; pistolets and short swords under their robes*' (5.4.68.2–4). The stage direction conveys to the reader the point the audience will get as soon as the dukes unmask and turn their pistols on Mendoza: the symbolism of music and costume is all very well, but power comes out of the barrel of a gun.

The use of weapons grounds the ending in practical reality. While affirming order, it discredits the notion that order is natural or providential. There are also curious overtones in the masque that pull against the celebration of Altofront's return, touching it with suggestions of death and melancholy. Though the Dukes come ostensibly to celebrate, they are led in by 'Cyllenian Mercury, the god of ghosts, / From gloomy shades that spread the lower coasts' (5.4.56–7); they are ambassadors of death. That may seem like a threat to Mendoza. But the revels that accompany the masque include Maria, who is under sentence of death, and Aurelia, who enters in mourning. Altofront takes Maria to dance, and she tells him, 'why then you dance with death' (5.4.72); Pietro offers to dance with Aurelia, and she asks, 'What, wouldst thou court misery?' (5.4.82). Altofront and Pietro are among the nominal winners at the play's end, but one has danced with death and the other with sorrow. The women, no longer trophies, seem to exemplify the longing for retreat from the world that the play has not altogether shed, and that pulls against the triumph of Altofront's return.

In a sense the most vital figure at the end is Ferneze. Wounded and apparently dead after being discovered with Aurelia, he has returned to life, received a lecture against lust from Malevole and joined Altofront's counter-revolution. But any impression that he is born again is wiped out when we find him in the last scene dancing with Maquerelle and trying to seduce Bilioso's wife Bianca (5.6.87–8). If Ferneze is incorrigible, perhaps the court is incorrigible. If so, Altofront will simply be in charge of a brothel. Yet with Maria celebrating her impending execution – 'Die like a bride, poor heart, thou shalt die chaste' – and Aurelia declaring *'Life is a frost of cold felicity, / And death the thaw of all our vanity'* (5.6.44–6), chastity and penitence seem associated with the rejection of life, and if life is to go on there may be something to be said for Ferneze's impenitence.

Nominally, the play attacks a corrupt present, longs for a good old order, and celebrates that order's return. If its date is 1604, it could be an early example of nostalgia for Elizabeth. But the impression of conservatism and moral firmness is vitiated in ways I have indicated: the instability of the central character, the cynical pragmatism that touches the play's politics. There is also an air of unreality over the whole play that allows a pervasive irony. The local disruptiveness of *Pyramus and Thisbe* breaks out all over *The Malcontent* in a persistent, self-mocking meta-theatricality. Marston, presenting the play to the reader, insists it is really a theatrical experience: 'only one thing afflicts me, to think that scenes invented merely to be spoken should be enforcively published to be read ('To the Reader', 26–8). Even granted the general extravagance of Jacobean drama, there are passages in which the theatricality seems self-mocking:

Malevole. ... Pistols and poinards! pistols and poinards!
Pietro. Death and damnation!
Malevole. Lightning and thunder!
Pietro. Vengeance and torture!
Malevole. Catso!
Pietro. O, revenge!   (1.3.101–7)

Imagining this in what Marston calls 'the soul of lively action' ('To the Reader', 36–7), it is impossible to imagine it played seriously. Self-parody of this kind creates metatheatrical awareness in the audience. Such awareness is more explicit when Malevole warns Pietro, 'O do not rand [rant], do not turn player; there's more of them than can well live one by another already' (4.4.4–5). We may recall the reference in *Hamlet* to the way the boy actors (like the Blackfriars company) are driving the adults (like the Globe company) out of business. Whether metatheatrical awareness was automatically triggered by the boy actors, childishly imitating adult passion, is a matter of controversy;[17] but in this case there are moments when the text itself invites such awareness. Webster's Induction ensures the effect is carried over into the public playhouse by bringing several of the Globe actors onstage in their own persons.

When Malevole exclaims gleefully on Mendoza's failure to murder him, 'poisoned with an empty box!' (5.4.88), he suggests not just the fakery of all stage deaths (we will do no harm with our swords) but the basic unreality of the play's action. There is also an air of sheer fun in the intrigue: when Malevole and Pietro are hired to kill each other, the former exclaims, 'Cross capers, tricks!' (4.4.13). Satire can be a serious business, but the satire of this play is regularly deflated by flippancy. Malevole follows his grim warning about adultery leading to incest with a glib joke about simony (1.3.140–7). There are bursts of speed in the writing that add to the flippancy, as when Malevole tells Pietro, 'Maquerelle is a cunning bawd; I am an honest villain; thy wife is a close drab; and thou art a notorious cuckold. Farewell, Duke' (1.3.89–91). He seems to be saying, so what?

John Scott Colley complains, 'The pervasive mood of unreality that critics note about the play interferes with its political message, and detracts from its sense of moral urgency.' He sees this as 'a failure of nerve, or a failure of vision'.[18] According to R.A. Foakes, Marston offers 'a sort of cartoon version of a corrupt court, in which revenge motifs are deployed for comic and melodramatic effects'.[19] This cartoon quality is nowhere more apparent than in Malevole–Altofront's final speech:

> [*To the courtiers*][20] You o'er-joyed spirits, wipe your long-wet eyes.
> (*Kicks out Mendoza*) Hence with this man: an eagle takes not flies.
> (*To Pietro and Aurelia*) You to your vows; (*To Maquerelle*) and thou unto the
>   suburbs.
> (*To Bilioso*) You to my worst friend I would hardly give;
>   Thou art a perfect old knave. All-pleased live
> (*To Celso and the* Captain) You two unto my breast; (*To Maria*) thou to my
>   heart.
>   The rest of idle actors idly part.
>   And as for me, I here assume my right,
>   To which I hope all's pleased. To all, good night.
> > *Coronets, a flourish. Exeunt omnes.*
> > (5.6.159–67.1)

Order is at once restored and trivialized. The discordant music that opens the play is succeeded by the music of triumph. Malevole and Altofront are integrated as the Duke enforces the judgements of the satirist. With Maquerelle sent where she belongs, the court may no longer be a brothel. But Altofront does not seem to notice what Ferneze is up to, and while he insults Bilioso he does not explicitly banish him. More important, the sheer speed of the speech deflates its seriousness. Mendoza is hardly a formidable villain if he can be despatched with a simple kick, and Altofront's victory over him is accordingly less impressive. In the drama of the period, last speeches generally *feel* like last speeches and create a metatheatrical awareness that the play is nearly over. This awareness is particularly strong here, as Altofront dismisses 'the rest of idle actors' (the other courtiers, the audience?) and bids us good night.

The restoration of order seems as trivial as the rest of the action.[21] This has been anticipated earlier in the play, when Malevole compares 'the state of humanity' to buckets rising and falling in a well (3.3.63–6) and Maquerelle talks of playing favourites with her two dogs: 'Now I, like Lady Fortune, sometimes love this dog, sometimes raise that dog, sometimes favour Watch, most commonly fancy Catch' (5.2.49–52). From this perspective the rise of Altofront and the fall of Mendoza are drained of moral significance. They may also be drained of reality. When, to a flourish of cornets, Mendoza's enemies reveal themselves, he exclaims,

> What strange delusions mock
> Our senses? Do I dream? or have I dreamt
> This two days' space? Where am I?   (5.6.117–19)

Was his time of power unreal, or is this present (and highly theatrical) moment unreal? Or both? His confusion is like that of the lovers in *A Midsummer Night's Dream* waking from their night in the forest. But while in Shakespeare's comedy distancing the action into a dream was a form of consolation, making trouble seem unreal, here the effect is to make everything seem unreal. Early in the play Malevole complains that he cannot sleep but he dreams anyway:

methinks I see that signior pawn his footcloth, that metreza her plate; this madam takes physic, that t'other monsieur may minister to her; here is a pander jewelled; there is a fellow in a shift of satin this day, that could not shift a shirt t'other night. Here a Paris supports that Helen; there's a Lady Guinever bears up that Sir Lancelot – dreams, dreams, visions, fantasies, chimeras, imaginations, tricks, conceits!   (1.3.49–56)

He is speaking to Pietro, and so at the end he slips into images of adultery. But the general effect of the speech is that he sees the ordinary world going about its business as a waking nightmare. He sees no lurid violence, no horrific crimes; just trivial corruption, changes of fortune signalled by changes of clothing and trips to the pawnbroker, material transactions of the sort we shall see in *Michaelmas Term*. It is normal life that is fantastic and unreal.

If there is seriousness behind the play's flippancy it may lie in this suggestion of life as a play, a dream, a fantasy as unreal as the cartoon action of the court of Genoa. Marston's epistle to the reader, as we have seen, endorses established order; the play registers a longing for a calm, settled life. But as its central character, unstable and even unreal in himself, sees the world as a waking nightmare, the Latin tag that ends the epistle declares, '*Sine aliqua dementia nullus Phoebus*' (38): there is no poetic power without some madness. The madness in question may be, initially, poetic inspiration. But it may also be the dislocated, alienated vision that sees the world not as fundamentally ordered but as fundamentally unreal.

Notes

1 All references to *The Malcontent* are to the Revels edition, ed. George K. Hunter, London, 1975.

2 *John Marston of the Middle Temple*, Cambridge, Mass., 1969, p. 38. On the

larger tradition of festive abuse the boys' companies inherited, see Michael Shapiro, *Children of the Revels*, New York, 1977, p. 40.

3 Hunter, Introduction, pp. xxviii–xxx.

4 Hunter surveys the evidence, noting 'a convergence of arguments on 1603': Introduction, pp. xli–xlvi.

5 Keith Whigham, 'Flattering Courtly Desire', *The Theatrical City: Culture, Theatre and Politics in London, 1576–1649*, ed. David L. Smith, Richard Strier and David Bevington, Cambridge, 1995, pp. 138–9. The general edginess of the transitional period is indicated by the report of a contemporary observer in London that in March 1603, as the old Queen lay dying, 'many men, both nobles and others, have made very great provision of armour, munitions and victuals': quoted in Derek Hirst, *Authority and Conflict: England 1603–1658*, London, 1986, p. 96.

6 '*The Malcontent* and "Dreams, Visions, Fantasies"', *Essays in Criticism*, XXIV, 1974, 269.

7 Lloyd Davis has noted that in this play male anxiety about political instability is transformed into attacks on female inconstancy: *Guise and Disguise: Rhetoric and Characterization in the English Renaissance*, Toronto, Buffalo and London, 1993, p. 83.

8 Donald K. Hedrick notes that while satirists are bad sleepers so are princes: 'The Masquing Principle in Marston's *The Malcontent*', *English Literary Renaissance*, VIII, 1978, 41. This is a valid point, but Malevole does not make the connection himself. Hedrick's argument that Altofront is like a prince in a masque, adopting a role but with his own identity always clear, is one of the most interesting readings of the character's disguise (pp. 27–34).

9 Michael Scott, *John Marston's Plays: Theme, Structure and Performance*, London and Basingstoke, 1978, p. 29; Finkelpearl calls the character 'a true malcontent posing as a malcontent'(*John Marston*, p. 185).

10 Wharton, '*Malcontent*', p. 271.

11 *John Marston*, p. 184.

12 David Underdown, *Revel, Riot, and Rebellion: Popular Politics and Culture in England 1603–1660*, Oxford and New York, 1985, p. 111.

13 *Plays*, pp. 28–9. For a reading of Altofront as the character's essential identity, not just one more role, see Robert Beale Bennett, 'The Royal Ruse: Malcontentedness in John Marston's *The Malcontent*', *Medieval and Renaissance Drama in England*, I, 1984, 81–2.

14 Marston may be recalling the decay and demolition of the old monastic churches in the late Tudor period; see D.M. Palliser, *The Age of Elizabeth: England under the Later Tudors 1547–1603*, 2nd edn, London and New York, 1992, p. 431.

15 Scott, *Plays*, p. 32.

16 Hunter, commentary, p. 145.

17 Shapiro, *Children*, sees metatheatrical awareness as a feature of the boys'

companies (pp. 103–12). For a contrary view see Ann Blake, '"The Humour of Children": John Marston's Plays in the Private Theatres', *Review of English Studies*, XXXVIII, 1987, 471–82.

18 *John Marston's Theatrical Drama*, Salzburg, 1974, p. 126.

19 'On Marston, *The Malcontent*, and *The Revenger's Tragedy*', *The Elizabethan Theatre VI*, ed. G.R. Hibbard, Toronto, 1978, p. 69.

20 This is Hunter's emendation; in the original the line is addressed to Pietro and Aurelia. See Hunter, commentary, p. 158.

21 Michael Scott makes a similar point, but he seems to imagine 'real' people and situations behind the role-playing, regarding Altofront as a character who can be criticized for his shallowness (*Plays*, pp. 30–1). I am less certain that we are to imagine an underlying reality.

6

Middleton, *Michaelmas Term*

W HILE the Children of the Blackfriars performed satiric comedies with topical references that regularly got them into trouble, the Children of Paul's mined a vein of city comedy in which sexual and financial intrigue followed rules so conventional that there was generally no need for the standard disclaimer against personal satire. This was not their only fare – they also performed Chapman's demanding tragedy *Bussy d'Ambois*, for example – but if they had a specialty it was the sort of play in which gallants and usurers, city wives and courtesans, involve themselves in cheats and intrigues. The years 1604–5 saw them perform a cluster of such plays: Dekker and Webster's *Westward Ho* and *Northward Ho*, depicting the frustrated sexual adventures of gallants courting city wives, and Middleton's *A Trick to Catch the Old One*, *A Mad World, My Masters* and *Michaelmas Term*, all of which combine sexual intrigue with chicanery involving money and land. The close concentration of these plays in a relatively short period suggests that Middleton, a busy professional writer, was playing on a fashion, and aiming at a market with clearly defined tastes. This was, nominally, Lyly's old company; but it was hardly performing in Lyly's style. Besides the cynical, prosaic manner of the plays themselves, the theatrical occasion was changing. Music (still important for Marston in the Blackfriars *Malcontent*) was becoming marginal at Paul's; and, assuming a certain continuity in the company, which had re-formed in 1599, many of the principal children would now be young men: there is is a reference in 1606 to 'the youths of Paul's'.[1] Closer to the ages of the characters they were playing, they could tilt the performance away from stylization and towards realism.

The fascination with London as a dramatic subject runs through all these plays, none more than *Michaelmas Term*. Middleton subjects the city to the kind of scrutiny Marston had fixed on the court. Though the Induction promises nothing more than a portrait of the city going about its business, 'those familiar accidents which happen'd in town in the circumference of those six weeks whereof Michaelmas Term is lord' (71–3),[2] the action is in fact shaped around one central idea: the flow of people from the country into the city. Between 1550 and 1700, while the population of England 'less than doubled', the population of London quadrupled.[3] The excitement, danger and tension of being where everybody else wants to be preoccupied English drama (comedy in particular) in a variety of ways throughout the seventeenth century. Middleton's vision, like Lyly's and Marston's and unlike Greene's and Shakespeare's, is centred, not dispersed. His centre is a place.

The main story lines concern three characters who come to London and, with varying degrees of literalness, lose themselves. Andrew Lethe (formerly Andrew Gruel) forgets his name and humble origins and with the help of fancy clothes tries to live the life of a gentleman with court ambitions. A Country Wench, who has no proper name, comes to London to live as a gentlewoman, and fulfils her ambition by becoming a prostitute; she makes no distinction between the roles. She is transformed, like Lethe, by new clothes. Richard Easy, a gentleman of Essex, loses not his name but the source of his social identity, his land. In an elaborate intrigue that makes up the central action he is fleeced by the usuring linen-draper Quomodo. The importance of changing clothes in London is signalled in the Induction, where Michaelmas Term himself appears in '*a whitish cloak, new come up out of the country*' (0.1) and then formally, allegorically, lays it aside:

> Lay by my conscience,
> Give me my gown, that weed is for the country;
> We must be civil now, and match our evil;
> Who first made civil black, he pleas'd the devil.
> So, now I know where I am.   (1–5)

That last touch suggests that by changing gowns he is not just creating a role, he is creating a place. Black, the devil's colour, is also the colour of lawyers and city officials; Middleton seems to be anticipating Shelley's claim that Hell is a city much like London.[4]

The one character who appears to have a moral purpose in London is the Country Wench's father, who has come to rescue his daughter from a life of sin. He is driven by his own memory of the city as the place where he literally lost himself:

> Woe worth th'infernal cause that makes me visit
> This man-devouring city, where I spent
> My unshapen youth, to be my age's curse,
> And surfeited away my name and state
> In swinish riots, that now, being sober,
> I do awake a beggar. (2.2.20–5)

The dream-motif returns, as London's pleasures become a delusion from which one awakes to cold reality. The Father goes on to see his rescue mission as a kind of Harrowing of Hell: 'Such is my care to fright her from base evils, / I leave calm state to live amongst you, devils' (2.2.37–8). We shall see that as moral agent and rescuer the Father fails. But his reference to London as a place that devours 'unshapen youth' has a force that resonates through the play. While the wood near Athens is a place of transformation, London is a place of dissolution, of unshaping, where people and actions lose their distinctive forms.

In both language and action, sexual and financial transactions collapse into each other. As Marston's court is a brothel, Middleton's London is a place of exchange where money, goods, land and women are all in play together. Quomodo sums up the class war between citizens like himself and gentry like Easy as 'our deadly enmity, which thus stands: / They're busy 'bout our wives, we 'bout their lands' (1.1.106–7). Enmity notwithstanding (and other forms of trade include mutual hostility), he seems to be describing a barter system. He is also anticipating the action of the play, in which he gets Easy's land and Easy gets his wife. As a prostitute, the Country Wench is in business. Encouraging her new career, the pander Hellgill advises, 'Virginity is no city trade' (1.2.43). She later offers a punning defence of her business and insists that it is not confined to the brothels: 'Is not wholesale the chiefest merchandise? Do you think some merchants could keep their wives so brave, but for their wholesale?' (4.2.13–15). The pun (holesale) gives a limited, strictly pragmatic sense of what she and the merchants' wives are selling. Hellgill points to the paradox that men and women have different sources of credit. In a man's business, ruin is ruin; in a woman's, ruin is success: 'Let a man break, he's gone, blown up, / A woman's breaking sets her up' (1.2.41–2). Given the air of calculation in the puns, the effect of such passages is not to make business seem erotic but to make sex seem businesslike.

Sex is conflated with law when Andrew Lethe sees a pair of gallants chatting up the Country Wench, whom he thinks of as his property: 'what do they but ... like two crafty attorneys, finding a hole in my lease, go about to defeat me of my right?' (3.1.144–7). As in the 'wholesale' pun, the discovery of the hole turns the property from something owned to something transferable.[5] The Country Wench equates her body with the law year, and points out that she is equipped to do more business even than the lawyers: 'our Term ends once a month; we should get more than the lawyers, for they have but four Terms a year, and we have twelve' (3.1.50–2). She has none of her father's sense of her trade as destructive; she thinks of it only as brisk. It is the gallant Salewood, losing at dice, who speaks for the ruined client:

> I'll be damned, and these be not the bones
> Of some quean that cozened me in her life,
> And now consumes me after her death.   (2.1.127–9)

Law, business, gaming and sex are the means by which the man-devouring city claims its victims, and one trade keeps shading into another.

There is no equivalent here for the fixed, chaste devotion of Marston's Maria, and there are no permanent values for such a character to guard or exemplify. There is not even an equivalent, among the women at least, of Aurelia's penitence. Middleton's women are as ready to be used as coins, and as unconcerned. They fall quickly. As the Father puts it, invoking conventional sexual standards, 'One minute, and eternally undone' (2.2.30). Quomodo, chagrined at the speed with which his wife has given herself to Easy, goes further. When the Judge comments that 'oft a minute does it' he retorts, 'Less, a moment, / The twinkling of an eye, a glimpse, scarce something does it' (5.3.53–4). Early in her career the Country Wench makes a brief attempt to see herself as the victim of temptation, but Hellgill retorts, 'I know you are all chaste enough, / Till one thing or another tempt you' (1.2.31–2). Even outwardly respectable women have quick imaginations, betrayed by their language. Quomodo's daughter Susan, warned that if she dines with Lethe she will have to eat standing, replies, 'methinks it does me most good when I take it standing' (2.3.66–7). Her mother rejects Lethe's advances not out of chastity but out of social discrimination: ''tis for his betters to have opportunity of me' (2.3.7–8). Even the conventional greeting of the social kiss is enough to arouse her: kissing Easy, she comments, 'Beshrew my blood, a proper springall and a sweet gentleman' (2.3.403–4), and her interest in his body becomes as keen as Quomodo's interest in his land. Lethe gives the gallants Rearage and Salewood leave to kiss the Country Wench and is chagrined at the results: "Slid, they both court her at once, and see, if she ha' not the wit to stand still and let 'em! I think if two men were brew'd into one, there is that woman would drink 'em up both' (3.1.85–8). In *The Malcontent* promiscuity and chastity were signs, respectively, of cynical power politics and established loyalty. In *Michaelmas Term* everything and everyone is for sale, and there is only promiscuity.

There are faint hints of the country as a place where old values are preserved, as they are in the citadel in *The Malcontent*. Easy's fall begins when Quomodo's assistant Shortyard, in his disguise as Blastfield, claims a common acquaintance in another Essex gentleman, Alsup. Alsup's name suggests old-fashioned country hospitality, the pleasure and pastime we saw in *Friar Bacon*; Easy remarks, 'I should keep Christmas with him' (2.1.24). But as Shortyard's alias (Blastfield) indicates, this is simply part of a ploy to deprive Easy of his land. The real function of the country in *Michaelmas Term* is to feed the relentless appetite of the city. As Michaelmas Term himself puts it in the Induction: 'what by sweat from the rough earth they draw / Is to enrich this silver harvest, Law' (9–10). The labour of the country is not romanticized here: it is real and hard. But (in a variation on Titania's complaint that the ploughman has lost his sweat) only the lawyers gain. As workers lose their labour, gentry lose their rent. Easy gambles away his income at dice, losing 'all my rent till next quarter' (2.1.67). The next, natural stage is to lose the land itself, breaking the continuity of country property. Rearage laments his losses at dice: 'Consumption of the patrimony! … Forgive me, my posterity yet ungotten!' (2.1.119–21). He and Salewood are relieved (and Salewood does not yet have to face the implications of his name) when they learn that some of their country tenants are looking for them, presumably to pay rent (2.1.165–8). The far-fetched coincidence makes a symbolic point: as the land yields only a silver harvest for the lawyers, the rent goes straight to the gaming-house. Greene in *Friar Bacon* gives us images of country feasting; Lethe invites the gallants to partake of some venison, which they will then vomit up again. As Cockstone comments, 'First dogs take pains to make it fit for men, / Then men take pain to make it fit for dogs' (1.1.193–4). The flow of wealth from the country to the city is not a sign of healthy trade; it is simply waste.

Andrew Lethe, coming to the city, takes pains to destroy his old identity, to become no more recognizable than the vomit that used to be venison. His original name, Gruel, his cowardly scruples about fighting Englishmen (3.1.100–1), and Quomodo's expectation that Lethe can introduce him at court (2.3.38–47), make him part of the unpopular invasion of Scots who accompanied James I to his new kingdom. Middleton soft-pedals these suggestions, however. (In the previous year some anti-Scottish jokes in Chapman, Jonson and Marston's Blackfriars city comedy *Eastward Ho* landed the authors in trouble: Chapman and Jonson were imprisoned and Marston fled.) Middleton's real concern is with the implications of 'Lethe', the river of forgetfulness in Hades: the son of a tooth-drawer, Lethe forgets 'His father's name, poor Walter Gruel, that begot / Him, fed him, and brought him up' (1.1.145–6). His forgetfulness extends to people he met the previous night, particularly if they have given him gifts (1.1.164–74). He is so concerned to fashion himself that he tries to stay independent not just of those who nurtured him but of those who try to involve him in transactions. The result is a complete alienation, even from himself. As Rearage comments, his acquaintances 'no more know him than he knows himself' (1.1.149). Listing Lethe's vices, Rearage puts forgetfulness first as the one that leads to the others: 'Forgetfulness, lust, impudence, and falsehood' (1.1.152). To construct a social and moral self is an act of memory, of holding people and principles in mind. Lethe, abandoning memory, is engaged in a social and moral deconstruction of himself.

He is chiefly re-made by his clothes. Rearage comments that while he used to wear cast-offs he now 'shines bright / In rich embroideries' (1.1.64–5). Appropriately, his nemesis comes through a character who is playing a similar game, the Country Wench. She too is a social climber made by new clothes, and she fools Lethe. He prides himself on acquiring her as a trophy: 'a gentlewoman of a great house, noble parentage, unmatchable education, my plain pung [punk]' (3.1.73–4). Arrested with her on the morning of the day he was to marry Quomodo's daughter Susan, he is forced to marry the punk instead. His other principal relationship is with his mother. He panics when she appears in London – 'Does she come up to shame me, to betray my birth, and cast soil upon my new suit?' (1.1.236–7) – but the suit itself has done its work. She fails to recognize him. When he asks, 'Know you not me, good woman?' her reply is not quite the *non sequitur* it sounds: 'Alas, an't please your worship, I never saw such a glorious suit since the hour I was kersen'd' (1.1.261–4). Not knowing the suit, she does not know the man.

He finds a use for his mother as a go-between. He wants to marry Quomodo's daughter Susan; while Susan wants him and Quomodo endorses the match, her mother Thomasine holds out in favour of Rearage. Lethe, assuming this is because Thomasine wants him herself, writes to assure her that marrying her daughter will give him access to her; he hires Mother Gruel to deliver the letter. His sense of shame is very selective:

> I may employ her as a private drudge
> To pass my letters and secure my lust,
> And ne'er be noted mine, to shame my blood,
> And drop my staining birth upon my raiment. (1.1.268–71)

His final punishment includes not just marriage but whipping (his fate recalls that of Lucio in Shakespeare's near-contemporary comedy about another city, *Measure for Measure*); he will be let off this punishment only if someone he has abused pleads for him. He appeals to his mother, and she refuses to recognize him: 'Call'st me mother? Out, / I defy thee, slave!' (5.3.145–6). Convinced only by the authority of the judge that this is her son, she passes her own judgement: 'How art thou chang'd! / Is this suit fit for thee, a tooth-drawer's son?' (5.3.156–8). Marriage and parent–child reunions are the stock in trade of romantic comedy; they presuppose the value of relationships. For Lethe, who has denied that value, they are turned into judgements.

The Country Wench, who came from 'the bosom of a barn, and the loins of a hay-tosser' (3.1.23), wants to pass for a gentlewoman and, once she has been wearing her new clothes for only a few minutes, calls herself 'a gentlewoman born' (3.1.171). We watch her new identity being assembled, as we watch a tailor and a tirewoman working at her dress and hair. Hellgill asks, 'Why should not a woman confess what she is now, since the finest are but deluding shadows, begot between tirewomen and tailors? For instance, behold their parents' (3.1.3–6). (The best in this kind are but shadows.) The Country Wench claims to be a gentlewoman born; Hellgill's point is that as we watch her being assembled – the tailor ties up her gown, the tirewoman adjusts her hair and Hellgill applies cosmetics – we watch that birth take place.

We are also watching her prepared for the sexual marketplace, where, as Hellgill promises her, 'The gilded flies will light upon thy flesh'. (It is a sign of the moral stupidity that affects the dupes in this play, and in Middleton generally, that to this threatening image she replies, 'Beshrew

your sweet enchantments, you have won' (2.1.48–9). All that matters is
that the flies are gilded.) The fact that we are also watching a boy actor
being dressed as a woman may explain the tirewoman's suggestion that
she is being prepared for sodomy: 'you shall wear your hair still like a
mock-face behind; 'tis such an Italian world, many men know not before
from behind' (3.1.16–18). To the complex that includes commerce and
prostitution we may add theatregoing when it becomes voyeurism and
sexual fantasy. When Rearage and Salewood, to Lethe's annoyance, start
to lavish attention on her, and Shortyard (disguised as Blastfield) demands
his share, Shortyard's complaint picks up the Hell associations we have
seen elsewhere but drains their seriousness by suggesting that the real
problem is unfair business practice: 'How can it appear in you but
maliciously, and that you go about to engross hell to yourselves? Heaven
forbid, that you should not suffer a stranger to come in; the devil himself is
not so unmannerly' (3.1.156–9). In a more conventional use of the image,
she might be like Hell because she is hot and foul-smelling; here, she is like
Hell because many men enter her.

Her father has the true right of paternity that the tailor and tirewoman
parody, and a claim of affection that counters the casual promiscuity of her
new life:

> She was my joy,
> And all content that I receiv'd from life,
> My dear and only daughter.   (2.2.4–6)

But, if we are expecting a moral and sentimental reunion, Middleton fools
us as his tricksters fool their dupes. Hellgill, once the Country Wench is
dressed and made up, declares her own father would not know her;
confirming the link with Lethe, she replies, 'I think no less. How can he
know me, when I scarce know myself?' (3.1.30–1). Moments later her
father enters in disguise, and there is no recognition on either side. Like
Mother Gruel he sees only the clothing, and he is profoundly impressed.
Immediately after her bawdy speech comparing women's terms to
lawyers', he exclaims, 'A mistress of a choice beauty! Amongst such imperfect creatures I ha' not seen a perfecter; I should have reckoned the
fortunes of my daughter the happiest, had she lighted into such a service'
(3.1.54–7). He seems to be looking, not listening, and not even looking
very carefully. It is only when he sees how many men cluster around her
that he realizes (unconsciously picking up Hellgill's gilded-fly image) that
he is in a meat market: 'I scarce like my mistress now; the loins / Can ne'er

be safe where the flies be so busy' (3.1.108–9). He punishes her and Lethe
together by having them arrested; since this leads to their marriage, he has
in a sense taken a father's prerogative of disposing of his daughter. He is
even marrying her to the man she wants: unlike Lethe she is keen on the
marriage, claiming he promised it to her from the beginning (5.3.103). But
the play ends with the father and daughter still unknown to each other, and
far from feeling punished or repentant she is quite satisfied with what she
has got. The fact that what she has got is Andrew Lethe is the play's final
judgement on her.

Lethe and the Country Wench figure in a succession of symbolic
scenes rather than a fully developed story. It is appropriate that these
scenes should be disconnected and episodic, given the disconnectedness
of their own relationships; and it is equally appropriate that for them the
traditional comic endings – marriage, parent–child reunions, recovery of
identity, judgement – should be either suspended or parodied. Having
denied their own identities, they are denied any return to moral or
personal reality. Easy, on the other hand, is involved in an elaborately
developed plot. His original identity is based not on his parentage (as is
the case with Lethe and the Country Wench) but on his possession of
land.[6] In a long, detailed intrigue, that land is stripped from him by
Quomodo and his assistants Shortyard and Falselight. Easy's new friend
Blastfield (Shortyard in disguise) loses money at dice, and tries to borrow
from Quomodo; Quomodo, having no money at hand, pays him in cloth
which he re-sells for a fraction of its value; Blastfield then disappears,
leaving Easy, who co-signed the loan as a matter of form, responsible for its
payment. A pair of officers (Shortyard and Falselight) come to arrest him.
A pair of substantial citizens (Shortyard and Falselight again) charitably
bail him out; in return he signs over his land to them, and they sign it over
to Quomodo. At every stage his deceivers claim innocence and reluctance.
Quomodo does not want him to co-sign the loan, and has to be persuaded;
the citizens, having been stung before, are reluctant to bail him; Quomodo
does not really want his land, he would rather have his money back. While
Lethe and the Country Wench precipitate themselves instantly into what
London offers – the loss of self – Easy is drawn step by careful step into
ruin, and there is a macabre fascination in watching the scam at work.

As for the Country Wench sex is business, for Quomodo and his
assistants business is sex. Early in the play Cockstone describes Easy as
'somewhat too open / (Bad in man, worse in woman …)' (1.1.53–4),
implicitly equating his openness with that of Thomasine, Susan and the

Country Wench. Playing on this equation, Quomodo instructs Shortyard,

> Keep foot by foot with him, out-dare his expenses,
> Flatter, dice and brothel to him;
> Give him a sweet taste of sensuality;
> Train him to every wasteful sin, that he
> May quickly need health, but especially money;
> Ravish him with a dame or two, be his bawd for once,
> I'll be thine forever;
> Drink drunk with him, creep into bed to him,
> Kiss him and undo him, my sweet spirit.   (1.1.120–8)

The sexual pleasures that are part of the temptation blend into the pleasure of the temptation itself. Shortyard describes their relations: 'in a word, w'are man and wife; they can but lie together, and so do we' (2.3.155–6). There is no need to assume they have literally had sexual relations; equally, there is no need to allow our reading of such moments to be restricted by the information that 'Elizabethan men slept together as a habit of friendliness'.[7] There is more than friendliness here. The gulling of Easy is as lovingly detailed, as closely attentive to his desires and his vulnerable points, as a seduction. Even its false starts and hesitations, the moments when the cheaters pretend to draw back, partake in the 'sweet, reluctant, amorous delay' that is Eve's contribution to sex in Milton's Eden. They make the pleasure last. Here at least, business is erotic.

While Lethe and the Country Wench want to pass themselves off as members of a higher class, the social insecurity that makes Easy vulnerable is subtler. He is a gentleman by virtue of his land; what he does not know is how a gentleman ought to behave in London. Shortyard, as Blastfield, insists there are all sorts of rules, known only to initiates like himself, and it is vital to follow the rules because everyone is watching: 'Then, for your observances, a man must not so much as spit but within line and fashion. I tell you what I ha' done: sometimes I carry my water all London over, only to deliver it proudly at the Standard; and do I pass altogether unnoted, think you?' (2.1.92–6). Esoteric rules for every action, and every action under public scrutiny: it is the perfect recipe for social insecurity. (Which knife do you use? What do you do with the cherry stones?) Having warned Easy, 'You must always have a care of your reputation here in town' (2.1.36–7), Shortyard-Blastfield persuades him that at gaming no gentleman lets himself end on a winning streak: 'None will do so but those have base beginnings' (2.1.47); no gentleman forswears dice (2.1.105–7); it is laughable to repent at one's losses (2.1.122–5); and if he does *not* lose everything he will be socially disgraced: 'what would gentlemen say of you? "There goes a gull that keeps his money!" I would not have such a report go on you for the world, as long as you are in my company' (2.1.112–14). That Easy accepts such doctrine without protest is a sign not just of his stupidity but of his anxiety to look right in London. His dependence on Shortyard–Blastfield is such that his claim 'Methinks I have no being without his company' (3.2.6) seems the literal truth; Blastfield makes him over as the tailor and tirewoman make over the Country Wench.[8] The class touchiness Blastfield creates is a key factor in Easy's fall; he is insulted when Quomodo refuses to accept him as co-signer of the loan: 'I hope you will not disparage me so. 'Tis well known I have three hundred pound a year in Essex' (2.3.257–8). It is at his own insistence, over Quomodo's protests, that he signs the document that loses him his land.

The gulling of Easy is completely understandable in social terms, greed playing on snobbery. But Middleton also surrounds the cheaters with supernatural suggestions. Quomodo calls Shortyard and Falselight his spirits,[9] and as he commands them he sounds at times like a magician producing transformations: 'Go, make my coarse commodities look sleek'; 'Shift thyself speedily into the shape of gallantry' (1.1.81, 118). Falselight's response when called on – 'I am nimble' (1.1.80) – might have come from Robin Goodfellow or Ariel. Their shape-shifting abilites are uncanny. In one scene Falselight is himself, a porter and a neighbouring merchant, Master Idem. Easy laments the disappearance of Blastfield (Shortyard) to the sergeant who arrests him (also Shortyard) and the friendly citizen who bails him (Shortyard again). As in *Friar Bacon*, this is magic with a touch of the demonic. Shortyard says of his shape-shifting ability: 'Spirits can change their shapes, and soonest of all into sergeants, because they are cousin-germans to spirits; for there's but two kinds of arrests till doomsday: the devil for the soul, the sergeant for the body' (3.3.1–5).

The darkness of Quomodo's shop (conveyed in Falselight's name) suggests the darkness of Hell; it also aids the disguises (3.4.182–4) and generally creates a setting, both symbolic and practical, for deception and self-deception. Quomodo may boast, 'my shop is not altogether so dark as some of my neighbours', where a man may be made cuckold at one end, while he's measuring with his yard at tother' (2.3.32–5). But while Quomodo is cheating Easy he does not notice his wife is watching, and becoming smitten with his victim; by the end of the play he, like his neighbours, will be a cuckold. His shop is darker than he thinks. As Hellgill sees the make-over of the Country Wench as symbolic of how all women are created, Quomodo speaks on behalf of a nation of shopkeepers: 'Your worship must pardon me, 'tis always misty weather in our shops here; we are a nation the sun ne'er shines upon' (2.3.97–9). The imagined darkness Robin creates to produce the final confusion in the forest of *A Midsummer Night's Dream* has come to London, and the pattern of order in the city and confusion in the country is reversed.

Quomodo shares the pride, and the ultimate vulnerability, of the stage magician. His reasons for wanting Easy's estate seem at first prosaic enough. It will be a source of supplies: 'Methinks I am felling of trees already; we shall have some Essex logs yet to keep Christmas with, and that's a comfort' (2.3.338–40). Easy imagined keeping Christmas in the country with Alsup; Quomodo will keep Christmas in London with Easy's wood, which for him is a practical commodity. (If you put Quomodo in the wood near Athens he would start calculating what the timber would fetch.) But as his pride swells he thinks of his own prestige as Friar Bacon thinks of his fame:

> Now shall I be divulg'd a landed man,
> Throughout the Livery; one points, another whispers,
> A third frets inwardly, let him fret and hang!   (3.4.5–7)

He imagines excited conversations among his neighbours: 'Whither is the worshipful Master Quomodo and his fair bedfellow rid forth? – To his land in Essex! – Whence comes those goodly load of logs? – From his land in Essex! – Where grows this pleasant fruit? says one citizen's wife in the Row. – At Master Quomodo's orchard in Essex' (3.4.13-17).[10] It may be a danger sign that, concerned with his social standing and imagining himself the centre of attention in London, Quomodo is becoming like his dupe, Easy.

Like actual Londoners known to social historians, he is committed to the city and has no interest in retiring to the country.[11] His celebration of his wealth can be seen as a comic version of the civic pride Middleton would later appeal to, with a perfectly straight face, when he earned money as pageant-writer to the city.[12] But Quomodo does not stop there. As there is something erotic in the cheating of Easy, there is something erotic in Quomodo's fantasy about his land: 'Oh, that sweet, neat, comely, proper, delicate parcel of land, like a fair gentlewoman i'th' waist, not so great as pretty, pretty; the trees in summer whistling, the silver waters by the banks harmoniously gliding' (2.3.82-5). Critics have found this fantasy unreal, the product of an urban imagination, with the whistling of the trees (Roma

Gill suggests) recalling the rustling of silks.[13] As the land is unreal, so is the gentlewoman; she is the slightly wistful fantasy of a middle-aged shop-keeper with two grown children.

In a later scene the sexual side of Quomodo's fantasy develops, as he imagines an excursion (what for his descendants would be a bank holiday) with his fellow citizens:

> A fine journey in the Whitsun holidays, i'faith, to ride down with a number of citizens and their wives, some upon pillions, some upon sidesaddles, I and little Thomasine i'th' middle, our son and heir, Sim Quomodo, in a peach-colour taffeta jacket, some horse-length or a long yard before us – there will be a fine show on's, I can tell you – where we citizens will laugh and lie down, get all our wives with child against a bank, and get up again.   (4.1.70–7)

The context for this dream is a statement that recurs through the play, presented as though it had the force of natural law, that the power to get money and the power to get children are incompatible. Michaelmas Term himself declares in the Induction, 'Where bags are fruitful'st, the womb's most barren; / The poor has all our children, we their wealth' (22–3). Shortyard, impersonating a rich citizen, explains why he and his kind are childless: 'We could not stand about it, sir; to get riches and children too, 'tis more than one man can do' (4.1.33–4). Shortyard's name becomes appropriate here; throughout the play there are reminders of its bawdy significance, as when Quomodo claims he would trust him with his wife (1.1.86–7) or when Shortyard himself, sentenced to banishment in the final judgement scene, declares, 'Henceforth no woman shall complain for measure' (5.3.166). Unusually gifted at deception and shape-shifting, Shortyard is disabled elsewhere. It may be the reference to Sim riding 'a long yard before' that by association makes Quomodo's dream of a holiday excursion turn erotic. With his own son highlighted (he is the only character whose clothes Quomodo imagines) and more children on the way, the slander that financial success and procreation are incompatible is disposed of.

Given the existence of Susan and Sim, Quomodo may seem to be an exception to the principle in any case. He has proved that he can get money, lands *and* children. Yet he, like Shortyard, is the target of slurs on his sexual ability, and they come from his wife. Lamenting his cruelty to Easy, Thomasine asks, 'Why am I wife to him that is no man?' (2.3.206). She complains to Easy, 'he ne'er us'd me so well as a woman might have been us'd' (4.3.54–5), and after Quomodo's apparent death she finds Easy a more satisfying husband: 'What difference there is in husbands, not only in one thing, but in all' (5.1.50–1). The reference to 'one thing' shows that she has begun with a strictly practical comparison. Determined to get her back, Quomodo threatens to demonstrate his sexual prowess: 'You shall feel, wife, whether my flesh be dead or no' (5.1.121–2).

Leaving aside the consideration that paternity is always potentially doubtful, Quomodo has shown himself a successful procreator on at least two occasions. Yet that does not seem to free him from jokes that equate his ability with Shortyard's. The reason may be that, whatever he used to be capable of, he is now past it. But I think Quomodo is subject to a deeper anxiety than this. Parenthood is for him a sign of power because it is a way of securing the future; and it is on that point that he fails. Susan marries against his wishes, finally picking Rearage instead of Lethe. More important, Quomodo wants Sim to inherit his land, and no sooner has Sim done so than Shortyard cheats him of it. Both developments lie towards the end of the play, after Quomodo has faked his own death. He plays that trick in order to test his hold over the future, a point on which he seems as anxious, as insecure, as Easy is about his social appearance.

Sim is crucial. If, as Quomodo claims, gentry are 'busy 'bout our wives, we 'bout their lands', Shortyard suggests why citizens get the better of the bargain: 'To be a cuckold is but for one life, / When land remains to you, your heir, or wife' (1.1.109–10). When with pretended reluctance Quomodo accepts Easy's land in discharge of his debt, he claims it is for his son's sake (4.1.39–47). Even in his private reveries he confesses to the same motive: 'an excellent place for a student, fit for my son that lately commenc'd at Cambridge'. But when he adds, 'Thus we that seldom get lands honestly, must leave our heirs to inherit our knavery' (2.3.86–9), he hits on a difficulty that will return to haunt him. He wants to secure the future through the continuity of inheritance. But in cheating Easy of the land he himself violates that continuity. Shortyard's alias, Blastfield, suggests that land thus acquired is as good as destroyed. It may have as much financial value as ever, but its symbolic value is gone. Thomasine, as she watches the crucial stages of Easy's gulling, describes Quomodo as an executioner, killing Easy as he kills his land. The melodramatic extravagance of her language – 'Now is he quart'ring out; the executioner / Strides over him; with his own blood he writes' (2.3.341–2) – may say more about her own infatuation with Easy than about the actual seriousness of the scene. But the basic point fits with the general charge of procreative disability: Quomodo is more adept at taking life than at giving it.

Quomodo's dream of the Whitsun holiday, which highlights Sim and ends with a fantasy of procreation, leads directly into the unravelling of his achievement. Like Easy, but more finally and completely, he destroys himself through anxiety. Trying to grip the future, he overreaches. As though it is taking revenge, the land itself gives him the idea:

To see how the very thought of green fields puts a man into sweet inventions! I will presently possess Sim Quomodo of all the land; I have a toy and I'll do't. And because I see before mine eyes that most of our heirs prove notorious rioters after our deaths, and that cozenage in the father wheels about to folly in the son, our posterity commonly foil'd at the same weapon at which we play'd rarely ... being awake in these knowings, why should not I oppose 'em now, and break destiny of her custom, preventing that by policy, which without it must needs be destiny?   (4.1.79–91)

He is trying to face the fact that land gained by cozenage and folly could be lost the same way, and this anxiety triggers a host of others, about his wife, his children, his real hold over the world around him. Pretending to die, he will see

how pitiful my wife takes my death, which will appear by November in her eye, and the fall of the leaf in her body, but especially by the cost she bestows upon my funeral, there shall I try her love and regard; my daughter's marrying to my will and liking; and my son's affection after my disposing; for, to conclude, I am as jealous of this land as of my wife, to know what would become of it after my decease.   (4.1.105–12)

Once again the land is eroticized, and this time the distinction between wives and lands collapses, as Quomodo fears he will lose both. Confident and expansive up to this point, Quomodo shrinks before our eyes into a bundle of anxiety and suspicion. He will not even trust Shortyard and Falselight, but determines to act completely alone (4.1.103–4). He has had complete confidence in his spirits, and they know all his secrets; now, suddenly, his suspicion turns on them as it does on his family.

He plans his deathbed as a parody of the lurid end of a despairing sinner: 'Then will I begin to rave like a fellow of a wide conscience, and, for all the world, counterfeit to the life that which I know I shall do when I die: take on for my gold, my lands, and my writings, grow worse and worse, call upon the devil, and so make an end' (4.1.95–9). The casualness of his admission that one day he *will* die like this shows a remarkable complacency. Yet the torment he suffers is arguably worse than a conventional sinner's death: he has to go on living to watch helplessly as

Shortyard cheats Sim of the land, Susan marries against his will and Thomasine breaks all speed records in her eagerness to marry Easy. The *'confused cry within'* (4.3.0.1) that greets his death is not so much a sign of mourning as a symbol of the sudden ruin of everything he has achieved, the confusion of all his hopes. It anticipates the strange, hollow and confused noise with which Prospero's wedding vision vanishes.

The gulling of Easy is slow, carefully detailed, fully dramatized. Middleton seems prepared to take all the time in the world, and to explain every turn as it happens. The collapse of Quomodo's fortunes is unnaturally swift, with foreshortened action that cuts off explanations. We never know how Shortyard gulls Sim; it just happens, and Shortyard reports it in a brief speech that presents a *fait accompli* (5.1.1–12). He in turn loses the land even more quickly to Easy, who has suddenly seen through all the disguises – 'Rogue, Shortyard, Blastfield, sergeant, deputy, coz'ner' (5.1.20) – and who claims that the lands have returned to him of their own will, with a kind of homing instinct: 'the lands know the right heir' (5.3.76). Shortyard emphasizes the speed of his loss: 'When, no sooner mine, / But I was glad more quickly to resign' (5.3.87–8). One look at Lethe under arrest with the Country Wench, and Susan switches to Rearage, having seen the difference 'Bewtixt a base slave and a gentleman' (5.2.10). Rearage, however, prefers to see the switch as a sign not of her discrimination but of 'How soon affections fail' (5.2.12). This insults both himself and Susan, and drains their match of any significance other than its speed. The play seems to be hastening to its conclusion at whatever cost to the seriousness of its characters or the credibility of its action. Sometimes we can tell, or guess, why the plot twists have taken place; but how Quomodo, acting on his own, manages to fake his own death and escape from the house leaving a counterfeit corpse to be buried, remains unexplained and inexplicable.

What matters is the demonstration that Quomodo, who had seemed to be master of his world, knowing himself and knowing how to manipulate others, is as empty as Easy, Lethe and the Country Wench. His relationships collapse. Having declared, 'What a belov'd man did I live!' (4.4.1), he hears both Sim and his fellow citizens denounce him as a cozener (4.4.17–42). Thomasine calls herself 'the happiest widow that ever counterfeited weeping' (4.3.39–40) and Shortyard greets the news of Quomodo's death, 'The happiest good that ever Shortyard felt!' (4.3.6). Quomodo also suffers internal collapse as his wit deserts him. Clinging to the fantasy that Thomasine is a grieving widow, he thinks to delight her by returning from the dead. Disguised as a beadle, he signs with his own name a discharge for the money he has received for the funeral expenses. He realizes too late that by the wording of the discharge he has just signed all his property over to Easy: 'What have I done? Was I mad?' (5.1.108). He really does seem mad when in the last scene he sees Lethe and the Country Wench brought into the courtroom under arrest and declares, 'Here's master Lethe comes to wed my daughter; / That's all the joy is left me' (5.3.94–5). His bizarre misreading of Lethe's entrance shows him clutching at straws.

His funeral included '*A counterfeit corse*' and 'Thomasine *and all the Mourners equally counterfeit*' (4.4.51.1–2). Once Quomodo has returned to life Easy describes the funeral as a fake commemoration of a fake life:

> The Livery all assembled, mourning weeds
> Throughout his house e'en down to his last servant,
> The herald richly hir'd to lend him arms
> Feign'd from his ancestors, which I dare swear knew
> No other arms but those they labour'd with,
> All preparations furnish'd, nothing wanted
> Save that which was the cause of all: his death.   (5.3.4–10)

Quomodo has tried to give himself a social identity by contriving the external signs of class and family, grasping at that continuity he hoped to find in land.[14] Easy, who really is a gentleman, sees through it. It is the judge who ferrets out the true source of Quomodo's identity, as the latter tries to authenticate his return from the dead:

Judge.   I'll try you.
　　Are you the man that liv'd the famous coz'ner?
Quomodo. Oh, no, my lord.
Judge. Did you deceive this gentleman of his right,
　　And laid nets o'er his land?
Quomodo.   Not I, my lord.
Judge. Then you are not Quomodo, but a counterfeit.   (5.3.20–5)

Threatened with arrest and whipping as an impostor, he is reduced to admitting he did all this; like Lethe, he simply forgot. Quomodo is, in short, the accumulation of his deeds; and his deeds are cheats.

He loses Easy's land, and his own wealth; he intends to disinherit Sim (5.3.44–5); and, though his marriage to Thomasine is still legally valid, she retorts, when Lethe calls her 'Mistress Quomodo', 'Inquire my right name / Again next time' (5.3.140–1). So far as she is concerned, she is still

Thomasine Easy. The Judge does not even bother to banish Quomodo as he banishes Shortyard and Falselight. His sentence is, 'Thou art thine own affliction, Quomodo' (5.3.164). Easy's statement early in the trial casts doubts on Quomodo's identity that sound like doubts about his reality:

> We are not certain yet it is himself,
> But some false spirit that assumes his shape
> And seeks still to deceive me.   (5.3.12–14)

This is the upshot of all the shape-shifting: Quomodo now seems a ghost, a counterfeit, an imitation of himself.

One could argue that the play's vision is fundamentally conservative. Won from Easy only by great effort, the lands return to him by nature. Upstarts like Lethe and the Country Wench never fool the audience; and with the failure of Quomodo's ambition everything returns to its original state. According to Gail Kern Paster, the circling action of city comedy 'ironically produces the illusion of bewildering change without affecting any real change at all'.[15] This does not mean, however, that we end the play with solid earth beneath our feet. If the conservatism of the satire recalls *The Malcontent*, so does the final air of unreality. London is a place of shadows and deceptions, and all we have seen is London. The land that seems to matter so much is seen only as it appears from the London perspective, something to be won or lost, at most a source of prestige for a Londoner. It has value, but no reality. Social identity is for Lethe and the Country Wench a matter of clothing; for Easy it is a matter of self-destructive behaviour, which he learns from a disguised shop-assistant. When we look for the true gentlefolk, or the true town sophisticates, these characters are impersonating, we find no one; or at most the shadowy figures of Rearage and Salewood. Easy's restoration, like his fall, is more Quomodo's doing than his own. Quomodo, the most solid and vital character for most of the play, is simply an accumulation of dishonest actions, and when he tries to give himself permanence by extending his power into the future he crumbles. What is real is the market, where anything can be faked, anything can be negotiated, and anything, whether a piece of land or a woman's body, can be sold. The speed with which the action unravels shows how unstable that market is. Middleton's world is more down to earth and closer (literally) to home than Marston's;[16] but his exposure of the emptiness of the means by which the characters try to construct their social reality is no less searching.

Notes

1 Reavley Gair, *The Children of Paul's: The Story of a Theatre Company, 1553–1608*, Cambridge, 1982, pp. 153–5. This impression that the boys were growing up works against the reference in Webster's Induction to *The Malcontent* to the Blackfriars company playing 'Jeronimo in decimo-sexto' (78–9). That reference (implying childishness) may be a year or so earlier; and the Paul's company had been operating a little longer than the Blackfriars company. But the inconsistency may also suggest that the boys generally were at that stage of development where child and adult are confusingly mixed.

2 All references to *Michaelmas Term* are to the Regents Renaissance Drama edition, ed. Richard Levin, Lincoln, 1966.

3 Roger Finlay and Beatrice Shearer, 'Population Growth and Suburban Expansion', *London 1500–1700: The Making of the Metropolis*, ed. A.L. Beier and Roger Finlay, London and New York, 1986, p. 38.

4 George E. Rowe, Jr, *Thomas Middleton and the New Comedy Tradition*, Lincoln and London, 1979, lists some of the play's allusions to Hell (p. 64); on the other hand, for Theodore B. Leinwand, *The City Staged: Jacobean Comedy, 1603–1613*, Madison, Wis., 1986, the play is too conventional for its Hell references to carry real force (pp. 51–2). Ben Jonson produces an ironic variation on the London-as-Hell motif in *The Devil Is an Ass* (1616), where Pug, an incompetent junior devil, finds London worse than Hell.

5 As W. Nicholas Knight sees the play's equation of law and sex, both reflect a desire for continuity, through property and procreation: 'Sex and Law Language in Middleton's *Michaelmas Term*', *'Accompaninge the Players': Essays Celebrating Thomas Middleton, 1580–1980*, ed. Kenneth Friedenrich, New York, 1983, p. 94.

6 On the importance of land as establishing the honour, credit and wealth of a gentleman, see D.M. Palliser, *The Age of Elizabeth: England under the Later Tudors 1547–1603*, 2nd ed., London and New York, 1992, p. 119.

7 Levin, commentary, p. 13. The homoerotic level of the play is elaborately expounded by Theodore B. Leinwand, 'Redeeming Beggary/Buggery in *Michaelmas Term*', *English Literary History*, LXI, 1994, 53–70.

8 As Leinwand puts it, Easy lets others write his part for him (*City*, p. 100).

9 'Fly' can mean 'spirit', and this may add a supernatural suggestion to the recurring image of flies buzzing about the Country Wench.

10 'Master' was a title given to gentlemen; city councillors indicated their social aspirations by insisting that the title be applied to them. See Palliser, *Age*, pp. 82, 86.

11 R.G. Lang, 'Social Origins and Social Aspirations of Jacobean London Merchants', *Economic History Review*, 2nd series, XXVII, 1974, 28–47.

12 Susan Wells, 'Jacobean City Comedy and the Ideology of the City', *English Literary History*, XLVIII, 1981, 54.

13 'The World of Thomas Middleton', in *Accompaninge*, p. 25. See also Gail Kern Paster, *The Idea of the City in the Age of Shakespeare*, Athens, Ga, 1985, p. 174.

14 On the importance of funeral pageantry in establishing the status of the deceased and affirming the social order to which he belonged, see Michael Neill, '"Exeunt with a Dead March": Funeral Pageantry on the Shakespearean Stage', *Pageantry in the Shakespearean Theater*, ed. David M. Bergeron, Athens, Ga, 1985, pp. 154–61.

15 *Idea*, p. 158.

16 Quomodo ('how' in Latin) may have been based on a real person, a broker named Howe who in 1596 was convicted in Star Chamber of 'a swindle similar to Quomodo's' (Levin, Introduction, pp. xi–xiii).

7

Shakespeare, *The Tempest*

MODERN criticism has put *The Tempest*, along with *Pericles*, *Cymbeline* and *The Winter's Tale*, among Shakespeare's 'romances'; but that category is a recent invention. *The Tempest* appears in the Folio of 1623 at the head of the comedies, making it the first play in the collection. It has also acquired a kind of mythic status as the last play in Shakespeare's career, his summing-up, though in fact it could have been written before *The Winter's Tale*, and Shakespeare went on afterwards to collaborate with Fletcher, possibly on *Henry VIII*, certainly on *Two Noble Kinsmen* and the lost *Cardenio*. In recent years the habit of seeing it as Shakespeare's meditation on his art has been replaced by what is virtually a critical industry treating the play as a document in the history of colonialism.[1] The play has generally seemed to be making an important statement about *something*; yet in practice it has had some difficulty living up to its reputation as a masterpiece. In performance it is generally disappointing. Peter Brook, who has tackled *The Tempest* several times both in conventional productions and in experiments, has noted that 'if you were to describe it to someone who did not know it then it would appear to be the greatest play in the world', yet 'the text itself never seemed able to deliver what it promised'.[2]

In order to free the play from its reputation, and simply see what it is doing, it may be useful to take it back to its first performances, in 1610 or 1611. Then it would have appeared not as one of Shakespeare's last romances, or as an attempt, successful or otherwise, at a world-class masterpiece, but as the King's Men's latest comedy, part of its repertory at the Globe and the newly acquired Blackfriars. In terms of the plays we have been studying, it returns to an interest in the power of magic we have seen in *Endymion, Friar Bacon and Friar Bungay* and *A Midsummer Night's Dream. Friar Bacon* also centres on a magician who renounces his power. More immediately, it is a Jacobean comedy, in line with *The Malcontent* and *Michaelmas Term,* offering a sceptical, sardonic examination of the fantasies that surround power – political, economic and domestic.

It opens with the stage representing a storm-tossed ship on which a group of well-dressed aristocrats, angry and in a panic, are interfering with the work of the sailors who are trying to save the ship, and their lives. The social order has been inverted (or, if we prefer, has been revealed in its true light): everything depends on the workmen, and the best thing the aristocrats can do, and are singularly failing to do, is keep out of the way.[3] As the Boatswain tells them, 'You mar our labour. Keep to your cabins' (1.1.13–14).[4] Reminded that one of his passengers is the King of Naples, he is no more impressed than the sea is: 'What cares these roarers for the name of king?' (1.1.16–17).

This inversion opens the way for a period of experiment. The stage becomes an island, a natural identification at the Globe in particular, where it would be surrounded by the audience as an island is surrounded by the sea. On this island stage political events, displaced from reality, are acted out by performers. In an obvious sense this is the normal condition of theatre: kings, lords and rebels are impersonated by paid professionals, well down the social scale. The scripts they follow may (like *The Malcontent*) include sardonic suggestions that the great folk they impersonate are acting too. *The Tempest*'s sense of displacement depends not just on conscious theatricality but on the stage's own impersonation of an island: cut off from society, where power struggles might seem to be *about* something, the characters, high and low, go on struggling for power, acting out rebellions that are reduced by the emptiness of the surroundings to pure performance, political comedies rendered ironic by the setting as the power struggles of *The Malcontent* are rendered ironic by the style.

From More's *Utopia* to Golding's *Lord of the Flies*, islands have been places to try out models of society. The honest old lord Gonzalo sees this island as a chance for a fresh start. If it were his to rule,

> I'th'commonwealth I would by contraries
> Execute all things, for no kind of traffic
> Would I admit; no name of magistrate;
> Letters should not be known; riches, poverty,
> And use of service, none; contract, succession,

Bourn, bound of land, tilth, vineyard, none;
No use of metal, corn, or wine, or oil;
No occupation.   (2.1.145–52)

He has created his ideal society by taking normal society and adding the
word 'no'; his speech is a catalogue of nouns evoking the social world.
Besides the obvious irony (which Antonio and Sebastian are quick to
point out) that this free society depends on Gonzalo's ownership and
sovereignty, the play has already shown through the relations of Prospero
and his servants that on this island, even with its meagre population,
contract, service, territorial bounds, occupation and the exploitation of
nature are matters of hot dispute. Even the idealized vision of nature
Prospero presents for the lovers includes images of agricultural labour.[5]
Gonzalo's ideal commonwealth is like Oberon's vision of the imperial
votaress untouched by love: no action could be founded on it, and *The
Tempest* is full of action.

At once grave and playful, Gonzalo's speech toys with an attractive
impossibility. At the opposite end of the scale is the carnivalesque
absurdity of the rebellion conducted by Stephano, Trinculo and Caliban.
They have a mini-tempest of their own at the beginning of 2.2, as though at
this point a counter-play is beginning with a parody of the storm that
opens the main play, transformed into low-life comedy by Trinculo's
observation, 'Yon same black cloud, yon huge one, looks like a foul
bombard that would shed his liquor' (2.2.20–1). New birth, a serious idea
when Prospero's victims come alive out of the sea, is acted out before our
eyes when Stephano seems to pull Trinculo out of Caliban's body,
equating birth with passing a bowel movement: 'How cam'st thou to be
the siege of this mooncalf?' (2.2.101–2). Led into the horse-pond by Ariel,
the conspirators suffer their own version of death by water: as Trinculo
complains, 'Monster, I do smell all horse-piss, at which my nose is in great
indignation' (4.1.198–9). Prospero speaks of drowning his book in the sea;
Stephano's source of power is his bottle, also called his 'book' (2.2.124),
and when he loses it in the horse-pond he determines to dive in after it
(4.1.212–13).

Thinking he and his fellows are three-fifths of the island population,
Trinculo remarks, 'if th'other two be brained like us, the state totters'
(3.2.6). Gonzalo wants to dispense with the state and the offices that go
with it, to create a peaceful life; Stephano wants to create a state that is all
offices, and founded on violence: 'Monster, I will kill this man. His
daughter and I will be king and queen – save our graces! – and Trinculo

and thyself shall be viceroys' (3.2.104–6). Caliban already knows the state will be not just founded on violence but kept in order by it: watching Stephano beat Trinculo, he demands, 'Beat him enough. After a little time / I'll beat him too' (3.2.82–3). He knows how subjects are kept in line; Prospero has taught him.

Gonzalo imagines a world without commerce. For Stephano and Trinculo, as for the characters of *Michaelmas Term*, everything has market value. That includes Caliban: Stephano declares, 'If I can recover him and keep him tame, I will not take too much for him;[6] he shall pay for him that hath him, and that soundly' (2.2.73–5). Trinculo plans to display Caliban as a sideshow freak and thinks of England as a particularly lucrative market: 'When they will not give a doit to relieve a lame beggar, they will lay out ten to see a dead Indian' (2.2.31–2) – a disquieting joke for an audience that has just paid money to see *The Tempest*. Stephano's response to Caliban's stunning description of the island's music is 'this will prove a brave kingdom to me, where I shall have my music for nothing' (3.2.142–3). This commercialism is one of their links with Antonio and Sebastian. Prospero's 'Two of these fellows you / Must know and own' (5.1.274–5) follows hard upon the lords' mockery of the mutineers: 'Will money buy 'em? … Very like. One of them / Is a plain fish, and no doubt marketable' (5.1.265–6). Humiliated themselves, Antonio and Sebastian are trying to find someone more degraded. Their mockery, they think, opens a gap between themselves and the lower orders; Prospero's remark, triggering our awareness of the actual resemblance, seals it up.

Antonio and Sebastian resemble Stephano and Trinculo not just in their commercial mind-set but in their history of rebellion. Antonio has already usurped Prospero's dukedom, and in the process parodied his art. Recalling how Antonio wormed his way into power, Prospero thinks of his brother as a black magician who 'new created / The creatures that were mine, I say: or changed 'em' (1.2.81–2). As Prospero deals in deceptive illusions, Antonio fooled himself, making himself believe 'He was indeed the Duke' (1.2.103). And as Caliban rebels only to get a new master, Antonio won the dukedom at the cost of submission to the King of Naples. By tempting Sebastian to kill Alonso and become King in his stead, Antonio plans to solve that problem. Sebastian promises to release him from paying tribute (2.1.290–2), and, given that Antonio is clearly the more decisive of the two, the prospect is that from now on Milan will dominate Naples.

But he is also tempting Sebastian into a re-enactment of his own crime, and in that re-enactment there is not just something second-hand but something absurd. Given that they have no prospect of returning to Naples, this is a palace revolution without a palace. If the murder will make Sebastian king of anything, it will make him king of an island he and Antonio have already insisted is barren – as bare, in fact, as the stage of the Globe. One recalls Fortinbras conquering a tiny patch of Poland, not worth farming, or Voltaire's gibe about Britain and France fighting over a few arpents of snow (Canada). As there is something dream-like about the world of *The Malcontent*, there is something dream-like about this conspiracy: Sebastian speaks more truly than he knows when he jokingly accuses Antonio of talking in his sleep (2.1.209–10). Believing in the power of the sword, Antonio insists that all it will take for Sebastian to become king is 'three inches' of 'obedient steel' (2.1.281). But steel in this play is disobedient. When in the show of the disappearing banquet the courtiers try to draw their swords, they are unable to lift them and, recalling the Boastwain's 'What cares these roarers for the name of king?', Ariel tells them they might as well fight the sea (3.3.61–8). Prospero's power, like Bacon's, renders the weapon of the aristocrat useless.

The disappearing banquet introduces another strand in the play's sardonic deflation of power and its symbols. Much has been made of *The Tempest*'s relation to the court masque, mostly because the show Prospero puts on for Ferdinand and Miranda, with its allegorical dialogue and its celebratory dance, recalls the masques of the Jacobean court.[7] Ben Jonson's *The Masque of Queens* (1606) is a classic example of the form; it begins with an antimasque of hags, who stage a grotesque dance in the midst of which, to a single loud note of music, the setting, a smoky hell-mouth, is miraculously transformed into the gorgeous House of Fame. The hags vanish; the masque continues with a celebration of famous queens of legend and a tribute to James's consort Anne. It concludes with a series of dances, which would have been followed by a banquet. But the relation of *The Tempest* to shows like *The Masque of Queens* is far from straightforward. While the actual Jacobean masques, with texts by Jonson and designs by Inigo Jones, depended on the presence of the real court with King James in the place of honour in the audience, Prospero's wedding show, if it is a masque at all, is a masque within a play. As Lyly's Cynthia is (at times) an onstage imitation of Elizabeth, but hardly Elizabeth herself, this is an onstage imitation of a masque, imperfect and truncated, displaced from its natural setting as the political struggles are displaced from theirs, on to the island which is also a stage. Jones's spectacular scenery, a key element in the court masque, is missing. There is no monarch in the audience to be celebrated as the source of light, order and power, as James is in the typical masque; if any power is celebrated here it is that of the maker, Prospero. The only transformation scene is the sudden, confused and confusing breakup of the vision.

It is worth noting that in *The Tempest* as a whole the usual sequence of a court celebration – antimasque, masque, banquet – is reversed. The banquet comes first. The courtiers think they are being welcomed to a feast by courteous islanders. Instead, to the noise of thunder and lightning, the table vanishes;[8] then Ariel appears as a harpy and lectures them on their sins, reversing the flattery courtiers could expect when they were addressed by mythical figures in a masque. Jonson's *Oberon*, performed around the same time as *The Tempest*, paid tribute to Prince Henry as James's heir; Ariel says of the powers he serves, 'Thee of thy son, Alonso, / They have bereft' (3.3.75–6). The spirits, parodying their initial courtesy, then reappear and remove the banquet, with rude gestures ('*mocks and mows*' (3.3.82.2)). The betrothal masque also breaks up in disorder when in the middle of the dance Prospero recalls Caliban. Caliban and his fellow conspirators then appear as antimasque figures, embodiments of comic disorder. The difference is that antimasque figures normally appear first, to be transformed or banished as the true masque begins; but Caliban and his cohorts have in effect banished the masque.

The language of the masque included rich costumes, and fine clothing was an important part of the courtly ethos.[9] As the courtiers are fooled with a banquet, Stephano and Trinculo (like Lethe and the Country Wench) are led astray by '*glistering apparel*' (4.1.193.1) that the uncourtly Caliban recognizes as 'trash' (4.1.223). Again there is an ironic link with Antonio, who sees his successful usurpation as a chance to dress better: 'look how well my garments sit upon me, / Much feater than before' (2.1.270–1). Ariel describes how he has supplied suitable music and dance for the antimasque:

> Then I beat my tabor,
> At which like unbacked colts they pricked their ears,
> Advanced their eyelids, lifted up their noses
> As they smelt music …
>   At last I left them,
> I'th' filthy-mantled pool beyond your cell,
> There dancing up to th'chins, that the foul lake
> O'erstunk their feet.   (4.1.175–84)

The symbolic language of the masque, culminating in dancing, celebrated the power of the court. *The Tempest* comically subverts that language. The business of the masque was to mystify power by turning it into music, dance and spectacle. As master of illusion Prospero can do that too; but the play is also clear about how much his power depends on the use of force, even of torture. The masquing Dukes of *The Malcontent*, we remember, had weapons under their costumes. Prospero threatens Caliban, 'For this be sure tonight thou shalt have cramps, / Side-stitches that shall pen thy breath up' (1.2.325-6). He has Caliban and his cohorts hunted as though they were animals, and commands Ariel,

> Go charge my goblins that they grind their joints
> With dry convulsions, shorten up their sinews
> With agèd cramps, and more pinch-spotted make them
> Than pard or cat o'mountain. (4.1.259-62)

To an audience used to seeing public torture – whipping, branding and mutilation, not to mention hanging, drawing and quartering – this might seem mild; but it would not seem fanciful. This was how they were used to seeing criminals dealt with.[10] Punishment seems to have a salutary effect on Stephano, who by the last scene has lost his identity in pain – 'I am not Stephano, but a cramp' – and who replies to Prospero's challenge, 'You'd be king o'the isle, sirrah?' with a rueful pun, 'I should have been a sore one then' (5.1.286-8). To put it one way, he is reformed; to put it another way, he has been brought to self-contempt by torture.

Incarceration is another stock punishment. Prospero, reminding Ariel that Sycorax imprisoned him in a pine, threatens to imprison him in an oak (1.2.274-96). Caliban complains,

> here you sty me
> In this hard rock, while you do keep from me
> The rest o'th' island. (1.2.342-4)

The play is full of images of bowed bodies: Prospero threatens Ferdinand, 'I'll manacle thy neck and feet together' (1.2.462), recalling Sycorax, 'who with age and envy / Was grown into a hoop' (1.2.257-8). Caliban repeatedly stoops as he tries to kiss Stephano's foot, making literal the action of Antonio when he submitted to Alonso and bent 'The dukedom yet unbowed – alas, poor Milan! – / To most ignoble stooping' (1.2.115-16).

The free movement and shape-shifting of Ariel may seem to contrast with these images of stooping and imprisonment; but Ariel too is in bondage, against which he chafes. His initial dispute with Prospero, in which each accuses the other of forgetting the terms of their contract and Prospero is reduced to Sycorax-like threats, is a burst of surprising anger on both sides.[11] There is arguably something of the whipped dog in Ariel's later question, 'Do you love me, master? No?', though the tone of Prospero's reply, 'Dearly, my delicate Ariel' (4.1.48-9), suggests real affection and warns us not to reduce the relations of these two characters to a mere power struggle. Like Robin Goodfellow when he recounts his practical jokes, Ariel describes a shape-shifting power that would be hard to show on stage: 'Sometimes I'd divide / And burn in many places' (1.2.198-9). The shape-shifting we see, like that of Quomodo's spirits, is a mastery of stage disguise: Ariel becomes a sea-nymph, a harpy and (assuming the same actor is used) Ceres. When in his mockery of Stephano and company he plays the tabor and pipe, he would recall the famous Elizabethan clown Richard Tarlton. If we can imagine Ariel doing a Chaplin impersonation we may get something like the original effect. What we never see is Ariel's true form. When he celebrates his coming freedom –

> Where the bee sucks, there suck I,
> In a cowslip's bell I lie;
> There I couch when owls do cry;
> On the bat's back do I fly ...   (5.1.88-91)

– we realize that this is the true Ariel, and all we have seen is the form he adopts when appearing to Prospero, the form of a life-sized actor. As Ariel was imprisoned in the pine, he is now imprisoned, temporarily, in the body of the actor who plays him. We never see him released.[12] Singing of his freedom, he uses the present tense, while, in his adopted body, he is helping dress Prospero. It is as though he is simultaneously free and bound, as he is when darting around in different shapes on Prospero's orders.[13]

The paradox of bondage in freedom, and freedom in bondage, is explored more overtly through Caliban and Ferdinand. Caliban's cry as he rebels against Prospero – 'Freedom, high-day! High-day, freedom! Freedom, high-day, freedom!' (2.2.181-2) – is a drunken frenzy made sharply ironic by the way he grovels to his new master Stephano. As Ariel sings of his freedom while dressing Prospero, Caliban sings of his, while proclaiming, ''Ban, 'Ban, Ca-Caliban / Has a new master' (2.2.179-80).[14] The next thing the audience sees is Ferdinand carrying a log, doing the job Caliban has rejected. He makes it an image of his service to Miranda:

> The very instant that I saw you did
> My heart fly to your service, there resides
> To make me slave to it, and for your sake
> Am I this patient log-man.   (3.1.63–6)

When the lovers exchange vows they promise service to each other, and Ferdinand, kneeling, offers himself as husband to Miranda 'with a heart as willing / As bondage e'er of freedom' (3.1.88–9). The idea of love as service, which can be a dead metaphor, is given life by the literal servitude Ferdinand is performing. For him the service of love is freedom. The final revelation of the lovers playing chess may give us a last image of the bent body, as they bow toward each other over the chessboard.

Accepting bondage gives the lovers, and Ariel, the freedom they want. Physical pain seems to do Stephano good, and emotional pain seems good for Alonso. Prospero succeeds with Alonso because, through the apparent death of his son, he can make him suffer; unlike Antonio and Sebastian Alonso cares for someone other than himself, and this means he can be hurt. Punishment has wrought in Caliban only resentful submission, but, when he sees Prospero dressed as Duke of Milan, he is impressed as he never was by Prospero the magician: 'How fine my master is!' (5.1.262). The glistering apparel did not impress him, but, when clothing becomes part of the language of power, it works on him as the sight of the Count's boots works on Jean in Strindberg's *Miss Julie*. He determines to 'be wise hereafter, / And seek for grace' (5.1.294–5). So far the play seems to be endorsing the wisdom of punishment and extolling the virtue of submission.

But there is one set of characters unaccounted for: Prospero's spirits. Like Ariel they appear only in the forms in which Prospero conjures them up – nymphs, reapers, hounds. Giving Ariel power over them, Prospero calls them 'the rabble' (4.1.37); he speaks of releasing them 'from their confines' (4.1.121) to perform for him, as though backstage in his magic theatre is a row not of dressing rooms but of prison cells. Caliban, thinking Trinculo is one of the spirits, cries, 'Thou dost me yet but little hurt; thou wilt anon, I know it by thy trembling. Now Prosper works upon thee' (2.2.76–7). This suggests the agony of the spirits as Prospero's power moves through them, a kind of demonic possession in reverse. When Caliban says of the spirits, 'They all do hate him / As rootedly as I' (3.2.92–3), there is no reason to disbelieve him. (Caliban, so far as we can tell, never lies.) Prospero's surrender of his magic presumably releases them, but the play makes no particular point of this, as it does about Ariel's freedom. This reflects Prospero's own relative indifference to them: in plantation terms, Ariel is his personal servant, who works with him in the house, and with whom he develops a close relationship; the spirits are the field hands. In his final song, Ariel gives a brief glimpse of his independent life in his own words; the only glimpse we have of the spirits' independent life comes in the speech in which Prospero surrenders his magic (5.1.33–40). He describes them as free nature spirits, like Ariel; but it is his description, not theirs. Readings of *The Tempest* as a play about colonialism naturally concentrate on Caliban as oppressed native. But Caliban is an islander in the same sense that (for example) I am a Canadian – born there of a mother who was born elsewhere. It may be that the spirits are the true natives, and that the play's refusal or inability to see them in anything other than the shapes they take for the imaginations of the invaders replicates the European understanding, and misunderstanding, of the natives of what for them was the new world.

The Tempest, like the court masque, celebrates order in music and dance. But this vision is in tension with images of disorder, and the play is full not just of music but of confused noise. As *The Malcontent* begins with jarring, out-of-tune music, *The Tempest* begins with '*A tempestuous noise of thunder and lightning*' (1.1.0.1); and as the ship sinks we hear '*A confused noise within*' (1.1.59.1).[15] The mariners' cry, 'We split, we split!', conveys both the breaking of the ship and the breaking of human ties in death: '"Farewell, my wife and children!" "Farewell, brother!"' (1.1.60–1). Things fall apart. We hear also of the groaning of the imprisoned Ariel, the roaring of the hunted mutineers, the 'strange and several noises / Of roaring, shrieking, howling, jingling chains' that wake the mariners (5.1.232–3). The 'hollow burst of bellowing, / Like bulls, or rather lions' (2.1.309–10) that Sebastian and Antonio claim to have heard is their own invention, but it confirms the general impression that the isle is full not just of noises but of noise. The climax of the play's vision of order is the wedding masque; and as it breaks up we hear what may well be the natural sound of the spirits when their forms and voices are not being shaped by Prospero: '*to a strange, hollow and confused noise, they heavily vanish*' (4.1.138.4–5). This is a play full of order, a play full of meaningful symbols, a play that responds almost too readily to allegorical readings. But at this moment we hear the sound of chaos, of unmaking, of non-meaning. Like the sound of the echo in the Marabar caves in *A Passage to India* it flattens meaning into absurdity. Prospero forces the spirits to mean something, on his terms. The confused noise we hear is the sound of his control relaxing.

It may be their own natural language, perfectly meaningful to them; but we will never know.

Friar Bacon controls, initially with confidence, demonic forces from a familiar, popular Hell. His spirits are devils, and appear as such. Prospero controls, with palpable effort, powers whose true nature we never quite see. He determines the way they appear to us, and in that way his hold over the audience is greater than Bacon's; but his power in the long run is no less problematic. Up to a point, he has unusual control over the audience. He fools us as he fools the other characters, revealing that the shipwreck we thought we saw in 1.1 was an illusion.[16] In *A Midsummer Night's Dream* the lovers express in their own words what it feels like to wake up after their night in the forest, poised between dream and reality. At the equivalent point in *The Tempest*, as the courtiers come out of his spell, it is Prospero who describes for us what they are feeling (5.1.64–8). His magic may be dissolving, but his quasi-authorial control of the narrative remains. Yet his own nature is curiously fissured. Like Malevole–Altofront he is a displaced ruler, and this gives him a split identity. As Duke, magician and father he has different roles, each with its own kind of authority. While Malevole–Altofront seems unable to keep his roles apart, Prospero seems unable to hold his roles together. Before he tells Miranda the story of the loss of his dukedom, he takes off his magician's robe, with the words, 'Lie there, my art' (1.2.25). Here as in *Michaelmas Term*, garments create identity, and before putting on the father and exiled ruler Prospero has to put off the magician. At the end of the play he puts off the magician again and dons a hat and rapier to become 'As I was sometime Milan' (5.1.86). He makes Miranda sleep before he calls up Ariel, as though she is not allowed to watch the magician at work. It is striking that Miranda and Ariel, the two characters with whom Prospero has the closest relationships, have no relationship with each other. Ariel never refers to Miranda, and Miranda shows no knowledge that Ariel exists. Prospero's most acute problems come from his inability to be ruler and magician at once: concentrating on magic lost him his dukedom, and he surrenders that magic before he resumes office. Prospero's claim as he interrupts the masque that he simply forgot Caliban's conspiracy is startling; but it takes its place with other lapses of attention that reveal disconnections in his own nature. Miranda exclaims she has never seen him so angry (4.1.144–5); perhaps his inattention to Caliban recalls his inattention to Antonio.[17]

As he describes that first lapse, his own language suggests that he did

more than create a vacuum that made Antonio's evil possible: he actually
created that evil:

> my trust,
> Like a good parent, did beget of him
> A falsehood in its contrary as great
> As my trust was.   (1.2.93–6)

In that respect his magic was positively dangerous, and he was
responsible. This may explain the lingering anger that makes him couch
his forgiveness of Antonio in such vindictive language:

> For you, most wicked sir, whom to call brother
> Would even infect my mouth, I do forgive
> Thy rankest fault – all of them – and require
> My dukedom of thee, which perforce I know
> Thou must restore.   (5.1.130–4)

There is an unresolved tension here, as though the person Prospero really
cannot forgive is himself.

As he reviews the power of his magic just before he surrenders it, he
conveys again a sense of its danger. His speech draws on a speech of
Medea in Ovid's *Metamorphoses*, linking what we may have seen as
Prospero's white magic with the black magic of the witch, collapsing
Cynthia into Dipsas. He speaks not of the harmony he has created but of
the destruction he has caused with storms and earthquakes, and he rises to
a startling climax:

> Graves at my command
> Have waked their sleepers, oped, and let 'em forth
> By my so potent art.

It is at this point that he reins himself in, and declares, 'But this rough
magic / I here abjure' (5.1.48–51). Though some Renaissance texts saw
raising the dead, when performed by a true magus doing the will of God,
as a legitimate miracle,[18] Sir Walter Raleigh gave the conventional
Protestant view when he warned that those who think they are raising the
dead are really raising the Devil.[19] By one interpretation that is what
Marlowe's Faustus is doing when he conjures up Helen of Troy; and
Greene's Bacon deals quite frankly with devils. We never see Prospero go
so far; but as he surrenders his magic he lets us glimpse its link with the
demonic.

Dangerously powerful in some directions, Prospero's magic is limited in others. He depends on Caliban for the most ordinary tasks: 'We cannot miss him. He does make our fire, / Fetch in our wood' (1.2.311–12). Prospero's magic, we gather, could produce the illusion of fire, but not a fire that would actually cook anything. He can produce illusions and torments for his victims; but he cannot get right into their minds and transform them. If they respond to external experience, as Alonso and possibly Stephano do, they can change themselves. But the silence of Antonio and Sebastian suggests they have resisted. In the last scene, as the courtiers wake, Ariel leaves the stage, and from that point Prospero deals with the others not as magician to victim but as man – and occasionally father or ruler – to man, drawing on that common humanity Ariel's compassion made him acknowledge (5.1.17–30). But while he embraces Alonso and Gonzalo (it is the touch of a human pulse that makes Alonso feel his sanity restored (5.1.113–15)) he means to keep Antonio and Sebastian under control by the ordinary art of blackmail:

> But you, my brace of lords, were I so minded,
> I here could pluck his highness' frown upon you,
> And justify you traitors. At this time
> I will tell no tales. (5.1.126–9)

In effect, he has a file on them; his magic gone, he is learning the tougher arts of politics. If he cannot reform them, he can at least intimidate them. Marston rendered the ordered ending of *The Malcontent* ironic by speeding it up. Shakespeare slows down the ending of *The Tempest*, exploring the failures and limitations of the final order as well as its real successes, making it not too swift to be true but too real to be simple.

Matters of political power – who loses and who wins, who's in, who's out – are not, however, the only issues the play explores. The story of how Prospero came to the island, a story we have to piece together from the words of different speakers each of whom has an interest in telling it his way,[20] involves a whole network of relationships. Prospero, telling the story to his fellow Europeans, claims he 'was landed' on the island 'To be the lord on't' (5.1.161–2), as though his authority rests on a kind of Manifest Destiny. Caliban tells another story:

> This island's mine by Sycorax my mother,
> Which thou tak'st from me. When thou cam'st first,
> Thou strok'st me and made much of me; wouldst give me
> Water with berries in't, and teach me how
> To name the bigger light and how the less,

> That burn by day and night; and then I loved thee,
> And showed thee all the qualities o'th'isle.   (1.2.331-7)

Though he begins by asserting his own territorial claim through inheritance (a claim perhaps as arbitrary as Prospero's), Caliban goes on to describe a lost community of mutual support and co-operation. He taught the newcomers about the island, and they taught him the names and uses of things (though he has either forgotten the words 'sun' and 'moon' or is stubbornly refusing to use them). Each had something to give the other, and their mutual need seems to have been touched with mutual affection.

But somehow this Edenic existence, this time of naming, discovery and mutual help, went wrong, and the community was replaced by a rigid power structure:

> I am all the subjects that you have,
> Which first was mine own king, and here you sty me
> In this hard rock, whiles you do keep from me
> The rest o' th' island.   (1.2.341-4)

As Prospero does not say how he came to master the island, and has to be reminded, Caliban does not say what went wrong, what produced the fall in this Eden. Prospero does:

> I have used thee –
> Filth as thou art – with humane care, and lodged thee
> In mine own cell, till thou didst seek to violate
> The honour of my child.

Caliban is unrepentant:

> O ho, O ho, would't had been done!
> Thou didst prevent me – I had peopled else
> This isle with Calibans.   (1.2.345-50)

He and Prospero read the event quite differently. Their languages are different: Prospero uses words – violate, honour, child – that seem to mean nothing to Caliban. Caliban was following a breeding instinct so impersonal he uses the passive voice for it ('would't had been done'). Prospero centres his accusation on the threat to Miranda; Caliban ignores her. Even their offspring would be simple reproductions of him, and him alone. Miranda's own version is cryptic and general:

> But thy vile race –
> Though thou didst learn – had that in't which good natures
> Could not abide to be with.   (1.2.357-9)

It was Miranda who taught Caliban language;[21] but her own language lapses into generalization when she recalls, or refuses to recall, what he tried to do to her in return.

The biblical sense of the word 'know' implies that one's first sexual experience is an initiation into a new kind of understanding. It is, in effect, learning a new language. This is the terrible irony of the relationship of Caliban and Miranda, as her initiation of his mind is met with his attempted initiation of her body. Miranda conveys what she did for Caliban:

> When thou didst not, savage,
> Know thine own meaning, but wouldst gabble like
> A thing most brutish, I endowed thy purposes
> With words that made them known.   (1.2.354–7)

Without language, he knew nothing; he in turn tried to 'know' her. Miranda's claim recalls the assumption of European explorers that the natives were speaking meaningless gabble.[22] But Caliban never claims he had a language before Miranda taught him hers; it was a strange, hollow and confused noise he himself did not understand. His stinging retort –

> You taught me language, and my profit on't
> Is, I know how to curse. The red plague rid you
> For learning me your language!   (1.2.362–4)

– shows that teaching him language was, from his point of view, an injury. It lets him shape, feel and understand his torment.

Power, knowledge, sex and language – all these things are bound up in the tangle of mutual resentment and misunderstanding that binds these three characters. Caliban is now so trapped in the mind-set thus created that when he encounters Stephano and Trinculo he can only replicate his relationship with Prospero and Miranda, even as he thinks of himself as rebelling. Giving him drink – and perhaps forcing the bottle into his mouth, hinting at the violation with which Caliban threatened Miranda – Stephano orders, 'Open your mouth – here is that will give language to you, cat' (2.2.78–9). Caliban in return offers service and teaching:

> I with my long nails will dig thee pig-nuts,
> Show thee a jay's nest, and instruct thee how
> To snare the nimble marmoset.   (2.2.162–4)

He is trying to restore something like the original community. But the subjection Prospero has forced on him he now offers voluntarily and abjectly to Stephano; and while he still thinks of Miranda as good breeding stock he offers her to his new master: 'she will become thy bed, I warrant, / And bring thee forth brave brood' (3.2.102–3). Paying tribute to her beauty, he has advanced (or declined) in his view of Miranda far enough to see her as a trophy. Like the women of *The Malcontent*, she is a political trophy, the legitimate prize of whoever wins the island.

Caliban's return to his old master is distasteful to modern readers who would rather see him as a successful rebel. (For that, we must turn to Aimé Césare's *Une Tempête* (1969), where Prospero remains on the island, doomed to lose the power struggle with Caliban.) But there is some question about what that return means. Caliban grovelling and seeking for grace is not all that happens. Caliban not only has problems with language, he creates problems of language for others. What is he? Stephano and Trinculo see him variously as fish, monster and devil. Is he human? Miranda counts him as human, calling Ferdinand 'the third man that e'er I saw' (1.2.446). His mother was Sycorax, and witches are human. Prospero's accusation that his father was the Devil (1.2.319–20) is open to question on two counts: it may be Prospero's own anger talking, and in any case paternity is unprovable. In the end Prospero accepts and acknowledges Caliban in a manner that raises more questions still: 'this thing of darkness I / Acknowledge mine' (5.1.275–6). 'Thing of darkness' keeps Caliban's identity unsettled; 'mine' opens many possibilities. Has Caliban found his true, or at least adopted father? Is Prospero acknowledging Caliban as the darkness, the cursing anger and unbridled desire in himself, including his own incestuous feelings for Miranda?[23] (As he and Caliban cursed each other on Caliban's first entrance, they sounded disconcertingly alike.) Or does 'mine' simply mean 'my slave, my responsibility'? Prospero's final order to Caliban suggests the old master–servant relationship restored, but with a difference:

> Go, sirrah, to my cell;
> Take with you your companions. As you look
> To have my pardon, trim it handsomely.   (5.1.291–3)

He puts Caliban in charge of the work party, as he put Ariel in charge of the spirits; he gives him responsibility. And this is not just the brute labour of carrying logs: he expects Caliban to show a bit of taste. In some way a new relationship is beginning, as each character reaches out to the other. It remains incomplete: Caliban's response when Prospero acknowledges him is 'I shall be pinched to death' (5.1.276); he is still fixed in the old fear.

When he comes out of it with his promise to 'be wise hereafter, / And seek
for grace' Prospero replies, 'Go to, away' (5.1.294–7). But on one point
there is a connection: ordered to trim the cell, Caliban replies, 'Ay, that I
will' (5.1.294). Whatever remains to be negotiated, the master–servant
relationship is restored, and for the first time Caliban obeys an order
without complaining.

But we have had hints that this relationship is not all there is between
the characters, and the affinities between Prospero and Caliban are not
confined to Prospero's dark side. In his tribute to the music of the island,
'The isle is full of noises' (3.2.133–41), Caliban has not only shown he can
do more with Miranda's language than curse; he reveals a link between his
imagination and Prospero's:

> then in dreaming
> The clouds methought would open and show riches
> Ready to drop upon me, that when I waked
> I cried to dream again.   (3.2.138–41)

Two scenes later Prospero declares,

> like the baseless fabric of this vision,
> The cloud-capped towers, the gorgeous palaces,
> The solemn temples, the great globe itself,
> Yea, all which it inherit, shall dissolve,
> And, like this insubstantial pageant faded,
> Leave not a rack behind. We are such stuff
> As dreams are made on, and our little life
> Is rounded with a sleep.   (4.1.151–8)

What for Caliban is a dream is for Prospero life itself; Caliban wants to
possess the dream, Prospero is willing to surrender it.[24] What links them is
a sense of vanishing glory. They do not hear each other's speeches; but if
Prospero seems to be moving, however tentatively and incompletely, back
towards Caliban at the end of the play, it may be because they both know
what it is to be dispossessed.

The relationship Prospero and Miranda have with Caliban is a dark
version of the relationship they have with Ferdinand. As Caliban is the
central figure in the story of how they came to the island, Ferdinand is
equally crucial to their leaving it. Though he appears in the first scene he
does not speak, and this means that on his entry in 1.2 he is virtually a new
character, embodying a fresh start.[25] Miranda has no point of reference for
him: 'What is't? – a spirit?' (1.1.410). She herself, after spending most of

her life with only her father and Caliban, is ready for a fresh start. In her
first scene, she seems to be rebelling against her father, demanding that he
stop the tempest and rebuking him for his cruelty:

> Had I been any god of power, I would
> Have sunk the sea within the earth or ere
> It should the good ship so have swallowed, and
> The fraughting souls within her.   (1.2.10–13)

This anticipates the way Ariel rebukes Prospero for his treatment of his
victims: 'if you now beheld them, your affections / Would become tender
… Mine would, sir, were I human' (5.1.18–20). A gap between Miranda
and her father opens when, as he tells the story of his life, he keeps
checking her level of attention: 'Dost thou attend me? … Thou attend'st
not!' (1.2.78, 87). She is presumably listening as hard as she can, but it can
never be hard enough for Prospero; the story can never matter to her as it
does to him. When she actually meets the characters of Prospero's story
her exclamation, 'How many goodly creatures are there here! / How
beauteous mankind is!' (5.1.182–3) confirms his suspicion that she was not
really paying attention.[26] But it is, appropriately, in her relationship with
Ferdinand that Prospero's control over her weakens most obviously. She
lets her name slip out: 'Miranda. – O my father, / I have broke your hest to
say so' (3.1.36–7). She is too excited to follow the model of conventional
female behaviour he has taught her:

> But I prattle
> Something too wildly, and my father's precepts
> I therein do forget.   (3.1.57–9)

In a play full of forgetting Miranda's acts of forgetfulness are creative,
freeing her from her father's control.

She has an instinctive rapport with Ferdinand. Even as she watches
the ship sink she laments it 'had, no doubt, some noble creature in her'
(1.2.7). She knows there was more than one passenger, but her imagination
already senses that one in particular matters. When they first meet he
addresses her as 'O you wonder!' (1.2.427), sensing her name before he
literally knows it. It is only in 3.1, long after he has fallen in love and
proposed marriage, that he goes through the formality of asking her name.
(Hello, I love you, won't you tell me your name?) The rapport is more
remarkable in view of the wide gap of experience between them. The
cultural gap between Prospero and Caliban over his attempt on Miranda
(social code versus natural behaviour) is duplicated when Ferdinand

refuses to let Miranda carry logs for him, claiming it would be dishonour. She replies that she's just as capable of carrying logs as he is, and, if she feels like it, why shouldn't she? (3.1.25–31). There is also a wide disparity of sexual experience. Miranda has known no member of the opposite sex apart from her father and Caliban; Ferdinand admits to having loved 'Full many a lady' (3.1.39).

When they first meet, the interwoven ideas of language, teaching and sex, so crucial to her experience with Caliban, are recalled and transformed:

> *Ferdinand.* Vouchsafe my prayer
> May know if you remain upon this island,
> And that you will some good instruction give
> How I may bear me here. My prime request,
> Which I do last pronounce, is – O you wonder! –
> If you be maid or no?
> *Miranda.* No wonder, sir,
> But certainly a maid.
> *Ferdinand.* My language! Heavens! (1.2.423–9)

As he knows her name, they know each other's language. We can imagine a wide gap closing slowly and painfully as Miranda taught Caliban words. Here the gap closes instantly. His marriage proposal, which comes only a few lines later, makes her virginity the only condition (1.2.448–50). His frankness makes him seem as direct as Caliban, but unlike Caliban he cares about the codes of society. Like the wood of *A Midsummer Night's Dream*, the island (popular fantasies about islands notwithstanding) is no place for free love. Even in Gonzalo's back-to-basics commonwealth the women will be 'innocent and pure' (2.1.153); and Miranda, ignorant about so much, knows that her 'modesty' is 'The jewel in my dower' (3.1.53–4). Ferdinand evidently agrees. He and and Caliban both get straight to business; but the business is radically different.

Prospero has a curious relationship to the lovers. While they seem to be falling in love on their own initiative, his aside, 'It goes on, I see, / As my soul prompts it' (1.2.420–1), suggests that his desire for the match is so great he is somehow making it happen; or at least he would like to think so. In 3.1, imagining they are alone, they have a long, frank conversation, on which Prospero eavesdrops. It is hard to separate benevolent interest from distasteful prurience. At the same time he admits a gap between himself and the lovers: 'So glad of this as they I cannot be, / Who are surprised withal' (3.1.92–3). Here again there is a double effect: Prospero's control and prescience make this affair something he has expected, even created. But as there is no surprise in it for him, he also recognizes that he can never experience the delight of first love as they do. In that way they have the edge over him. The author, and the audience, may be closer to Prospero at this point. We always seem to be looking at Ferdinand and Miranda from a distance, as though the author of *The Tempest* could not write so directly of young love as could the author of, say, *As You Like It*.

Prospero also imposes a narrative design on a love that seems too straightforward to need it, as though following, arbitrarily, the dramatist's principle that a love story needs a complication:

> They are both in either's powers; but this swift business
> I must uneasy make lest too light winning
> Make the prize light.   (1.2.451–3)

It is not enough for them to be in each other's powers; they must also be in his. Yet Prospero's interference is not purely arbitrary. The fact that he gives Ferdinand Caliban's job of carrying wood shows he is testing the Caliban in him. There is a sharp juxtaposition of the two characters, as Ferdinand's first appearance on the island follows immediately on Caliban's exit, and the song that brings the prince on to the stage runs backwards from the final harmony of the joining of lovers – 'Come unto these yellow sands, / And then take hands' – to a warning of approaching danger – 'Hark, hark! ... The watch-dogs bark!' and a suggestion of phallic impudence, 'The strain of strutting Chanticleer' (1.2.374–85).[27] Making Ferdinand unable to use his sword, Prospero seems to be inducing impotence, as witches were sometimes accused of doing: 'I can here disarm thee with this stick / And make thy weapon drop' (1.2.473–4).[28] Even when Prospero relents and accepts Ferdinand, he gives him not just one lecture on premarital chastity but two. Ferdinand seems a decent young man who hardly needs this treatment. But Caliban's attempt on Miranda has created an anxiety in Prospero that he finds hard to shake – another reason why the sudden memory of Caliban makes Prospero so angry, and destroys the wedding masque.

The vision of harmony and fertility that the masque creates is oddly sexless: it is all about the land and the crops, 'Earth's increase, foison plenty, / Barns and garners never empty' (4.1.110–11). Venus and Cupid are explicitly banished, and Cupid, like Ferdinand, is reduced to infancy, his weapons broken (4.1.99–101). As it imagines a year without a winter – 'Spring come to you at the farthest, / In the very end of harvest!' (4.1.114–15)

– the masque seems to imagine fertility without sex, as though Ferdinand and Miranda could have children without doing what Caliban wanted to do. Sex in *Michaelmas Term* was a crude commercial transaction, hole-sale. To Prospero it seems more a dangerous, magic power, which can easily become black magic if the timing is wrong. As Prospero is aware of the importance of timing in his own magic (1.2.180–4), he warns Ferdinand that if he anticipates the wedding night

> barren hate,
> Sour-eyed disdain, and discord shall bestrew
> The union of your bed with weeds so loathly
> That you shall hate it both.
>
> (4.1.19–22)

(In George Lamming's novel *Water with Berries* (1971), the character who corresponds to Miranda is gang-raped, leaving her both sexually frigid and compulsively promiscuous.) Ferdinand's assurance of premarital chastity embodies not coldness but an eagerness like that of Theseus. He too knows the importance of timing; by waiting he will make the magic more powerful. No temptation, he promises, will

> take away
> The edge of that night's celebration
> When I shall think or Phoebus's steeds are foundered,
> Or night kept chained below.
>
> (4.1.28–31)

Prospero replies, 'Fairly spoke', but it may be this frank expression of desire that a few lines later leads him to give Ferdinand a second lecture (4.1.51–6).

The court party have come from a political marriage, that of Claribel and the King of Tunis, that seems to have been unpopular with everyone including the bride (2.1.121–9). There is of course a political dimension in the linking of Ferdinand and Miranda, but it goes far beyond that. Chess is a game of sex and power;[29] it is a game of seduction (Middleton uses it this way in *Women Beware Women* (c.1621)); and it gives the players an ability to toy with kings and other potentates that recalls the power of Prospero. The lovers, bent over the chessboard, are showing control over the political world (unlike Claribel, who was a political puppet) and over their own sexuality. Even their quarrel is significant: Miranda accuses Ferdinand of cheating – 'Sweet lord, you play me false' – and, when he denies it, instead of accepting his denial she claims it doesn't matter: 'Yes, for a score of kingdoms you should wrangle, / And I would call it fair play' (5.1.172–5). She began the play listening to her father brood at length on past injuries;

she offers to treat any betrayal by Ferdinand as fair play, to wipe out any offence as though it had never happened. This may be naive or just playful; but it dramatizes a power of forgiveness far greater than Prospero's, and the contrast between the lightness and speed of her response and the sheer length of Prospero's opening narrative is an important part of the effect. It is more than their youth that suggests the lovers can give the world a fresh start.

Even Sebastian seems for a moment impressed: 'A most high miracle!' (5.1.177). Alonso sees in Miranda a power greater than Prospero's: 'Is she the goddess that hath severed us, / And brought us thus together?' (5.1.187–8). When, learning her true identity, Alonso asks Miranda's forgiveness, Prospero tells him to leave the past behind: 'Let us not burden our remembrances with / A heaviness that's gone' (5.1.199–200). He cannot, we have seen, do this with Antonio. But, given the fresh start the lovers represent, he can do it with Alonso, and Alonso himself, thinking his son and Prospero's daughter were both drowned, has already pointed the way:

> O heavens, that they were living both in Naples,
> The king and queen there! That they were, I wish
> Myself were mudded in that oozy bed
> Where my son lies.   (5.1.149–52)

Prospero shows at times a similar willingness to give up his own life and make way for the future, but in him it is characteristically less straightforward. Giving his daughter to Ferdinand, he claims to be giving away 'a third of mine own life, / Or that for which I live' (4.1.3–4). Throughout 4.1 he speaks only to Ferdinand, suggesting he has indeed let Miranda go. But this also gives him a new role as Ferdinand's mentor; he is not letting go that easily. His surrender of his magic seems a deeper, more radical surrender. In the Epilogue he turns to prayer, an admission of his dependence on a higher power, like Friar Bacon's turning to God. In this he repeats the action – a socially levelling one – of Alonso, Ferdinand and the mariners, who in the face of imminent death turned to prayer. Behind his declaration, 'And my ending is despair / Unless I be relieved by prayer' (5.1.333–4) lies the simple cry of the mariners, 'All lost! To prayers, to prayers!' (1.1.51).

It seems an appropriate ending for a play that has so radically examined the danger and the emptiness of power. In the end we are all equally helpless, and can only pray. But this is not really how the play ends; Prospero has not quite let go. In two time signals, he and Ariel equate the action of the play with an afternoon at the playhouse. Near the start of the play they check the time and find it is two o'clock, time for the performance to begin. (Of course it is already under way.) Allowing a little more than the usual two to three hours, Prospero declares, 'The time 'twixt six and now / Must by us both be spend most preciously' (1.2.240–1). Later, the metatheatrical reference is seemingly completed when Ariel announces it is 'the sixth hour, at which time, my lord, / You said our work should cease' (5.1.4–5). But if we think the play is over we have been fooled; this is the beginning of Act 5, and there is a whole act to go.

Even so Prospero may surrender his magic, but he does not quite surrender the narrative control that went with it. He prays, it would seem, not to God but to the audience, and in turning the story over to us he tells us what to do with it:

> Now 'tis true
> I must be here confined by you,
> Or sent to Naples. Let me not,
> Since I have my dukedom got,
> And pardoned the deceiver, dwell
> On this bare island by your spell,
> But release me from my bands
> With the help of your good hands.   (5.1.321–8)

Now the stage itself is a trap, and Prospero's plea is the play's final image of release from bondage. A play full of confinement, restriction and imprisonment ends with the words, 'set me free' (5.1.338). Our 'hands' will do it, meaning our applause. What audience will not applaud (especially since, if they do not, the play will never end and they will never get out of the theatre)? As the audience applauds, Prospero leaves the stage which is also the island; the last word of the Folio text is '*Exit*'. Prospero's last command has been obeyed.

Critics who have taken up his invitation to complete the story have tended to stress Prospero's ongoing power. The marriage of Ferdinand and Miranda may seem to duplicate Antonio's offence of submitting Milan to Naples; but it can also be seen as expanding Prospero's dynastic influence, as King James did by uniting England and Scotland;[30] and it effectively cuts Antonio out of the line of inheritance.[31] If these completions of the story are valid, Prospero achieves the control over the future that eluded Quomodo. His vision of the final dissolution of all pomp and power, of the world ending like a play or masque –

> The cloud-capped towers, the gorgeous palaces,
> The solemn temples, the great globe itself,
> Yea, all which it inherit, shall dissolve,
> And, like this insubstantial pageant faded,
> Leave not a rack behind.   (4.1.152–6)

– should be seen in its dramatic context. He attributes it to a moment of stress: 'Bear with my weakness, my old brain is troubled' (4.1.159). The response of the lovers, speaking together, 'We wish your peace' (5.1.163), may be the response of the audience when out of compassion they release the tired old man from the island. But no sooner have the lovers left the stage than Prospero, no longer complaining of weakness, calls up Ariel and mounts his last, violent attack on Caliban and his company. *The Tempest* ends, seemingly, with a moving image of the surrender of power; but with enough of its pervasive scepticism in place to leave us wondering how far we can believe it.

Notes

1 There is no point in attempting a full listing, but a few examples may be mentioned. John Gillies, in 'Shakespeare's Virginian Masque', *English Literary History*, LIII, 1986, points out that the double image of the island as a rich paradise and a place of danger and deprivation parodies the contemporary double image of Virginia (p. 682). In *New Perspectives on the Shakespearean World*, tr. Janet Lloyd, Cambridge, 1985, Richard Marienstras argues that Caliban combines the 'Indian', who 'must be dominated and overcome' with the 'Black', who 'was seen as a domestic animal, one necessary to the exploitation of the continent and the domination of nature by the White man' (pp. 177–8). Barbara Fuchs, in 'Conquering Islands: Contextualizing *The Tempest*', *Shakespeare Quarterly*, XLVIII, 1997, proposes that colonialist readings should include the British subjugation of Ireland, and equates Caliban's cloak with the Irish mantle (pp. 45–54). There is a full and balanced discussion of the whole issue in Meredith Skura, 'Discourse and the Individual: the Case of Colonialism in *The Tempest*', *Shakespeare Quarterly*, XL, 1989, 42–69.

2 Albert Hunt and Geoffrey Reeves, *Peter Brook*, Cambridge, 1995, pp. 136–7.

3 Francis Barker and Peter Hulme see this as the first of a series of 'actual or attemped usurpations of authority': 'Nymphs and Reapers Heavily Vanish: the Discursive Con-texts of *The Tempest*', *Alternative Shakespeares*, ed. John Drakakis, London and New York, 1985, p. 198. On the ship's crew, see M.M. Mahood, *Playing Bit Parts in Shakespeare*, London and New York, 1998, pp. 205–22.

4 All references to *The Tempest* are to the Oxford Shakespeare edition, ed. Stephen Orgel, Oxford and New York, 1987.

5 Gillies, 'Virginian', p. 689.

6 Orgel glosses, 'No price will be too high for him'.

7 See Orgel, Introduction, pp. 43–50.

8 After *The Masque of Blackness* (1605) there was such crowding and confusion that the table holding the banquet was overturned; see *Ben Jonson*, X, ed. C.H. Herford and Percy and Evelyn Simpson, Oxford, 1950, p. 449.

9 R. Malcolm Smuts, 'Art and the Material Culture of Majesty in Early Stuart England', *The Stuart Court and Europe: Essays in Politics and Political Culture*, ed. R. Malcolm Smuts, Cambridge, 1996, pp. 91–3.

10 In a discussion of state-sanctioned torture as part of the play's context, Curt Breight notes that pinching could mean removing pieces of flesh with red-hot pincers, and Caliban's fear of being 'pinched to death' (5.1.276) is not hyperbole: '"Treason Doth Never Prosper": *The Tempest* and the Discourse of Treason', *Shakespeare Quarterly*, XLI, 1990, 24–6.

11 According to K.M. Briggs, Prospero's 'rude, peremptory and unconciliatory' manner is the one magicians normally adopted to keep control over the spirits they had raised: *The Anatomy of Puck*, London, 1959, p. 54.

12 Productions sometimes manage a spectacular exit for him; at Stratford, Ontario in 1962 he ran off up the centre aisle of the theatre. In Peter Greenaway's film *Prospero's Books* (1991) he runs towards the camera, through a series of rooms, getting younger as he goes. But in the 1982 Royal Shakespeare Company production, Prospero, giving his last orders to Ariel, looked around and found he was already gone. He hadn't seen him go, and neither had the audience. Since the last order is for calm seas and auspicious gales, and since Prospero in the Epilogue turns to the audience to release him from the island and send him to Naples, one implication of this staging is that Ariel neither hears nor obeys the last command. We have to take over.

13 This paradox was captured in Giorgio Strehler's production for the Piccolo Teatro di Milano (revised 1977). Ariel (played in this case by a woman) was in a flying harness that let her soar freely; but during her quarrel with Prospero she struggled on the end of the wire like a fish on a line. At the end Prospero released Ariel by freeing her from the harness (Orgel, Introduction, p. 27). This brilliant production was an exception to the rule that the play generally fails in performance.

14 In the 1976 production at Stratford, Ontario, Caliban sang his song of freedom while marching on all fours, with a collar round his neck and Stephano holding the leash.

15 It is not clear that the exact wording of the stage directions is Shakespeare's; it may be that of the scribe Ralph Crane, reporting a performance he saw (Orgel, Introduction, p. 58). But at least it can be said that the effects described are part of the play as Shakespeare's company performed it.

16 Anne Righter [Anne Barton], Introduction to the New Penguin Shakespeare edition of *The Tempest*, Harmondsworth, 1968, pp. 7–9.

17 Margareta de Grazia, '*The Tempest*: Gratuitous Movement or Action without Kibes and Pinches', *Shakespeare Studies*, XIV, 1981, 259.

18 John S. Mebane, *Renaissance Magic and the Return of the Golden Age*, Lincoln and London, 1989, pp. 178, 180. Mebane gives a positive reading of Prospero (pp. 174–99), in contrast to the rough handling he gets in much late twentieth-century criticism. The latter is exemplified by de Grazia's listing of the parallels between Prospero and Sycorax ('Gratuitious', pp. 255–6).

19 K.M. Briggs, *Pale Hecate's Team*, London, 1962, p. 44.

20 According to Barker and Hulme, Prospero's 'Here in this island we arriv'd' suppresses the full story, and it takes the objections of Ariel and Caliban to re-open it ('Nymphs', pp. 199–200).

21 The speech that gives this information (1.2.350–61) used to be transferred from Miranda to Prospero, by editors who found its harsh tone unsuitable to the Miranda of their imaginations. The result was a generation of texts in which Prospero taught Caliban language, and the assumption that he was the teacher persists: in *Prospero's Books* we see Miranda and Caliban as children, studying side by side under Prospero's direction.

22 Stephen J. Greenblatt, *Learning to Curse*, New York and London, 1990, pp. 17–18.

23 This is the interpretation offered in the 1954 science fiction film *Forbidden Planet*, where the equivalent of Caliban is the 'monster from the id', a projection of the scientist himself.

24 John Gillies notes another difference: Caliban sees a 'strangeness and mystery' in the island that no other character expresses ('Virginian', p. 702).

25 In Derek Jarman's 1980 film version, Ferdinand emerges naked from the sea. The effect is more telling than the nakedness of the actors in *Prospero's Books*, which is so general that it becomes drained of meaning.

26 Righter, Introduction, pp. 10–11.

27 David Sundelson, 'So Rare a Wonder'd Father: Prospero's *Tempest*', *Representing Shakespeare: New Psychoanalytic Essays*, ed. Murray M. Schwartz and Coppélia Kahn, Baltimore and London, 1980, p. 46. David Lindley links the barking watchdogs with the hounds who hunt Caliban and his cohorts: 'Music, Masque and Meaning in *The Tempest*', *The Court Masque*, ed. David Lindley, Manchester, 1984, p. 49.

28 If Prospero's relations with Miranda include incestuous feeling, he is not just striking Ferdinand with impotence but demonstrating his own superior phallic power.

29 Bryan Loughrey and Neil Taylor, 'Ferdinand and Miranda at Chess', *Shakespeare Survey*, XXXV, 1982, 114–15.

30 David M. Bergeron, *Shakespeare's Romances and the Royal Family*, Lawrence, Kan., 1985, p. 201.

31 Orgel, Introduction, pp. 54–5.

8

Jonson, *Bartholomew Fair*

MOST of the authors whose work we have examined were professionals writing for a commercial theatre. Ben Jonson was that too; but more than any other playwright of his period he had aspirations to being a serious literary artist. To the amusement of some of his contemporaries, he published in 1616 a Folio collection of his plays, poems and masques, calling them his Works. Though it set the precedent for later Folio collections of Shakespeare and of Beaumont and Fletcher, it seemed at the time a daring, even arrogant gesture. It was also an attempt, of a sort no other playwright of the time had made, to shape and define his own canon, excluding works (like his early comedy *The Case is Altered*) that he did not wish to be remembered by. The prologue to the revised *Every Man in his Humour*, proclaiming a realistic theatre dedicated to 'deeds and language such as men do use', introduces the collection with a deliberate policy statement, given the pride of place *The Tempest* was to be given in the Shakespeare Folio.

Though it was written and produced two years earlier, in 1614, *Bartholomew Fair* did not appear in the Folio. Jonson's plans for an edition of the play in 1631 did not materialize (it was printed but not published), and the play was not available to readers until 1640, three years after Jonson's death. Yet *Bartholomew Fair* does not, at first glance, stand apart from the canon. Indeed it can be read as a consolidation of what Jonson had achieved up to that point: the close observation of human folly in plays such as *Every Man in his Humour* and *Every Man out of his Humour*, the fascination with chicanery in *Volpone* and *The Alchemist*, even the critical examination of power in the Roman tragedy *Sejanus* with its brilliant analysis of the politics of terror – all these, it could be argued, come together in *Bartholomew Fair*. The reasons for its exclusion from the Folio remain elusive: it is as though there is in the play something, somehow, that doesn't fit.[1] Even the auspices of its first performance were odd. Jonson's major plays had been acted either by the Chamberlain's–King's company at the Globe or by the children of the Blackfriars; Jonson went in each case for the leading company of its kind. Yet *Bartholomew Fair* was first performed at the Hope, a newly opened and rather down-market public playhouse that doubled as a bear-baiting arena; the actors were Lady Elizabeth's Men, a relatively minor company that had recently amalgamated with the Children of the Revels.[2] Jonson was slumming. (But then so was Mozart when he wrote *The Magic Flute* for a rough popular theatre.) For all his care to keep himself centre front in the contemporary theatre, he seems to have felt on this occasion a need to break his self-imposed control, to work on the margins.

If *The Tempest* shows Prospero's control exerted, more or less successfully, in the face of persistent disruption and rebellion, *Bartholomew Fair* privileges disruption. From its opening, the play itself seems out of control. The start of the performance is delayed: at the beginning of the Induction the Stage-keeper comes out and asks for the audience's patience: 'He that should begin the play, Master Littlewit, the Proctor, has a stitch new fallen in his black silk stocking; 'twill be drawn up ere you can tell twenty' (2–4).[3] The audience has time to tell much more than twenty before Littlewit appears and the play begins. Littlewit will later delay the start of the puppet play of which he is the author, by a fruitless search for his wife, who is already in the audience dressed as a prostitute. He is the first speaker of the main play, and the author of the puppet play; and he has a gift for creating delay that would make him a stage manager's nightmare. As the start of the performance is uncertain, so is the running time. In place of the standard two or three hours, the audience is promised (or threatened with) 'two hours and a half, and somewhat more' (Induction, 79–80). The question, when will this play begin? is succeeded by the question, when will it end? As *The Tempest* begins with an inversion of authority in which mariners count for more than princes, the Induction begins with an uppity stagehand who attacks the playwright: 'But for the whole play, will you ha' the truth on't? (I am looking, lest the poet hear me, or his man, Master Brome, behind the arras) it is like to be a very conceited scurvy one, in plain English' (6–9). He has already had a violent backstage row with the playwright over his criticisms, and now he comes to give the audience his views, heading off the play before it starts by telling us what a disappointment it will be.

The theatrical occasion is out of control; but of course the effect is carefully contrived by Jonson himself. The Stage-keeper's rebellion anticipates the disruption of authority that will be one of the key features of the Fair. It is the first of many equations between the Fair and the play itself. Yet, characteristically, the equation of play and Fair is itself disrupted just as it is being established. The agreement between the author and the audience that takes up the bulk of the Induction specifies the date of the performance: 31 October 1614. Early in the play Littlewit declares the date of the Fair: 'Today! the four and twentieth of August! Bartholomew Day!' (1.1.6–7). As Lyly's *Cynthia* is not Elizabeth but a partial imitation of her, displaced on to the stage, the Fair is likewise displaced to a different location, the playhouse, and a different time, where it is not recreated but imitated in the controlled conditions of the theatre.

The Hope itself, doubling as a bear-baiting arena, provides a striking basis for the imitation, 'the place being as dirty as Smithfield, and as stinking every whit' (Induction, 161–2). Because of the Hope's double function, its stage would have been a removable scaffold, recalling, Leah S. Marcus has suggested, the portable stages used in fairs.[4] The pig-woman Ursula, who is the dominating spirit of the Fair, recalls by her name the bears who shared space with the players. The Induction promises the play will be 'merry, and as full of noise as sport' (82–3). How much true merriment, or true sport, the Fair offers is a matter of debate; but there is, as in *The Tempest*, plenty of noise. Language itself becomes noise in the game of vapours, '*which is nonsense: every man to oppose the last man that spoke, whether it concern'd him, or no*' (4.4.28.1–2). The puppet play is not so much a play as a mindless shouting match. In the backstage row the Stage-keeper reports, the disputatiousness of the playhouse anticipates the brawling of the Fair: as he complains the author has kicked him about the tiring-house (27–30), Knockem and Whit kick the punk Alice off the stage (4.5.83–4), and the puppets Damon and Pythias kick the puppet Hero (5.4.325–6). Kicks are as it were passed down the line, from the author to the characters to the puppets. As the players in the vapours game '*fall by the ears*' (4.4.105.1), so the puppets '*quarrel and fall together by the ears*' (5.4.318.1). According to Ian Donaldson, 'Anger is the great informing idea' of *Bartholomew Fair*, 'driving the characters forwards and awry in much the same fashion that love and enchantment drive the characters of *A Midsummer Night's Dream*'. He adds that the anger, unlike the righteous anger of Jonson's earlier plays, is ridiculous.[5]

In its noise and persistent aggression the manner of the play embodies the manner of the Fair. The Fair's restless energy and resistance to control are also suggested by staging devices. Terry Hands, preparing his 1969 Royal Shakespeare Company production, called the play 'an enormous canvas with no particular focus'.[6] If Eugene M. Waith is correct in his speculation that the play was staged with booths, allowing several locations to be present simultaneously, the lack of a single focus would be reflected in the staging.[7] The characters keep shifting from one location to another, and the general restlessness reaches its climax in the mad Troubleall, who in his first scene (4.1) leaves and re-enters five times in little more than eighty lines.

This restlessness becomes an insecurity about the operation of justice when the watchmen Haggis and Bristle, about to put the disguised Justice Overdo in the stocks, think better of it and take him, together with the Puritan Zeal-of-the-Land Busy, to the court of Pie-powders, the court that deals with offences at the Fair, where he will be dealt with by – Justice Overdo. The judge they are looking for is the prisoner they have under arrest, and of course they cannot find him. They have to bring him back to the stocks, where for a few moments he sits with two other authority figures, Busy and Wasp (the servant in charge of the foolish squire Cokes), in a sharp image of authority brought low. Even that image does not last. We scarcely have time to admire the symbolism when Wasp (having slipped a shoe over his hand, and substituted his hand for his foot) escapes, and, in an ensuing fracas between the watch and the mad Troubleall, the stocks are left open and Overdo and Busy slip away. In *The Tempest* imprisonment is a serious business: even Sycorax could not release Ariel from the pine tree. In *Bartholomew Fair* the stocks cannot hold for more than a few minutes even the authority figures the play's satire has placed there.

Much of the play's (and the Fair's) restless energy is driven by sheer appetite. Littlewit, whose household is dominated by the Puritan Busy, manages to get his family to the Fair over Busy's initial objections by persuading his pregnant wife Win to long for roast pig. Having succeeded so far, and gorged on pig at Ursula's tent, he urges her to go further: 'long to see some hobby-horses, and some drums, and rattles, and dogs, and fine devices, Win. The bull with the five legs, Win; and the great hog: now you ha' begun with pig, you may long for anything' (3.6.5–9). Desire, once triggered, can expand indefinitely. Busy himself is easily persuaded, given his own appetite: even his denunciations of the Fair are fuelled by what he consumes there – 'I will eat exceedingly, and prophesy' (1.6.91–2) – and all his senses are in play: 'He eats with his eyes, as well as his teeth' (3.6.49). As a fanatical Puritan he is an iconoclast, denouncing a basket of gingerbread as a 'nest of images' (3.6.70) and attacking anything, from hobby-horses to puppets, that carries the taint of the visual. But in him appetite and anger are so fused that denunciation is a way of expressing desire. The playwright Peter Barnes, who directed *Bartholomew Fair* at the Round House Theatre in London in 1978, reports that while he had thought 'the fairground people were the picturesque characters', he discovered in working on the play that the visitors to the Fair were 'the true fantastics'.[8] Busy is the key example.

Quarlous, one of the saner visitors to the Fair, denounces Puritans in general as 'Fitter for woods, and the society of beasts, than houses, and the congregation of men' (5.2.41–2). The historian David Hirst, while cautioning that 'Puritan' is a loose term, notes that the Puritan (and to a lesser degree the general Protestant) emphasis on 'Bible-reading and sermon-going' constituted an attack on 'the old patterns of communal culture' embodied in social pastime and communal worship.[9] To that degree Busy is, in general terms, an enemy of society. Quarlous goes further, claiming Busy is 'ever in seditious motion' (1.3.135). The hint of sedition is confirmed when Busy challenges the puppets, Leatherhead as puppet-master replies that his performance (like the performance of *Bartholomew Fair* the audience is watching) is licensed by the Master of the Revels, and Busy retorts, 'The Master of the Rebels' hand, thou hast: Satan's!' (5.5.17). The authority of the Master of the Revels comes from the king, and that is the authority Busy is ultimately attacking. There was a real-life precedent in the bailiff Richard Wheatley, who in 1597 broke up a Sunday dinner party: 'When someone said that he hoped the queen would allow a group of friends to share a joint of meat, Wheately said: "If the queen do allow it, yet I will not allow it".'[10] Busy of course participates in what he attacks. He has been, like Ursula, 'A notable hot baker' (3.2.48), and he can easily match the noise of the Fair. When Leatherhead has him arrested, and commands the officers to 'Stop his noise', Busy retorts, 'Thou canst not: 'tis a sanctified noise. I will make a loud and most strong noise, till I have daunted the profane enemy' (3.6.98–101). Like the Fair he denounces, Busy is out of control.

Part of that loss of control is a blurring of categories, a loss of the distinctions that separate the human, the animal and the material. Busy, in quest of the pig-tent, *'scents after it like a hound'* and the animal noise he makes – 'huh, huh, huh' (3.2.79.1–83) is like the noise Win makes – 'uh, uh' (1.6.9, 23) – to show her longing for pig. Knockem refers to Ursula's 'litter of pigs' (2.3.2) as though she had given birth to them herself; when she scalds her leg with her own roasting pan, she calls for cream and salad oil 'as used to dress cooked pork'.[11] Ursula's tent doubles as a brothel, and Knockem makes no distinction between the kinds of meat sold there: 'Here you may ha' your punk and your pig in state, sir, both piping hot' (2.5.39–40). As the human and the animal blend, inanimate creatures come to life. In their slanging match early in the fair sequence Leatherhead denounces Joan Trash's 'ginger-bread-progeny' and she in turn taunts his 'stable of hobby-horses' (2.2.3–4, 14). Cokes and Leatherhead discuss the puppets as though they were real actors, with reference to actual performers including Richard Burbage and Jonson's protégé Nathan Field (5.3.48–99). Leatherhead even advertises the puppet Leander's sex appeal: 'He is extremely belov'd of the womenkind, they do so affect his action, the green gamesters that come here' (5.3.84–6). Cokes, handling the Hero puppet, assures Leatherhead, 'I will not hurt her, fellow; … I pray thee be not jealous: I am toward a wife' (5.4.6–8).

Gingerbread progeny, a roaster of pigs who provides her own litter, and puppets who are not just human but sexual: the material world of *Bartholomew Fair*, as evoked by the language, teems with unnatural life. It is as though Troubleall's recurring blessing, 'Quit ye, and multiply ye' (4.1.106–7), had been visited on the Fair at large; the more he utters it the more one imagines the sort of mad proliferation that haunts the plays of Ionesco: chairs, eggs, rhinoceroses. Yet at the heart of this vision of proliferating life is emptiness. Busy debates the legitimacy of theatre with the puppet Dionysius, who refutes the Puritan objection to theatrical cross-dressing by hoisting up his (its?) garment to demonstrate *we have neither male nor female amongst us* (5.5.97–8).[12] Flashing Busy, the puppet demonstrates that there is nothing to flash, and Busy's instant and total collapse reveals his own emptiness. Justice Overdo has already handed Quarlous (disguised as Troubleall) a blank sheet of paper with his hand and seal on it; the gesture seems to empty out his authority, letting Quarlous do anything he wants with Overdo's name. In the first act Wasp makes a great fuss about getting the box containing the licence for Cokes's marriage to Grace: but the cutpurse Edgeworth goes to work, and at the end of the play Wasp finds he is holding an empty box. The blank crotch, the blank legal document, the empty box: sex, authority and law all lose their distinguishing marks, and are drained of meaning.

So is identity. Cokes, losing his clothes, his material goods, his family and his fiancée at the Fair, tries to relocate himself by asking a perfect stranger, who just happens to be the mad Troubleall,

Friend, do you know who I am? Or where I lie? I do not myself, I'll be sworn. Do but carry me home, and I'll please thee, I ha' money enough there; I ha' lost myself, and my cloak and my hat, and my fine sword, and my sister, and Numps, and Mistress Grace (a gentlewoman that I should ha' married), and a cut-work handkerchief she ga' me, and two purses, today. And my bargain o' hobby-horses and ginger-bread, which grieves me worst of all. (4.2.79–86)

Cokes starts with a variation of Lear's question, 'Who is it that can tell me who I am?', asked in this case of a madman so that the bewildered question seems assured of a bewildering answer. In cataloguing all the things he has lost, and putting them all on the same level of importance, he implies that this miscellaneous collection of bric-à-brac – a hat, a sister, a basket of ginger-bread – is what constitutes his identity: once it is gone he does not know who he is. As Quomodo's identity is the accumulation of his deeds, Cokes's identity is an accumulation of junk, and of people listed as junk. There is no essential Cokes, merely a blank space in which the rubble has been piled. Wasp has already listed the contents of his head, 'all hung with cockle-shells, pebbles, fine wheat-straws, and here and there a chicken's feather, and a cob-web' (1.5.92–4), and Edgeworth has speculated that he has not a soul but 'a thing given him instead of salt, only to keep him from stinking' (4.2.54–5). In reply to Cokes's tale of loss Troubleall asks his standard question: 'By whose warrant, sir, have you done all this?' For Troubleall what matters is not identity but the authority behind one's actions. Cokes gives Troubleall's question the only effective reply it ever gets: 'Warrant? thou art a wise fellow, indeed – as if a man need a warrant to lose anything with' (4.2.87–9). The result is a standoff in which the nature of identity and the legitimacy of action seem equally meaningless problems.

Edgeworth's claim that Cokes is simply meat, who would stink without a preservative, takes us back to Ursula's pig-tent, one of the focal points of the Fair. It is the regular meeting place of the play's rogues, its brothel and its privy. Win Littlewit and Mistress Overdo both linger there to answer the call of nature, and as a consquence both are put on the game, equating one lower bodily function with another that uses the same organ.[13] Ursula herself is an expanding lump of matter, bursting its bounds like the play itself. Her name evokes the legendary shapelessnes of the bear-cub. She complains to her servant Mooncalf, 'did not I bid you should get this chair let out o'the sides, for me, that my hips might play?' (2.2.63–4). Talking makes her expand: Mooncalf says of her exchange of insults with Knockem, 'it makes her fat, you see. She battens with it' (2.3.37–8). If other characters represent the word made noise, Ursula is the word made flesh. However, she maintains an equilibrium, dissolving as well as expanding: 'I am all fire, and fat, Nightingale [is Jonson recalling Cleopatra's "I am fire and air"?]; I shall e'en melt away to the first woman, a rib, again, I am afraid. I do water the ground in knots as I go, like a great garden-pot; you may follow me by the S's I make' (2.2.49–53). *Bartholomew Fair*'s equivalent to *The Tempest*'s '*Enter Mariners wet*' is '*Ursula comes in again dropping*' (2.3.41.2).

Ursula's prediction that she will run human history backwards to the creation of Eve associates her with the Fall, and with the whole misogynist tradition that sees Eve as the cause of man's woe. To Quarlous she is a dangerous bog: 'he that would venture for't, I assure him, might sink into her, and be drown'd a week, ere any friend he had could find where he were' (2.5.88–90). (Male disquiet at the uncontrollable liquidity of the female body[14] surfaces again at the end of the play when Mistress Overdo spoils her husband's grand judgement scene by vomiting.) Full of flame, heat and frying bodies, the pig-tent recalls Hell, though Ursula insists, 'Hell's a cold cellar to't' (2.2.44).[15] She calls her attendant Mooncalf 'Thou arrant incubee' (2.2.84).[16] As in *Friar Bacon and Friar Bungay*, where Hell is a tavern and a devil appears with a joint of mutton on a spit, food and drink are comically associated with the demonic.

Throughout the play (as throughout the last paragraph) there is an itch to interpret Ursula, as though this will somehow bring her under control. When she enters with a firebrand, Winwife calls her 'Mother o'the Furies, I think, by her firebrand' (2.5.71). It is Busy who presents the most obvious interpretation: 'but the fleshly woman (which you call Urs'la) is above all to be avoided, having the marks upon her, of the three enemies of man: the world, as being in the Fair, the devil, as being in the fire; and the flesh, as being herself' (3.6.32–6). Time to take notes, we might think; but the fact that the speaker is Busy should give us pause. It is neat, pat and convincing, trapping Ursula into a formula, licking the bear-cub into shape. In the last analysis Ursula is Ursula, uncontrollably herself.

She is also a ruthless businesswoman. In *Friar Bacon* Miles imagined Hell as a tavern with a swinging piece of chalk, suggesting a reckoning that need never be paid. Ursula's tent may be Hell, but it is also a business where the customers have to pay and the management has calculated in detail how to bilk them:

threepence a pipeful, I will ha' made of all my whole half-pound of tobacco, and a quarter of a pound of coltsfoot mix'd with it too, to eke it out … Then, six and twenty shillings a barrel I will advance o' my beer, and fifty shillings a hundred o' my bottle-ale; I ha' told you the ways how to raise it. Froth your cans well i' the filling, at length, rogue, and jog your bottles o' the buttock, sirrah, then skink out the first glass, ever, and drink with all companies, though you be sure to be drunk; you'll misreckon the better, and be less asham'd on't. (2.2.90–101)

Greene's country feasting has been replaced by Middleton's urban marketplace. The customer loses: in the Fair 'real money is traded for more or less worthless goods'.[17] Leatherhead calls Joan Trash's ginger-bread people her progeny; but he also accuses her of making them of 'stale bread, rotten eggs, musty ginger, and dead honey' (2.2.9–10).

Pyramus and Thisbe is performed as a goodwill offering at Theseus's court; Flute hopes Bottom will get sixpence a day out of it, but he probably shouldn't hold his breath waiting. No one gets into the puppet play without paying twopence to the gatherers, Sharkwell and Filcher. Cokes recovers his lost identity by paying twelvepence, thus demonstrating that for all the losses he has suffered 'I am a gallant, as simple as I look now' (5.3.40–1). Having lost one identity he can buy another one. He is also, if we recall the Induction, buying a greater than usual right to judge the play, and he exercises that right, being the most voluble of its spectators until Busy arrives. In the agreement between author and audience the spectators of *Bartholomew Fair* have been told, 'it shall be lawful for any man to judge his six pen'orth, his twelve pen'orth, so to his eighteen pence, two shillings, half a crown, to the value of his place: provided always his place get not above his wit' (Induction, 88–92). Jonson liked to present himself as appealing to judicious spectators, and indifferent to or angry with the ignorant mob. He also claimed (in the face of occasional failure) that judicious spectators were hard to find. Here, with a kind of ironic despair, he gives up his search for the naturally judicious and puts the whole transaction on a cash basis, quantifying artistic judgement as Ursula quantifies her pigs: 'Five shillings a pig is my price, at least; if it be a sow-pig, sixpence more: if she be a great-bellied wife, and long for't, sixpence more for that' (2.2.110–13). Another distinction blurs, as we wonder briefly if the pig or the pregnant wife is for sale. Jonson has played the same trick, measuring the financial value not of his goods but of his clients.

Festivity is business; so is theatre; so is literary judgement, which is equally material. This prepares us for the play's treatment of love and sex, mostly the latter. Winwife, Quarlous, Grace and Purecraft all find mates in the Fair, giving it a function like that of the wood near Athens or the Forest of Arden; Michael Shapiro calls *Bartholomew Fair* 'an ironic "green world" comedy'.[18] The love-charm that affects Hero in the puppet play, however, is less romantic than that of *A Midsummer Night's Dream*. Cupid, disguised as a drawer, '*From under his apron, where his lechery lurks, / Puts love in her sack*' (5.4.282–3).[19] The wood near Athens and Prospero's island do not encourage free love as we might have expected; but Quarlous sees the Fair as a place where women become more available, urging Winwife to press his suit to the Puritan Dame Purecraft now that she has entered Ursula's tent: 'thou'lt never be master of a better season, or place; she that will venture herself into the Fair, and a pig-box, will admit any assault' (3.2.132–4).

One reason the pig-booth is auspicious is because it functions as a brothel. The transformation of Win Littlewit and Mistress Overdo into prostitutes provides an ironic parallel to the matchmaking that wins Grace for Winwife and Purecraft for Quarlous. While Mistress Overdo is tempted offstage, Win's temptation is acted out, and recalls the transformation of the Country Wench in *Michaelmas Term*. She too is drawn to lead 'the life of a lady' (4.5.27–8), and 'lady' quickly becomes another way of saying 'prostitute'. She too is tempted by clothes, 'her wires, and her tires, her green gowns, and velvet petticoats' (4.5.36–7). When Edgeworth invites Quarlous to the brothel it is to 'take part of a silken gown, a velvet petticoat, or a wrought smock' (4.6.17–19), as though he is going to copulate not with the woman but with the clothes. Whit and Knockem tell Win that a married woman is a bond-woman, but a 'lady' is free: for her the conventional categories do not exist: 'never to know ty husband, from another man ... Nor any one man from another, but i' the dark' (4.5.54–5). As Caliban is free to kiss Stephano's foot, Win will be free to copulate with any man who pays for her; the men's identities, and by implication hers, dissolve into an undifferentiated mass. In the Fair, as in Middleton's London, names and relationships vanish.

Though Win and Mistress Overdo reach the same point they come to it by very different routes. Win's new career ironically resembles her marriage. In the first act Littlewit fusses delightedly over her new clothing, and gets her to parade herself in front of him: 'This cap does convince! ... Sweet Win, let me kiss it! And her fine high shoes, like the Spanish lady!

Good Win, go a little, I would fain see thee pace, pretty Win! By this fine cap, I could never leave kissing on't' (1.1.20–6). 'It' leaves us wondering if he is kissing Win or the cap. Over her protests, he makes her accept kisses from Winwife and Quarlous, telling her 'Be womanly, Win' (1.3.39). This situation is echoed in the Fair when, again over her protests, he leaves her alone with Knockem and Whit, and they set to work. In a way he has prepared the ground for them, making her available and putting her on display. Her protests may have given the impression that she has a mind of her own, but that impression rapidly fades as, learning that a lady can wear fine clothes, cuckold her husband and still be honest, she declares, 'Lord, what a fool I have been!' (4.5.52). She is as gullible as Cokes, and with no more in the way of an essential identity.

Mistress Overdo seems to identify herself through her husband, constantly citing his authority even for points of language – 'though he be exorbitant, as Master Overdo says' (1.5.13) – and when at the end of the play she vomits and wakes from a drunken stupor, she bleats like a lost sheep, 'O lend me a basin, I am sick, I am sick; where's Master Overdo? Bridget, call hither my Adam ... Will not my Adam come to me? Shall I see him no more then?' (5.6.70–5). The new life, and the new identity, into which Win sinks with alacrity, leave Mistress Overdo feeling lost and disoriented. But she has succumbed to the same temptations. Jonson's point seems to be that in the pig-tent all men are alike, and so are all women. And not just in the pig-tent: when the professional punk Alice attacks Mistress Overdo, her complaint, 'The poor common whores can ha' no traffic, for the privy rich ones' (4.5.68–9), sounds like a comment about a larger world than that of the Fair. Grace is Overdo's ward, and she explains why her guardian has the power to make her marry Cokes: 'he bought me'. She calls this 'a common calamity' (3.5.275–6), and Jonson seems to be asking whether the Court of Wards, in which the king himself sold guardianships, is all that different from the pig-tent.

But at least Grace is protesting her fate. She and Winwife – and to a lesser degree Quarlous – seem to stand aloof from the Fair, and their story provides what in a more conventional play would be the love interest. Grace has no desire to go to the Fair, and stands on her dignity: 'there's none goes thither of any quality or fashion' (1.5.128–9). Winwife is offended when the people of the Fair offer their wares to him – 'That these people should be so ignorant to think us chapmen for 'em! Do we look as if we would buy gingerbread?' – though Quarlous is more tolerant and realistic: 'our very being here makes us fit to be demanded, as well as others' (2.5.12–17). The familiarity of Knockem's greeting, 'Ned Winwife? And Tom Quarlous, I think!' (2.5.19–20), suggests that Winwife's air of offended dignity is uncalled for: he is better known here than he likes to pretend. On the other hand Quarlous's tolerance has limits. When Edgeworth offers him a whore he retorts, 'Keep it for your companions in beastliness … the hand of beadle is too merciful a punishment for your trade of life' (4.6.21–7). Given that he has just used Edgeworth's services as a cutpurse, he is standing on a dignity as false as Winwife's.

In their relations with Grace the men are closer to the Fair's mentality than they pretend. Like Win, she is left alone with two strange men. As Littlewit assures his wife that Knockem and Whit are 'honest gentlemen' who will 'use you very civilly' (4.5.8–9), so Winwife tells Grace, 'I hope our manners ha' been such hitherto, and our language, as will give you no cause to doubt yourself in our company', and she replies, 'Sir, I will give myself no cause; I am so secure of mine own manners, as I suspect not yours' (3.5.295–300). Both parties sound a little defensive, and the real spirit in which the men approach her is betrayed by their bawdy puns, Winwife's 'How melancholy Mistress Grace is yonder! Pray thee let's go enter ourselves in grace, with her' (3.4.69–70), and Quarlous's regret that he is not more help in her legal difficulties: 'would I had studied a year longer i' the Inns of Court, an't had been but i' your case' (3.5.281–2).

Like Lysander and Demetrius, they find themselves rivals for the same woman. Entering with swords drawn, they seem prepared to settle the matter as between gentlemen; instead, Grace makes each of them write a name in her table-book, then asks the first passing stranger (Troubleall, of course) to pick one of the names. The ironies multiply. Though the names Quarlous and Winwife write, Argalus from the *Arcadia* and Palemon from *Two Noble Kinsmen*, evoke chivalric romance and idealized friendship,[20] the issue is settled not by a joust but by a lottery, and friendship here is not the high-minded affair described in *Endymion*. Quarlous fears that Winwife, left alone with Grace, will take the opportunity to backbite him; he would do the same himself (4.6.35–8). The ultimate comment on their friendship is the noisy quarrelling of Damon and Pythias, ideal friends in classical legend, but not in the puppet play.[21] Grace herself sounds sane and intelligent in her refusal to pick a husband from a field consisting of two men she has known less than two hours; but the impression collapses when she lets a passing madman do it for her, and her claim that they are 'both equal and alike' to her (4.3.34) relates her to Win, who in her new life as a prostitute will not tell one man from another.

Winwife gets her, but Quarlous uses Overdo's blank warrant to get control of her money. Despite her attempts, and the men's, to stand on their dignity, Grace has made herself the prize in a lottery and Quarlous treats her as Overdo does, as a ward with cash value.

Quarlous gets Dame Purecraft instead, and their match offers a similar combination of materialism and sheer craziness. Purecraft has been told by a cunning man that she must marry a madman within a week, giving her a motive for marriage about as reasonable as Grace's lottery. Seeing Quarlous disguised as Troubleall, she is immediately infatuated. Winwife has been paying court to her unsuccessfully, and Quarlous has given him racy lectures on the folly of marrying a widow, 'raking himself a fortune in an old woman's embers' (1.3.78). But when Purecraft offers herself to Quarlous he takes her, perhaps because she puts her strongest argument first: 'Good sir, hear me, I am worth six thousand pound; my love to you is become my rack' (5.2.49-50). Her proposal is a wonderfully odd combination of mad infatuation with a clear, realistic account of her own greed and hypocrisy: 'I am also ... a devourer, instead of a distributor of the alms' (5.2.54-5). In a way, that is part of her argument: if Quarlous takes her he will live richly off immoral earnings. He succumbs: 'Why should not I marry this six thousand pound, now I think on't? And a good trade too, that she has beside, ha? The tother wench, Winwife is sure of' (5.2.76-8). As men are alike to Win and Grace, women are alike to him; Grace is now 'the tother wench'. When Edgeworth offered him the chance to fornicate with a dress he got huffy; but he is willing to marry a sum of money.

The comedy of romantic courtship, essential to Lyly, Greene and Shakespeare, left Jonson indifferent or hostile. In *Bartholomew Fair* he gives it particularly rough treatment: men and women are brought together by chance, instinct and money. The distinction between marriage and prostitution, like other distinctions, becomes blurred. Jonson's treatment of authority, a key theme in *The Malcontent* and *The Tempest*, is equally ironic. There are no princes on stage: the highest authority is Overdo, who presides over a court that deals with petty local offences. The characters who have authority have it on a very small scale, but that does not make them any less obsessive about it. (H.L. Mencken observed that the reason academic politics are so nasty is because the stakes are so low.) Though Littlewit is the nominal head of his household it is Busy who 'governs all' (1.3.106) and the family cannot go to the Fair without his permission. Wasp uses political language to show his resentment of

Mistress Overdo's attempt to usurp his authority over Cokes: 'You think you are Madam Regent still, Mistress Overdo, when I am in place? No such matter, I assure you; your reign is out, when I am in, dame' (1.5.18–20). He uses similar language when Cokes's discovery that he has been in the stocks forces him to abdicate: 'Nay, then the date of my authority is out; I must think no longer to reign, my government is at an end' (5.4.94–6). Trying to stop the vapours game, Mistress Overdo sees herself as part of a chain of command that includes her husband and the king: 'Why gentlemen, why gentlemen, I charge you upon my authority, conserve the peace. In the king's name, and my husband's, put up your weapons; I shall be driven to commit you myself, else' (4.4.106–9). For Jonson and his contemporaries it would be particularly absurd to hear a woman talk like this. Bristle, when Troubleall addresses the Watch as 'the King's loving, and obedient subjects', bristles: 'His loving subjects, we grant you; but not his obedient, at this time, by your leave; we know ourselves a little better than so; we are to command, sir, and such as you are to be obedient' (4.1.3–8). But Bristle's authority collapses when his prisoners escape from the stocks and '*The watch, missing them, are affrighted*' (4.6.168.1). One of the sharpest terrors in an authoritarian society is that of the petty official who thinks he is in trouble.

The play's pervasive obsession with arrest touches even Littlewit's gloating over his wit: 'When a quirk, or a quiblin does 'scape thee, and thou dost not watch, and apprehend it, and bring it before the constable of conceit …' (1.1.13–15). This fussy vigilance becomes literal in Overdo. Like Malevole–Altofront he belongs to the tradition of disguised authority figures spying on and correcting the abuses of their societies, a tradition that includes the title character of Middleton's *Phoenix* and the Duke in Shakespeare's *Measure for Measure*.[22] Even Prospero, though he does not disguise himself, participates in the tradition through his mastery of surveillance and his tendency to keep his power hidden. But the offences Overdo spies on are petty ones, and his concern with them is out of proportion: the ordinary chicanery of the Fair is to him a series of 'enormities'. He needs to make them sound dramatic because it makes his role seem more impressive. Their importance to him is a measure of his importance to himself, which is considerable. His insistence on doing his own spying rather than depend on corrupt or foolish underlings (2.1.25–42) combines a public-spirited concern to have the job done properly with an assumption that only he can do it. Troubleall's mad reverence for Justice Overdo's warrant leads Overdo (at first) to call him 'a sober and discreet person' (4.1.26). To call Overdo's warrant 'the warrant of warrants' (4.1.19), as though he were the source of all authority, seems to Overdo himself entirely reasonable.

Bristle describes him as a peremptory judge who 'when he is angry, be it right or wrong, ... has the law on's side, ever' (4.1.75–6). Through the confusion of Bristle's language we take the point that when Overdo is in a temper, which seems to be much of the time, the law is whatever he says it is, even if it isn't. Overdo takes satisfaction in the fact that his name inspires terror (2.2.27–8). Even when he realizes that Troubleall is mad there is something self-centred in his pity: 'If this be true, this is my greatest disaster! How am I bound to satisfy this poor man, that is, of so good a nature to me, out of his wits' (4.1.58–60). Jonson avoids the easy options of showing Overdo born again, or simply incorrigible: the learning is real, the pity is real, but what makes it a convincing part of the character is Overdo's lament that this is *his* disaster. Hearing himself rebuked for anger, he reforms, but reluctantly: 'I will be more tender hereafter. I see compassion may become a Justice, though it be a weakness, I confess; and nearer a vice, than a virtue' (4.1.77–9). He is still hankering after his capacity to inspire terror.

He admires himself as the audience is directed to admire Middleton's Phoenix and Marston's Malevole–Altofront. But while their insights into the corruption of society are genuinely shrewd, Overdo thinks that the cutpurse Edgeworth is a civil young gentleman who needs to be rescued from bad company. While they do effective justice, Overdo finds himself unwittingly aiding the cutpurse by distracting the crowd, and his own wife, not recognizing him, denounces him as an enormity (3.5.209–12). Instead of giving him new, more effective authority, his disguise simply leaves his true authority vacant. Without his presence the Court of Pie-powders, which is supposed to do justice at the Fair, cannot meet, and its officers are left helpless and bewildered, not knowing what to do with their prisoners (one of whom is Overdo). Altofront and Prospero were forced from office; Overdo has irresponsibly abdicated.[23] His disguise as a preaching madman is a carnivalesque inversion, and on those terms might give him the authority Altofront enjoys as Malevole. But even as he boasts that his disguise is impenetrable, the effect is inadvertent self-mockery: 'They may have seen many a fool in the habit of a Justice; but never till now, a Justice in the habit of a fool' (2.1.7–9). More truly than he knows, he is playing the fool. His identification with the real Mad Arthur is so total that Mooncalf addresses him as an old acquaintance (2.2.126–31); at the same time Arthur's moralizing orations have so much of the real Overdo in them that as he denounces bottle-ale and tobacco Mistress Overdo and Cokes both comment on the madman's resemblance to Overdo (2.6.68–71). There seems not much to choose between his real identity and his assumed one: change places, and, handy-dandy, which is the justice, which is the fool?

Towards the end he works himself up for a grand scene of revelation and judgement of the sort that earlier disguised authority figures managed to pull off more or less successfully. He will have figuratively the power Prospero has literally: 'neither is the hour of my severity yet come, to reveal myself, wherein, cloud-like, I will break out in rain and hail, lightning and thunder, upon the head of enormity' (5.2.3–6). The great moment comes: 'Now, to my enormities: look upon me, O London! and see me, O Smithfield! the example of justice, and Mirror of Magistrates; the true top of formality, and scourge of enormity' (5.6.33–6). (Spotlight over here, please.) But this is around forty lines after he has first revealed himself; his attempts to take centre stage have been delayed and interrupted by the entry of fresh characters who keep pulling the focus away from him, and worse follows: '*Mistress Overdo is sick: and her husband is silenc'd*' (5.6.69.1). While Prospero is reminded by an airy spirit that he is human, Overdo is brought down to earth by gross physical reality, and Quarlous tells him, 'remember you are but Adam, flesh and blood! You have your frailty, forget your other name of Overdo, and invite us all to supper' (5.6.99–102).

The disruptions in Mistress Overdo's body, in Overdo's household, and in the action of the scene, form a multilayered image of rebellion and the breakdown of authority. The authority Overdo loses passes briefly to Quarlous, who lectures the Justice and reveals the truth about Edgeworth; but, having just made a crazy marriage of the sort he denounced at the beginning of the play, Quarlous is in no position to be the play's central spokesman. In fact there is no such character: the principle of dispersed attention holds, right to the end. No authority can govern the Fair, or the play. And yet the '*Fay ce que voldra*', do what you like, of Rabelais, could not quite be its motto. Its attitude to authority is double-edged. Its most scathing indictment of hierarchy lies in Troubleall, a figure Kafka might have invented, who embodies deference gone mad. He was an officer of the Pie-powders court, put out of his place by Overdo; the result was not to make him resentful but to make him madly dedicated to his old superior – even Caliban cringing to Stephano never goes this far – as though obedience is the centre of his life and he needs to cling to it at all costs: 'ever since, he will do nothing but by Justice Overdo's warrant: he will not eat a crust, nor drink a little, nor make him in his apparel ready. His wife, sir-reverence, cannot get him make his water, or shift his shirt, without his warrant' (4.1.53–7). Like the citizen of an authoritarian state suddenly and bewilderingly free, he is desperate to recreate his servitude, to fill in the blank that his life became when he fell out of the power structure. In that structure he could give orders as well as take them, and his demand of everyone he meets that they have Justice Overdo's warrant is his way of getting back the authority he lost. This is Jonson's sharpest indictment since *Sejanus* of the corrupting effect of power. Yet there are times when Troubleall's recurring question, what warrant have you?, is disconcertingly pointed. He asks it as Winwife and Quarlous write their chosen names in Grace's table-book; and he does well to ask it. He shakes the normally self-confident Edgeworth: 'Beshrew him, he startled me: I thought he had known of our plot. Guilt's a terrible thing!' (4.2.11–12). He intimidates the Watch into taking their prisoner (Overdo) before Justice Overdo instead of simply putting him in the stocks on their own initiative. At moments like these Troubleall has, however briefly, real authority: his demand that actions should have warrant suggests that even as it shows a world spinning out of control the play registers a need for some kind of meaning, some kind of legitimacy.

There are in fact two plays called *Bartholomew Fair*, and they weigh the issue differently. The first, the one performed at the Hope, may be called the people's play. It ends with the Fair unjudged and uncontrolled, spilling over into the lives of the visitors and even of the audience. Overdo invites *everyone* – and we have to think what that means – home to his house for supper. Jonathan Haynes finds this, as an image of communal festivity, unbelievable: 'Can Grace really sit down with Ursula? How will Winwife get along with Quarlous, who has just defrauded his fiancée of her inheritance?'[24] Good questions: and we might also note the pervasive self-absorption of the characters, which makes it hard to imagine them joining together as a community. Littlewit boasts of his wit, 'I ha' the luck to spin out these fine things still, and like a silk-worm, out of myself' (1.1.1–3); Busy 'affects the violence of singularity in all he does' (1.3.137). As Leo Salingar puts it, the play's characters form 'not a community but a crowd'.[25] Yet, as Anne Barton has noted, the Fair characters, unlike their visitors, are capable of surprising mutual loyalty and good will.[26] It may seem too much to hope that when the Fair comes to Overdo's house some of its communal spirit will brush off on the self-centred Londoners; but Busy, defeated by the puppet, has announced, 'I am changed, and will become a beholder with you!' (5.5.109–10). It is not that the puppets themselves exemplify any spirit of community: their play is a clash of screaming, competitive egos (or ids). But watching them is a communal exercise. What I have called the people's play ends with Cokes's line, 'bring the actors along, we'll ha' the rest o' the play at home' (5.6.117–18). Which actors, and which play? Is *Bartholomew Fair*, like *The Tempest*, being turned over to us? And if so, what does that mean? The Induction isolates individual spectators, demanding they judge for themselves, not as a group.[27] But by the time the play has worked on us, has that strategy of divide and conquer been replaced by a communal experience in which players and audience share? Or does having the play (Jonson's play or the puppet play or both) invade our homes mean that our polite lives will be broken up by noise, violence and chicanery, and, as the Fair's prostitution mirrors sexual relations in society at large, we will see our own lives disconcertingly reflected in it? The people's play ends with the play, and the Fair, spilling over the stage and out of the playhouse, and with no clear, certain interpretation of what that means.

Then there is the king's play. The day after its performance at the Hope, *Bartholomew Fair* was performed at court, with a prologue and epilogue addressed to the king. Instead of being lectured or bargained with like the playhouse audience, the king is simply greeted: 'Your Majesty is welcome to a Fair' (Prologue, 1). He is guided into the labyrinth of the action by being invited to notice one theme of special importance to him:

> the zealous noise
> Of your land's Faction, scandaliz'd at toys,
> As babies, hobby-horses, puppet-plays,
> And such like rage, whereof the petulant ways
> Yourself have known, and have been vex'd with long.   (Prologue, 3–7)

It has been said that the only way to read *Finnegans Wake* without going mad is to look for just one thing.[28] King James is to focus on the anti-Puritan satire, with its implicit endorsement of his own authority. That authority is confirmed by the epilogue:

> Your Majesty hath seen the play, and you
>   Can best allow it from your ear, and view.
> You know the scope of writers, and what store

> Of leave is given them, if they take not more,
> And turn it into licence: you can tell
> If we have us'd that leave you gave us, well ... (1-6)

By whose warrant do you do this? The king's.[29]

So far as we can judge Jonson's politics, he seems to have been torn between an instinctive republicanism and a desire to be known as the king's poet. *Bartholomew Fair* is in many respects Jonson's *King Lear*: a study of chaos and madness, full of carnivalesque inversion, in which people are kicked, beaten and put in the stocks, in which they lose their clothes and their identities, in which authority breaks down in the face of physical reality and the only sure truth seems to be that we have bodies. That is the play that sweeps over the Hope playhouse at full strength, uncontrolled by any final judgement; the play that somehow evaded even Jonson's own act of canon-formation, the 1616 Folio. At court the king's poet reins it in, and James becomes what Elizabeth was in shows like *The Lady of May*: the ultimate centre of an otherwise centreless occasion, the final arbiter of truth. The fact that a twelve-line prologue and an equally brief epilogue are enough to transform the people's play into the king's play may leave us impressed by the ease with which the king's power is brought to bear; or it may leave us wondering whether so slender a thread can really control this great dramatic leviathan.

Notes

1 In *Ben Jonson: To the First Folio*, Cambridge, 1983, Richard Dutton lists the play's reminders of Jonson's early work and suggests that it was excluded from the Folio for lack of space (pp. 156-7). Frances Teague, *The Curious History of Bartholomew Fair*, Lewisburg, London and Toronto, 1985, suggests that Jonson 'held his play back in order to rewrite it' (p. 59).

2 R.B. Parker, 'The Themes and Staging of *Bartholomew Fair*', *University of Toronto Quarterly*, XXXIX, 1970, 302-3, argues that this accounts for several passages in which characters are described as little, or called children.

3 All references to *Bartholomew Fair* are to the Revels editon, ed. E.A. Horsman, London, 1960.

4 *The Politics of Mirth*, Chicago and London, 1986, p. 43.

5 'Jonson and Anger', *Yearbook of English Studies*, XIV, 1984, 64-6; on Jonson's concern with the aggression that accompanies anger, see Helen Ostovich, '"Jeered by Confederacy": Group Aggression in Jonson's Comedies', *Medieval and Renaissance Drama in England*, III, 1986, 115-28.

6 Quoted in Teague, *Curious*, p. 124.

7 Introduction to the Yale edition of *Bartholomew Fair*, New Haven and

London, 1963, pp. 205–17. Similar staging has been postulated for *Endymion* (chapter 2, n. 17), though there it would be in play with the centralizing power of Cynthia.

8 'Still Standing Upright: Ben Jonson, 350 Years Alive', *New Theatre Quarterly*, III, 1987, 204. Barnes's title refers to the fact that Jonson is buried in Westminster Abbey in an upright position.

9 *Authority and Conflict: England 1603–1658*, London, 1986, pp. 65–8, 76.

10 Patrick Collinson, 'The Theatre Constructs Puritanism', *The Theatrical City: Culture, Theatre and Politics in London, 1576–1649*, ed. David L. Smith, Richard Strier and David Bevington, Cambridge, 1995, p. 163. On the king's power to license drama, see Marcus, *Politics*, pp. 59–60.

11 Brian Gibbons, *Jacobean City Comedy*, 2nd ed., London and New York, 1980, p. 147.

12 Debora K. Shuger notes the echo of Galatians 3.28, where Paul declares that in Christ there is 'neither male nor female': 'Hypocrites and Puppets in *Bartholomew Fair*', *Modern Philology*, LXXXII, 1984, 72.

13 Patricia Parker notes that 'pig' is 'an ancient slang term in Latin and Greek for the female genitals': *Literary Fat Ladies: Rhetoric, Gender, Property*, London and New York, 1987, p. 24.

14 On the female body's excessive production of fluids (with special reference to bladder incontinence) see Gail Kern Paster, 'Leaky Vessels: The Incontinent Women of City Comedy', *Renaissance Drama*, n.s. XVIII, 1987, 43–65.

15 R.B. Parker suggests that Ursula's booth could be 'on stage-left, the traditional "sinister" location of hell-mouth' ('Themes', p. 294).

16 Horsman glosses, '?the child resulting from intercourse with such a demon': this would link Mooncalf with Caliban, whom Stephano and Trinculo call 'mooncalf'. Caliban may also be recalled in the puppets, equally noisy and fractious: sideswiping Shakespeare in passing, the Induction notes the lack of a 'servant-monster' in the Fair but offers the puppets as compensation (128–35); Whit calls Leatherhead 'mashter o' de monshtersh' (5.4.8).

17 Jonathan Haynes, *The Social Relations of Jonson's Theater*, Cambridge, 1992, p. 123.

18 'The Casting of Flute: Planes of Illusion in *A Midsummer Night's Dream* and *Bartholomew Fair*', *The Elizabethan Theatre XIII*, ed. A.L. Magnusson and C.E. McGee, Toronto, 1994, 167.

19 In Richard Eyre's 1976 production at the Nottingham Playhouse, Cupid (who unlike the puppet Dionysius was anatomically correct) urinated into the sack. It would be more in tune with the reference to his lechery if he masturbated into it.

20 Anne Barton, *Ben Jonson, Dramatist*, Cambridge, 1984, pp. 208, 211–13.

21 In the Nottingham production (set in the nineteenth century) Damon and Pythias were dressed to look like Winwife and Quarlous, in identical officers' uniforms.

22 Barton, *Ben Jonson*, pp. 203–4.

23 Teague, *Curious*, p. 43.

24 *Social*, p. 138.

25 'Crowd and Public in *Bartholmew Fair*', *Renaissance Drama*, n.s. X, 1979, 143.

26 *Ben Jonson*, pp. 205–6. Haynes, *Social*, p. 124, notes that all the crimes of the Fair involve teamwork.

27 Haynes, *Social*, p. 132.

28 I owe this advice to William Blissett.

29 Marcus, *Politics*, p. 61, notes that, if spectators are entitled to judge according to what they have paid, the king's 'lavish' support of drama gives him the greatest right of all. (She has since revised her view of the play, regarding her interpretation in *The Politics of Mirth* as too narrowly centred on the king: see 'Of Mire and Authorship,' *Theatrical City*, p. 174.) On the implications of the licensing of theatre (and popular culture generally) by royal authority, with special reference to *Bartholomew Fair*, see Richard A. Burt, '"Licensed by Authority": Ben Jonson and the Politics of Early Stuart Theater', *English Literary History*, LIV, 1987, 529–60.

9

Caroline comedy: Shirley, *The Lady of Pleasure* and Brome, *A Jovial Crew*

THOUGH Ben Jonson lived and continued writing well into the reign of Charles I, he slipped from favour with both court and public. To his fellow writers he was either a respected mentor or simply a back number. The comedy of the Caroline period follows him in examining contemporary English society, but without his highly coloured imagination or his satiric rigour. It tends to be more relaxed, wider in focus and more varied in tone, combining satire and romance. The onstage societies of Jonson, Marston and Middleton are stylized for purposes of satire; in Caroline comedy the pressure of satire is lighter, the stylization relaxes and there is a greater sense of watching everyday social life.[1] James Shirley's *The Lady of Pleasure* (1635) looks at fashionable London while Richard Brome's *A Jovial Crew* (1641) is set in the country. Though both plays have, as we shall see, a critical edge, and neither can be described as straight reporting, the interest in single powerful (or would-be powerful) figures we have seen in earlier plays – the ruler, the magician, the magistrate – is replaced by an interest in the way people relate to each other in society at large.

Shirley was perhaps the best-known playwright of his time; just before the closing of the theatres in 1642 he succeeded Philip Massinger as leading dramatist of the King's Men. Brome was a protégé of Jonson; the commendatory verses to the first edition of *A Jovial Crew* include tributes to him for carrying on the master's tradition. Both plays were performed at a small private theatre, the Cockpit in Drury Lane. Shirley's was evidently a success; in his epistle dedicatory he calls it 'fortunate in the scene' (7–8).[2] Produced just before the closing of the theatres, Brome's play had no chance to establish itself in the repertoire; but it was revived shortly after

the Restoration, stayed in the repertoire well into the eighteenth century
and was adapted in 1731 into a comic opera that held the stage for the next
fifty years. Both plays proved themselves as audience entertainments; but
in each case an important part of the entertainment is a provocative view of
the state of English life.

While Middleton in *Michaelmas Term* shows London through a brisk
trade in money, land and sex, *The Lady of Pleasure* is a portrait of the
leisure-class life of the town, centred on the Strand in the fashionable West
End, a world of gossip, display and conspicuous consumption.[3] In this
respect the three key figures are the title character Aretina, a country lady
who has come to town with her reluctant husband Bornwell to lead the life
of a lady of fashion; her nephew Frederick, a university student corrupted
by learning town manners; and Celestina, a young widow who seems at
first to be using her new freedom to indulge in extravagant luxury, but who
reveals unexpected seriousness and self-control as the play goes on.

The country Aretina has left behind is not, as in Middleton, simply
real estate to be bargained for; it represents a way of life and a set of values
against which the town can be measured. The play opens with a debate
between Aretina and her Steward in which she complains of the boredom
and stupidity of rural life:

> The men
> So near the primitive making, they retain
> A sense of nothing but the earth, their brains
> And barren heads standing as much in want
> Of ploughing as their ground!

The sort of country pastime Greene celebrated in *Friar Bacon and Friar
Bungay* is for Aretina merely exhausting:

> To observe with what solemnity
> They keep their wakes, and throw for pewter candlesticks,
> How they become the morris, with whose bells
> They ring all into Whitsun ales, and sweat
> Through twenty scarves and napkins, till the hobbyhorse
> Tire and the Maid Marian, dissolved to a jelly,
> Be kept for spoon meat!   (1.1.4–16)

This may recall the dissolving into pure matter of Ursula in *Bartholomew
Fair*, but the scale is smaller: spoon meat is soft food for babies. To
Aretina country pastime is infantile. She has come to town, she claims, for
freedom and pleasure.

The Steward counters that in the country she had everything she needed:

> While your own will commanded what should move
> Delights, your husband's love and power joined
> To give your life more harmony, you lived there
> Secure and innocent, beloved of all,
> Praised for your hospitality, and prayed for;
> You might be envied, but malice knew
> Not where you dwelt.   (1.1.22–8)

He is vague about the 'delights' she could command, but clear in his views that her happiness rested on her husband's authority and that her key virtue was hospitality. It is precisely that authority against which she chafes, and she is now more interested in spending on herself than in giving to others. The tests this debate sets up are whether the town will provide Aretina with real pleasure and control over her own life; and whether its pastimes are in the last analysis any more intelligent than those of the country.

There is no Quomodo here to act as the single centre for a town-versus-country intrigue. Aretina is sucked in by the whole ethos of the town, exemplified in a range of characters. The Steward argues that in the country she was the object of prayer and gratitude, not gossip; but a key activity of the townspeople, as the play will emphasize, is talking about each other. Her husband Bornwell worries about their becoming 'the fable of the town' (1.1.66) and warns Aretina that her fondness for going to balls is giving her a bad reputation (1.1.111–17). Littleworth, a town gallant whose name tells us all we need to know, insists that the gossip is favourable: 'All tongues are so much busy with your praise / They have not time to frame other discourse' (1.1.234–5). (In the next line he offers her a sugar-plum: the progress from country to town is from spoon meat to candy.) Aretina believes in being talked about: she tells Bornwell that the way for him to rise to 'employment in the state' is by 'the popular vote and knowledge' (1.1.148–9). Celestina dominates the play's second scene as Aretina does the first. Her Steward warns her, 'Men's tongues are liberal in your character / Since you began to live thus high' (1.2.67–8). She counters that a reputation for extravagance is just what she wants, and there is something competitive in her ambition:

> I will
> Be hospitable, then, and spare no cost

That may engage all generous report
To trumpet forth my bounty and my bravery
Till the court envy and remove.

(1.2.80–4)

Celestina receives visits from perfect strangers who are drawn by her reputation. Haircut, who makes vague claims to high employment but is really a barber, excuses his calling on her:

He must live obscurely, madam
That hath not heard what virtues you possess;
And I, a poor admirer of your fame,
Am come to kiss your hand.

(1.2.111–14)

He goes on virtually to propose marriage. Bornwell, as part of a campaign to cure Aretina by making her jealous, likewise calls on Celestina as a perfect stranger and tries to start a love affair. The Lord, whose devotion to the memory of his late mistress isolates him at first from the intrigues of the town, is the subject of similar attentions. The bawd Decoy calls on him, hoping to set him up with Aretina: though she admits 'I am a stranger to your lordship' she presumes on the fact that 'you have much fame / For your sweet inclination to our sex' (3.1.14, 22–3). Offended, he threatens her with a bawd's punishments, whipping and carting; she has misread his reputation badly. Though not so obviously rebuffed, Haircut and Bornwell get nowhere with Celestina. This recurring device of the call from a stranger who has misread a character's reputation suggests that in the fashionable world people know about each other, but do not know each other.

The reputation for luxury that Celestina claims she wants reflects the main preoccupation of the town. In 1632 King Charles issued one of a number of proclamations against the rural gentry's abandoning their estates for a life of fashion in London, complaining in particular that their taste for imported luxury goods was enriching other nations at England's expense.[4] Bornwell's lecture to Aretina is comprehensive:

Your change of gaudy furniture, and pictures
Of this Italian master and that Dutchman's;
Your mighty looking-glasses, like artillery,
Brought home on engines; the superfluous plate,
Antic and novel, vanities of tires,
Fourscore pound suppers for my lord your kinsman,
Banquets for t'other lady, aunt, and cousins;
And perfumes that exceed all train of servants,

> To stifle us at home, and show abroad
> More motley than the French or the Venetian
> About your coach, whose rude postillion
> Must pester every narrow lane, till passengers
> And tradesmen curse your choking up their stalls,
> And common cries pursue your ladyship
> For hindering o' their market.   (1.1.74–88)

He goes on to complain of her lavish clothing and jewellery. In the country she exercised hospitality; here she feasts only her relations, and while she supports foreign trades her only contribution to London commerce is to block traffic. The foreignness of fashion is suggested in a later scene in which Aretina and Celestina converse at length in French, and Aretina's nephew Frederick sees the effect as one of visual display: 'This language should be French, by the motions of your heads and the mirth of your faces … 'Tis one of the finest tongues for ladies to show their teeth in.' He goes on to apologize that while he has Greek and Latin 'my tailor has not put me into French yet' (3.2.121–6).

As in other societies dominated by fashion, it is important to know what is In and what is Out. Bornwell asks Alexander Kickshaw, Littleworth's companion and another useless man-about-town, 'What exercise carries the general vote / O'th' town now?' Kickshaw replies that cockfighting 'now has all the noise' (1.1.220–2). The repeated 'now' suggests that next month it will be something else. Religion, on the other hand, is definitely Out. Kickshaw and Littleworth agree that praying is 'out of fashion' (1.1.324). Celestina complains to her Steward that her hangings and her newly ordered coach and sedan chair are not rich enough; she particularly objects to the religious subjects of her hangings, 'Jewish stories stuffed with corn and camels' (1.2.15). She wants something more temporary, 'Stories to fit the seasons of the year, / And change as often as I please' (1.2.23–4). She says of her coach, lined with camel hair instead of crimson plush, 'Some lady / Had rather never pray, than go to church in't' (1.2.39–40). Praying is in fashion only if accompanied by a proper show. There is, however, one religious subject that speaks to her: she wants her sedan chair decorated with 'all the story of the prodigal / Embroiderèd with pearl' (1.2.58–9). Presumably the appeal of the story lies not in its (all too relevant) warning but in the opportunity it gives for scenes of debauchery; and what finally matters is not the message but the richness of the medium. Marston used the decay of religious faith as a measure of the decadence of the Genoan court; Shirley, anticipating the jewelled cross of Belinda in *The Rape of the Lock*, shows religion turned into material display.

This is the life that Aretina finds more pleasurable and exciting than the country; but as she describes her day we see it has its own emptiness: 'A lady's morning work: we rise, make fine, / Sit for our picture, and 'tis time to dine' (1.1.322–3). Identities and relationships are empty or unsettled. Aretina's Steward can report the fashionable behaviour of Kickshaw and Littleworth, but has trouble recalling their names (1.1.178–98). Decoy calls on Aretina, but claims to be too busy to stay: she has many other calls to make (1.1.172–3). Even class is unstable, or a matter of dispute. Bornwell's name conveys his class dignity, and he insists that while Aretina also comes of a good family her position really depends on him: he is willing 'to give the dignity of your birth / All the best ornaments which become my fortune' (1.1.63–4). She in turn justifies her extravagance as befitting 'A lady of my birth and education' (1.1.58); each makes deliberate use of the word 'my', and Bornwell fears that if she does not get her way the house will be 'shook with names / Of all her kindred' (1.1.208–9). Ideally, he thinks, class should take second place to his own authority as her husband:

> I am not ignorant how much nobility
> Flows in your blood: your kinsmen great and powerful
> I'th' state. But with this lose not your memory
> Of being my wife.
> (1.1.59–62)

Class itself is unstable. Aretina's Steward reminds her that he is 'a gentleman, though now your servant' (1.1.37), not only trying to get an edge in their debate but suggesting that a class position can be lost. Haircut, like Middleton's Andrew Lethe, is a climber. In studiously vague language, he suggests he has a high position and even higher prospects (2.2.140–5); Celestina, knowing nothing about him, concludes, 'He has some great office, / Sure, by his confident behaviour' (2.2.102–3). We see the reality when he appears with the Lord, *preparing his periwig, table, and looking-glass* (3.1.0.1–2).

While Haircut is the only character who is exposed in quite this way, he is not the only one whose status is largely a matter of talk. The Lord (his title is never specified) represents the highest social reach of the play, and Celestina's account of his reputation for nobility, learning, wit, prudence, valour and bounty makes him sound like the ideal gentleman, the standard against which the rest of society can be measured (4.3.64–85). But this list of virtues remains disembodied; we never see them in action. If the Lord stands against the triviality of the town, it is because of his devotion to the memory of his late mistress Bella Maria, which suggests the Platonic love that Queen Henrietta Maria had made fashionable at court.[5] Like Maria in *The Malcontent*, he exemplifies a loyalty secluded from the world, and like her he annoys the creatures of the world. Decoy offers to 'Repair your loss' (3.1.37) by arranging an affair with Aretina, who is his kinswoman. Kickshaw and Sentlove tempt him to visit Celestina; as Kickshaw complains, ''Tis time he were reduced to the old sport; / One lord like him more would undo the court' (3.1.232–3). Celestina tries his virtue by tempting him; after holding out a while, he succumbs and offers himself to her, to be saved only by her refusal. There may be a danger signal in his first scene, when he describes his devotion not as an absolute ideal but as a loss of interest in sex: 'I do not find that proneness since the fair / Bella Maria died; my blood is cold' (3.1.69–70). Celestina warms that blood, then cools it again. In the end he promises to 'honour' Celestina 'with chaste thoughts' (5.3.159). But he needs Celestina's help; on his own, he betrayed the ideal we thought he stood for.

The moral authority the Lord loses by his apostasy is gained, surprisingly, by Celestina. At her first appearance she is a spoiled young widow bent on extravagance and testy with her Steward's attempts to restrain her; the parallel with Aretina's first scene is obvious. But while Aretina's surrender to the town culminates in a fall from chastity, which we shall examine later, Celestina holds out. Her early claim that she can rein in her extravagance when she pleases (1.2.104) is truer than we might at first have thought. Though men swarm around her, her own policy is 'jest, but love not' (2.2.17) and when she flirts she always keeps her guard up. She pretends to be impressed by Haircut, but with ironic reservations:

> You may be some young lord, and though I see not
> Your footmen and your groom, they may not be
> Far off, in conference with your horse.   (1.2.132–4)

His claim of devotion gets similar treatment:

> How long do you imagine you can love, sir?
> Is it a quotidian, or will it hold
> But every other day?   (1.2.151–3)

Bornwell's offer of love leads to a flirtation that is guarded on both sides, since neither really wants to go too far. Throughout their dialogue she reminds him that he is married, and finally challenges him, 'You dare not, sir, be virtuous' (2.2.252). He accepts the challenge. Having pretended to tempt the Lord, she congratulates him on holding out: 'I can / Now glory that you have been worth my trial' (4.3.170–1). When he returns and tries to tempt her she challenges him to sell his coat of arms; on his refusal she points out that what his arms are to him, her honour is to her. Their debate recalls the similar debate between Bertram and Diana in *All's Well that Ends Well* (4.2); her sexual honour becomes the equivalent of the aristocratic honour he does not quite succeed in exemplifying. Celestina supports her final dedication to chastity by evoking the truth and love of 'the two royal luminaries', Charles and Henrietta Maria (4.3.180). As in Oberon's vision of Elizabeth, though far more briefly, a royal embodiment of a high ideal is glimpsed beyond the borders of the play. While Aretina falls, Celestina, who had seemed to be at least her match in folly, comes to stand for a workable relation to the town, entertaining its pleasures but keeping a final self-control.

While Celestina preserves not only her own chastity but that of the men who attempt her, Aretina is largely responsible for her nephew Frederick's surrender to the town. Though Bornwell insists that education is necessary for a gentleman, and Frederick claims he was happy at his books (2.1.27–39), Aretina summons him to leave the university and come to London. Finding him dressed in simple black, she nearly faints, declaring, 'The boy's undone' (2.1.45); she wishes she had sent him to France to learn modish behaviour. Town manners have to be taught, and Kickshaw and Littleworth take over Frederick's training. Like the Middleton's Lethe and Country Wench, he is transformed by new clothes. Littleworth tells him,

> Your French tailor
> Has made you a perfect gentleman; I may
> Converse now with you, and preserve my credit.
> D'ee feel no alteration in your body
> With these new clothes?   (4.2.2–6)

But Frederick has been introduced to more than fashion. The Steward (whose role in Frederick's seduction is confusingly at odds with his opening lectures to Aretina) offers to supply the new-made gentleman with a pimp. He has already promised Frederick that if wine makes him feel like sex his aunt will not deny him 'Any of her chambermaids to practise on' (2.1.162). In fact he tries to practise on her. As the new-made prostitutes of *Bartholomew Fair* are told not to discriminate between men,

Frederick declares, 'My blood is rampant, too; I must court somebody. As good my aunt as any other body' (5.2.20–1). He tries to improve his education further: 'You have a soft hand, madam; are you so all over?' (5.2.35–6). When she refuses his invitation to join him on a couch, he is indignant: 'Are you so coy to your own flesh and blood?' (5.2.54).

Frederick's seduction by the town is mostly broad and farcical; but the final touch of incest as his debauchery becomes sexual has an uncomfortable edge. Though Aretina rejects him, she herself has already fallen. One of the characters who accompanies Frederick as he propositions his aunt is Kickshaw, with whom she has just committed adultery. Marston uses sex as a political barometer in *The Malcontent*; the fates of Middleton's Country Wench and the new-made prostitutes of *Bartholomew Fair* are signs of the seductive power of London and the Fair; and Shirley uses Aretina's sexual fall as the key symbol of her corruption by the town. The similarity of her name to that of the Italian writer Pietro Aretino, regarded in England as a pornographer, is a bad sign.[6] As Prospero's dire warnings to Ferdinand suggest, this was a culture in which female chastity had the power of a talisman. Female submission in marriage had a similar power to guarantee the social order; Aretina's resistance to Bornwell's authority goes so far that he starts complaining of his servitude to her (1.1.209–10). In the first scene the Steward summarizes the problem Aretina presents: 'Y'are a woman of an ungoverned passion, and I pity you' (1.1.44–5).

Much as he deplores her extravagant ways, Bornwell stops short of the final criticism: 'In the strict sense of honesty, I dare / Make my oath they are innocent' (1.1.156–7). Moments later, Decoy enters. Decoy insists she is not a bawd, but simply does 'honourable offices' (3.1.54). Her fake gentility includes pride in running a high-class establishment that appeals to sophisticated tastes:

> I have done offices, and not a few
> Of the nobility but have done feats
> Within my house, which is convenient
> For situation, and artful chambers,
> And pretty pictures to provoke the fancy.   (3.2.17–21)

The Lord tells her what she is, in the language of *Michaelmas Term*: 'Your ladyship, I conceive, / Doth traffic in flesh merchandise'. She replies, unperturbed, 'To men / Of honour, like yourself' (3.1.37–9). At this point 'honour' (a term much used and abused throughout the play) starts to acquire the ironic value it has in the mouth of Lady Fidget in *The Country Wife*. The Lord writes to Aretina, warning her against Decoy, but the warning misfires: learning what she is, Aretina decides to use her services. In Decoy the language of honour and fashion is a way of dressing up the old game, and Aretina's use of her suggests her own capacity for self-deception.

Instead of succumbing to some fascinating Don Juan of the town (there is no such character in the play) Aretina takes the initiative herself, making an assignation with the worthless Kickshaw. In her choice of partner, as in her choice of go-between, she offends against both chastity and taste. In a world where everybody talks about everybody else, she insists on secrecy to the point that Kickshaw will not know – and never does know – the identity of the woman he has sex with. This is part of a move from public to private space that Anne Barton has noted in the play,[7] and recalls the anonymity of prostitution in *Bartholomew Fair*. In the scene that leads to the actual encounter, Aretina herself is missing – withdrawn into the anonymity she desires, withdrawn even from the audience – and the point of view is Kickshaw's. Decoy appears to him, disguised as an old woman, claiming to be the lady he is to sleep with and embodying not sensual pleasure but comic horror. As Kickshaw puts it,

> She has no teeth
> This twenty years, and the next violent cough
> Brings up her tongue – it cannot possibly
> Be sound at root. I do not think but one
> Strong sneeze upon her, and well meant, would make
> Her quarters fall away.   (4.1.44–9)

Recalling the legend familiar to English readers from *The Wife of Bath's Tale*, Decoy promises that in bed, in the dark, she will seem young: 'my skin is smooth and soft / As ermine's' (4.1.76–7). Kickshaw is not reassured: he sees her not just as a crone but as a witch and a devil, asking anxiously 'Has she no cloven foot?' (4.1.63). Withdrawn into anonymity, Aretina is replaced by a male fantasy of the horror of the female body, recalling the fire and fat of Ursula and the crone-comedy of Dipsas in *Endymion*.

Confronted with this figure, Kickshaw beds her (in reality, he gets Aretina) not out of desire but out of fear:

> I must on,
> Or else be torn a-pieces; I have heard
> These succubi must not be crossed.   (4.1.81–3)

Decoy, as the crone, offers to make it worth his while:

> I grieved a proper man should be compelled
> To bring his body to the common market;
> My wealth shall make thee glorious.   (4.1.67–9)

This time it is the man who is prostituted. She gives him gold before the event, and in the next scene he appears in rich new clothes, juxtaposed with Frederick, who has just appeared similarly transformed. Aretina seems at first not to recognize him, and remarks aside, 'Now he looks brave and lovely' (4.2.143). She has not so much taken a lover as bought a sex-toy, and it amuses her to dress him up.

Given that the play has been centred on Aretina, the shift of focus to Kickshaw at this point is puzzling. His view that he is having sex with a combination of crone, witch and devil may be a displaced form of the self-disgust that conventionally Aretina ought to feel at her own act. But if so, it is displaced in more than one way. The person who arouses this disgust is not Aretina herself but Decoy, and Decoy in disguise at that. While Friar Bacon's devils, and even Ursula's pig-tent in its role as hell-mouth, retain a connection with a popularized hell that it seems just possible for an audience of the time to have believed in, the demonic associations of the Decoy–Kickshaw scene are so much a matter of disguise and artifice they seem to be not so much drawing on a real fear as constructing a conventional metaphor.

The question remains, what does Aretina herself feel about what she has done? After watching Kickshaw read the letter that sets up the assignation, she is left briefly alone on stage:

> I blush while I converse with my own thoughts:
> Some strange fate governs me, but I must on;
> The ways are cast already, and we thrive
> When our sin fears no eye or perspective.   (3.2.349–52)

She consoles herself for her initial shame by evoking something like the Calvinist sense of doom that touches certain Jacobean tragedies, notably Middleton and Rowley's *The Changeling*; but she expresses it lightly and takes comfort in the idea of secrecy. Encountering Kickshaw in his finery, she seems at first pleased at the transformation; but in a later scene Decoy notes a certain flatness in her mood: 'What, melancholy after so sweet a night's work?' (5.2.2). Kickshaw boasts complacently to her of his new-found wealth: 'I ha' sprung a mine' (5.2.111). He does not know that she is the mine. Feeling perhaps slighted and taken for granted, needing perhaps to know how he felt about their night together, she cross-questions him on the source of his wealth. Evasive at first, he finally tells what he thinks is the truth, and she hears herself described as 'a strange ill-favoured hag', 'a she-devil, too: a most insatiate, abominable devil with a tail thus long'; 'I did the best to please her, but as sure as you live, 'twas a hell-cat' (5.2.146, 157–8, 168–9). Once again she is left briefly alone, and looks at herself: ''Tis a false glass, sure, I am more deformed. What have I done? My soul is miserable' (5.2.178–9).

Assuming she is literally looking in a mirror, she sees nothing that corresponds to Kickshaw's fantasy, only her natural face.[8] Aretina is not in fact a witch or a devil but a woman who has made a mistake she now regrets. There is nothing here of the 'One minute, and eternally undone' (2.2.30) of *Michaelmas Term*. Shirley avoids the dramatic stereotyping that divided women into chaste maids (or wives) and whores, with nothing in between, and he spares Aretina the usual fates of fallen women in the drama of his time. She is not ruined, corrupted or publicly disgraced; she simply a woman who has had a bad experience.[9] And her glass tells her the truth: she is the same woman. Kickshaw is on stage when Frederick propositions her, suggesting that one misstep is leaving her open to others. In another kind of play this would be the start of a downward spiral into sin and death; here nothing more happens.

Like Marston's Aurelia, Aretina repents, submits to her husband, and prepares to retreat from the world:

> Heaven has dissolved the clouds that hung upon
> My eyes, and if you can with mercy meet
> A penitent, I throw my own will off
> And now in all things obey yours: my nephew
> Send back again to th'college, and myself
> To what place you'll confine me.   (5.3.174–9)

Instead of letting her grovel, he reaccepts her, and offers her freedom as a sign of trust that she will use it wisely: 'thou shalt please / Me best to live at thy own choice' (5.3.180–1). But Shirley leaves some doubt as to whether this is a full reconciliation, since we cannot be sure that Aretina has made a full confession. During the scene in which the Lord submits to Celestina, Aretina and Bornwell, at her request, have left the stage for the conversation from which she emerges as a penitent. When they return, nothing in his easy manner suggests that she has told him about herself and Kickshaw. For Bornwell to forgive her adultery would make him a striking, exemplary figure, of the sort Rowley and Webster dwell on in *A Cure for a Cuckold* (c.1625), where the forgiving husband Compass is paraded as a novelty. There is nothing of the sort here. From the beginning Aretina has insisted on secrecy; Kickshaw must never know her identity. In her final repentance, having dedicated her 'after life to virtue', she adds, 'pardon, heaven, / My shame yet hid from the world's eye' (5.3.193–4). It may be she is still hiding it from Bornwell.

How long she can hide is a question. Immediately after that last prayer, Decoy – who knows the truth – enters, and Aretina, in alarm, drives her from the stage: 'Not for the world be seen here: we are lost!' / I'll visit you at home', adding aside, 'But not to practise / What she expects. My counsel may recover her' (5.3.195–7). No sooner has Decoy left than Kickshaw enters, complaining that his devil has deceived him; she lectures him on sin, and brings him to repentance, still not revealing her identity. Her new role as reformer belongs to a conventional comedy of repentance and forgiveness; but the rapid, alarming entrances of Decoy and Kickshaw remind us that the full truth has not yet come out, and make us wonder if it can really be suppressed. Neither as fallen woman nor as exemplary penitent does Aretina quite fit the conventional pattern. We are catching English drama's treatment of sex at a transitional point between the idealism of the Renaissance and the realism of the Restoration, a realism in which something like the sexual pragmatism of New Comedy is restored.[10]

With his clear-eyed view of the folly of the town, his domestic authority and his name, Bornwell might seem the commanding centre of the play, taking the sort of role figures like Altofront, Prospero and Overdo aspire to. He comes close to this in the final scene, but the effect is qualified by our uncertainty as to what he knows about Aretina. Elsewhere his effectiveness is mixed. Determined to reform Aretina, he plans to 'fright her into thrift' (2.1.4) by pretending to extravagance himself, and to tame her flirtations by making her jealous of his relationship with Celestina. He is not fully in control of his design: in a brief soliloquy he confesses himself seriously attracted to Celestina, regrets his own chastity and seems, like the Lord, about to fall (4.2.216–20). Nothing comes of this; but his attempts to shock Aretina into repentance fail. She takes his flirtation as an excuse for her adultery (3.2.46–8), and when towards the end of the play he launches a competition to see which can claim the more desperate extravagance, far from being shocked into repentance she simply keeps up with him, each vying with the other in recklessness and indifference, each claiming to be unshockable. Even when he claims that the money will run out in a month, after which he will go for a soldier and she can be a whore, she merely replies, "Tis very pretty' (5.1.116).

In the end she is reformed not by his tricks but by her own shame at her encounter with Kickshaw. However, Bornwell has been a clear-eyed, witty critic of the town; his claims of extravagance may not work as he intends, but they function as satire. In the end his values prevail, and though he initially claims that they have cut off their hope of returning to the country by selling the estate (1.1.53-5) he is able to announce, 'we have wealth enough / If yet we use it nobly' (5.3.183-4). When he adds, 'I know not how my Aretina / May be disposed tomorrow for the country' (5.3.186-7), the tentative phrasing acknowledges he has left her free to make her own choices; but the direction of his thinking is clear. Her plan to reform Decoy, and her promise to find honourable court preferment for Kickshaw 'To encourage you to virtue' (5.3.206), may suggest that her own idea is to continue living in town, but to live better. Bornwell, having captured the spirit of the last scene by announcing, 'Our pleasures cool', then calls for a dance, and for more refined, Platonic pleasure to follow: 'in some new rapture to advance / Full mirth, our souls shall leap into a dance' (5.3.214-17). The play's satire on the extravagance of fashionable London is clear; so is its final drive toward repentance. It is less clear whether London is to be abandoned or reformed, whether pleasure is to be rejected or refined.

The Lady of Pleasure criticizes those who have too much. The title of *A Jovial Crew; or, The Merry Beggars* promises to romanticize those who have nothing. It takes us out into the country that we glimpse, satirized by Aretina and idealized by the Steward, beyond the borders of Shirley's London. The beggars of the title, wandering the countryside, present an alternative to living in society. Springlove, steward to the country gentleman Oldrents, feels an urge to join them every year when spring begins. When Oldrents rebukes him, 'I hop'd thou hadst abjur'd that uncouth practice,' he replies, 'you thought I had forsaken nature then' (1.1.154-5).[11] Uncouth or natural? In Brome's play, as in Shirley's, characters debate how to live; the issue in Shirley is extreme absorption into society, the issue in Brome extreme detachment from it.

One of the beggars' songs celebrates their freedom:

We have no debt or rent to pay.
No bargains or accounts to make;
Nor land or lease to let or take.

(1.1.485-7)

Oldrents, a careworn landowner, envies them: 'Our dross but weighs us down into despair, / While their sublimed spirits dance i'th' air' (2.2.189–90). The year 1641, when the play was first produced, was one of political crisis in England as Charles I confronted Parliament.[12] While Brome was no more likely than anyone else to have predicted the extraordinary events that would follow, he is clearly playing on the political anxiety of his times when Vincent, a gentleman who has joined the beggars, declares they suffer

> No fear of war, or state disturbances.
> No alteration in a commonwealth,
> Or innovation, shakes a thought of theirs.   (4.2.91–3)

At the same time, as Martin Butler has suggested, their insistence on freedom may mirror parliament's growing insistence on the liberty of the subject; if so, the beggars embody the growing spirit of independence that was beginning to disrupt the state.[13] There is something of that spirit in their insistence on doing things their way. When Oldrents thinks of throwing a lavish christening celebration for a beggar child, his servant Randall tells him not to bother: 'They'll never thank you for't. They'll not endure / A ceremony that is not their own' (2.2.147–8). The language suggests contemporary tensions over religious observance, notably the disastrous attempt by Charles and Laud to impose the Prayer Book on Scotland. There were others who would not endure a ceremony that was not their own.

However, the question of how seriously we can take the beggars is complicated by the air of fantasy that surrounds them. According to A.L. Beier, the very idea of a large wandering troop of beggars is at odds with contemporary reality; beggars may have gathered in large groups occasionally, but 'on the road they seldom travelled in groups of more than three'.[14] Within the play they are consciously theatricalized. They are first heard singing offstage, then Springlove 'opens the scene; the Beggars are discovered in their postures; then they issue forth' (1.1.362.1–2); this is followed by music and a dance. The effect is of a 'discovery' in a court masque, the lowest reaches of society presented by a device that entertained the highest. In a later scene they are similarly 'discovered at their feast. After they have scrambled awhile at their victuals, this song' (2.2.166.1–2). The Patrico, the beggar priest, introduces them as a showman would: 'See in their rags, then, dancing for your sports, / Our clapperdudgeons and their walking morts' (2.2.280–1). They seem to be not so much a troop of beggars free from society as a troop of singers and dancers who have a social (and subservient) role as entertainers.

Yet one of play's key effects is a sense of forced merriment, of pain beneath mirth.[15] Oldrents, as we shall see, participates in this; so do the beggars. At one point we hear '*A confused noise within of laughing and singing, and one crying out*' (2.2.120.1); Randall explains that the beggars are drowning out the cries of a woman in childbirth. As entertainers they have also a political edge: they mirror the estates of society. When they introduce each other, with a patterned formality that keeps up the artifice, we learn that one was a poet, one an attorney, one a soldier, one a courtier (1.1.375–427). They have no proper names, but the shadows of their professions remain, making them a representative cross-section of England.

The cringing deference they show to anyone who gives them money, in the repeated catch-phrase, 'Duly and truly pray for you', reflects the deference that runs through society at large: Oldrents's tenants 'pray for you morn and evening' (1.1.74). At the end of the play, restored to society by Oldrents, the Patrico promises to be 'your faithful beadsman, and spend my whole life in prayers for you and yours' (5.1.485–6). They are not free of society at all, but totally dependent on almsgiving and bound to pray for their benefactors. The notion that they are free from the cares of property is comically challenged when Oldrents's daughter Meriel, watching a beggar wedding, notes that even those who have nothing can still argue about it: 'How cautious the old contracted couple were for portion and jointure' (4.2.49–50). There is a sharper account of the reality of beggar life when the priest admonishes the couple 'to live together in the fear of the lash, … to escape the jaws of the justice, the clutch of the constable, the hooks of the headborough, and the biting blows of the beadle' (4.2.57–61). In a small-scale version of the breakup of the wedding masque in *The Tempest*, plans for the beggars' wedding entertainment are broken up when the constable and the watch appear, and the beggars flee.

The beggars are at once a show put on for the audience's amusement, a reflection of society and real vagrants who suffer real hardship. Oldrents's daughters Rachel and Meriel see the beggars simply as a means of escape, and persuade their lovers Vincent and Hilliard to join them in becoming beggars themselves. One thing they want to escape from is their fathers' melancholy; what they do not know until after their plans are formed is that he is brooding over a prophecy that his daughters will become beggars, a prophecy they will fulfil harmlessly. As Aretina seeks freedom in town, and chafes against her husband's authority, Meriel complains that they have liberty only 'in our father's rule and government, or by his allowance. What's that to absolute freedom, such as the very beggars have …?' (2.1.17–19). Hilliard describes the beggar life as something like Gonzalo's Golden Age commonwealth: 'they are the only people can boast the benefit of a free state, in the full enjoyment of liberty, mirth and ease, having all things in common and nothing wanting of nature's whole provision within the reach of their desires' (2.1.2–5). According to Meriel they

> observe no law,
> Obey no governor, use no religion,
> But what they draw from their own ancient custom,
> Or constitute themselves, yet are no rebels.   (2.1.173–6)

That last touch suggests that Meriel ultimately wants to play it safe; beggar freedom is politically innocent. Yet their refusal to recognize any authority makes the reservation sound illogical; in a very real sense the beggars *are* rebels, and the punishments regularly visited on their real-life counterparts reflected society's view that vagrancy was a felony and a challenge to the social order.[16] As in the paradox of Gonzalo's sovereignty over a free commonwealth, we sense the impossibility of constructing, even in imagination, a perfectly innocent society.

Attracted by the beggars' merriment, Meriel wants not just absolute freedom but perpetual mirth: 'We cannot live but by laughing, and that aloud, and nobody sad within hearing' (2.1.66–8). It sounds like a desire to live for ever in a really bad comedy. Revealingly, she will not be content with traditional communal pastimes. When Vincent asks if her desire for amusement means sports like 'Dover's Olympics or the Cotswold Games' she replies, 'No, that will be too public for our recreation. We would have it more within ourselves' (2.1.83–6). Like the beggars she will endure no ceremony that is not her own. Nor will she be content with living on the hospitality of her father's tenants (2.1.158–63); she wants pleasure that is outside the structure of authority altogether.

Of course the beggar world is no more a place of escape for the lovers than is the wood near Athens. As Springlove's decision to join the beggars is accompanied by the song of the nightingale, theirs is accompanied by the mocking call of the cuckoo (2.1.191). Their first uncomfortable night in a barn is an eye-opener, and Vincent observes, 'We look'd upon them in their jollity, and cast no further' (3.1.27). Far from being free of society they are on the bottom rung of the ladder, with all that that involves. The men learn that even if they are beaten they must cringe and fawn and not hit back. When they drive off a gentleman who had tried to rape the women, Vincent declares, 'He is prevented, and asham'd of his purpose' but Springlove retorts, 'Nor were we to take notice of his purpose more than to prevent it' (3.1.406–8). The freedom of the beggar life includes the freedom to be insulted, beaten and raped.

The gentry cannot change what they are, and as beggars they are comically out of their depth. The women retain the instinct to dress for the day; Springlove reports,

I left 'em almost ready, sitting on their pads of straw helping to dress each other's heads (the one's eye is the t'other's looking glass) with the prettiest coil they keep to fit their fancies in the most graceful way of wearing their new dressings, that you would admire.

(3.1.47–51)

Mentally, they are in Shirley's West End. The men have trouble grasping what a conventionalized activity begging is. Evoking contemporary debates on liturgy versus preaching, Hilliard insists, 'leave us to our own genius. If we must beg, let's let it go as it comes, by inspiration. I love not your set form of begging' (3.1.65–6). Unable to adjust to the scale of his new life, he asks a passing gentleman for ten or twenty pounds; Vincent, hearing the gentleman has insulted Hilliard, challenges him to a duel (3.1.207, 274–300). Springlove himself, though far more expert at leading the beggar life, is finally drawn from it by the reflection that 'this is no course for gentlemen' (4.2.262) and by his love for Amie, who has entered the beggar world during an unwise elopement and become attracted to Springlove instead. No less than the lovers, he belongs back in society.

The central figure of the society Springlove and the lovers have left is Oldrents, described in the dramatis personae list as '*an ancient esquire*' (p. 15). His name evokes the old, benevolent ways, a conservative nostalgia for a settled world. While Springlove and the lovers have an itch for freedom, Oldrents's servant Randall is uncomfortable to find himself on an estate that is not his master's: 'I was never twelve mile from thence i' my life before this journey. God send me within ken of our own kitchen smoke again' (5.1.156–8). The same homing instinct overtakes the would-be beggars by the end of the play. Oldrents himself stands for the country that Aretina's Steward evoked, a place of benevolence and hospitality. His friend Hearty, himself a decayed gentleman, praises Oldrents as an ideal landlord:

Whose rent did ever you exact? Whose have
You not remitted, when by casualties

> Of fire, of floods, of common death, or sickness,
> Poor men were brought behindhand? Nay, whose losses
> Have you not piously repair'd?   (1.1.80–4)

In return,

> Are you not the only rich man lives unenvied?
> Have you not all the praises of the rich,
> And prayers of the poor?   (1.1.67–9)

Oldrents is contrasted with Justice Clack, obsessed with his own authority, who cannot endure the sound of another person's voice, cutting off conversation with the formula, 'Nay, if we both speak together, how shall we hear one another?' (5.1.7–8); whose notion of justice is 'I would ha' found a jury should ha' found it so' (5.1.27–8); who punishes first and examines later; and whose hospitality is summed up by Oldrents and Hearty: 'To see how thin and scattering the dishes stood, as if they fear'd quarreling … And how the bottles, to 'scape breaking one another, were brought up by one at once' (5.1.270–3).

Clack is a caricature; but there is also something unreal about Oldrents. A long scene in which his servants celebrate his hospitality and kindness is made comically artificial by their recurring catch-phrase, 'he's no snail' or, as his Chaplain prefers, '*non est ille testudo*' (4.1.211). A catch is sung to celebrate the old ways: '*Old sack, and old songs, and a merry old crew, / Can charm away cares when the ground looks blue*' (4.1.226–7). The fact that '*the singers are all greybeards*' (4.1.223.1) picks up in its own way the comic stylization of 'he's no snail'. As the beggars are overtly theatricalized, Oldrents, more subtly, is made comic by association. His own merriment, like theirs, is forced. His initial mood is one of melancholy over the prophecy that his daughters will become beggars, and the play's opening line is his: 'It has indeed, friend, much afflicted me' (1.1.1). When they actually run away he tries to cover his feelings with a pretence of merry indifference which even Hearty, who has tried to cheer him up, finds upsetting: 'But this is overdone. I do not like it' (2.2.115). Moments later we hear the songs and laughter of the beggars, trying to drown out the cries of a woman in labour. Oldrents represents an ideal of social benevolence as the beggars represent an ideal of freedom: in both cases the ideal is vitiated by artifice and by a clear sense that all is not well within.

Surrounded by praise and prayers, Oldrents is in two cases touched by guilt, and in both there is a link with the beggars. At the end of the play the Patrico introduces himself to Oldrents as

> grandson to that unhappy Wrought-on,
> Whom your grandfather craftily wrought out
> Of his estate. By which, all his posterity
> Were, since, expos'd to beggary.   (5.1.411–14)

He is careful not to accuse Oldrents himself; but we have learned that the fortune which allows Oldrents to be so generous is tainted at its source. It is a bit like learning that Mr Pickwick made his money in the slave trade. We also learn that beggars do not simply exist: they are created, and the system that allows this to happen is the same system that allows the generosity of Oldrents.

Oldrents bears a more personal guilt with respect to the Patrico's sister. Though she had fallen to beggary, her gentle blood attracted love-suits and propositions, all of which she repulsed, until

> Only one gentleman
> (Whether it were by her affection, or
> His fate to send his blood a-begging with her,
> I question not) by her, in heat of youth,
> Did get a son, who now must call you father.   (5.1.425–9)

Oldrents is the father; Springlove is his son. This is the lost-child convention of New Comedy, and it carries a certain moral weight. The Patrico suggests that through this act the offence of Oldrents's grandfather is being visited on later generations, as it is in the prophecy that Rachel and Meriel will be beggars. We now know why Oldrents seemed anxious to offer a lavish celebration for the birth of a new beggar child (2.2.134–43); he was dealing with his own feelings of guilt. And we know why he was so upset when during a beggar entertainment the Patrico offered him a 'doxy, or a dell, / That never yet with man did mell' and he cried, 'Away! You would be punish'd. Oh!' (2.2.273–7).

Oldrents and the beggars seem to represent the extremes of social life, property and benevolence on the one hand, deprivation and dependence on the other. As Lear sees himself in Poor Tom, the play's final revelations collapse the distance society creates, revealing the inner links between the landlord and the beggars, and the responsiblity the former has for the latter. The revelations also come through the medium of a play-within-the play that closes the distance between artifice and reality. *Pyramus and Thisbe*, and Littlewit's version of *Hero and Leander*, are obliquely connected with the actions of the plays that surround them. Quince and company transpose the theme of thwarted love into a very different key, and much of the impact of their play depends on its stylistic differences from the rest of *A Midsummer Night's Dream*; Jonson's puppets are more integrated, reflecting in concentrated form the noise and energy of the Fair. Brome goes further: the beggar play is *A Jovial Crew* in miniature. The beggars, under arrest, are in effect acting for their freedom; Clack tells Oldrents, 'If they can present anything to please you, they may escape the law' (5.1.253–4). Oldrents, like Theseus, is offered a number of titles, which he rejects: *The Two Lost Daughters*, *The Vagrant Steward*, *The Old Squire and the Fortune-teller* and *The Beggar's Prophecy* are all too close to home; instead he picks *The Merry Beggars*, the subtitle of the main play. Every play he is offered, including the one he picks, tells his own story; there is no escape. With one exception the opening scenes of the beggar version of *A Jovial Crew* are a capsule version of the opening scenes of Brome's play. Springlove and the lovers play themselves, and the dialogue follows the original dialogue closely. It is the exception that makes all the difference. The beggar play begins with a new scene in which the Patrico, playing a fortune-teller, tells the Oldrents figure that because his grandfather drove another gentleman into beggary his own children will be beggars. The new scene disrupts the neat correspondence between inner and outer play, and in so doing reveals the truth behind the main action. When the Patrico breaks the inner play to reveal the truth directly, he is in effect continuing his role as the fortune-teller. When we saw how theatricalized they were, we began to wonder if we could take Oldrents or the beggars seriously. Brome now throws that process into reverse. The toy-theatre version of his own play is his most flagrantly artificial device; and he uses it as the medium to expose the uncomfortable reality of his characters' lives.

The beggar poet has contrived another entertainment, an allegorical show for the beggar wedding, that is never performed. As he describes it, it reflects the reality not of what has happened in the past of the play, but of what will happen in the future of England. His plan draws on the beggars' function of reflecting the estates of society:

I would have the country, the city, and the court, be at great variance for superiority. Then I would have Divinity and Law stretch their wide throats to appease and reconcile them; then would I have the soldier cudgel them all together and overtop them all.

The last character, the beggar, 'must at last overcome the soldier, and bring them all to Beggars' Hall' (4.2.207–17). If this 'apocalyptic fantasy'[17] were any closer to the truth one would suspect it of having been added when the play was first printed in 1652. Oldrents's past is guilt; England's future, if its political and social conflicts are not settled, is war and ruin.[18] The idea that the monarch is the single authority who can keep society together, embodied in the Cynthia of *Endymion* and touched on in the James of *Bartholomew Fair*'s epilogue, is no longer viable. The estates of society are in confict, the court is just one of those estates, and unless they can come together by mutual agreement England will be in trouble.

It was. The 1652 edition, three years after the execution of the King and one year after the publication of Hobbes's *Leviathan*, presents the play as a way of looking back at a lost society and a lost theatre. The playhouses had been closed in 1642, and Brome reports that *A Jovial Crew* 'had the luck to tumble last of all in the epidemical ruin of the scene' (Epistle dedicatory, 26–7). If not the last new play to appear, it may have been the last play performed. Referring to his subtitle, *The Merry Beggars*, he adds, 'since the times conspire to make us all beggars, let us make ourselves merry' (30–1). Yet as in the text itself mirth seems forced, now it seems out of place in what England has become; the Prologue, in what seems a reference to the time of printing rather than that of the first production, calls mirth 'a new / And forc'd thing in these sad and tragic days' (2–3). Brome has none of Milton's sense that England's republican experiment was an exciting glimpse of the New Jerusalem.

In both the Caroline plays we have examined, transgression has none of the exuberance it has in Jonson, liberty is revealed as a cheat, and those who sought it are only too glad to return to the settled order of society. With that order in ruins, Brome can offer his play only as a palliative to those, like himself, who feel they have been brought to Beggars' Hall. Both plays examine England, town and country, with a critical eye. Shirley takes the relatively easy route of exposing the emptiness and corruption of town pleasure; but the tentativeness of his ending suggests no very robust belief in the moral values and the social order the play tries to set against it. Having seen the worthlessness of London, the characters seem not quite certain about leaving it. Brome exposes the uncomfortable facts behind the benevolence of Oldrents and the real deprivation behind the holiday liberty of the beggars. While the gentry may rejoin the society over which Oldrents presides all they will gain will be staterooms on a sinking ship. Yet there is nowhere else for them to go. The prophecy that Oldrents's daughters will be beggars is fulfilled, but harmlessly; Brome's audience will not be let off so lightly.

Notes

1 On Caroline comedy as a reflector of social life, see C.V Wedgwood, *History and Hope*, London, 1987, pp. 172–97.

2 All references to *The Lady of Pleasure* are to the Revels edition, ed. Ronald Huebert, Manchester, 1986.

3 On the importance of the Strand as a fashionable place to lodge in the early seventeenth century, see Emrys Jones, 'The First West End Comedy', *Proceedings of the British Academy*, LXVIII, 1982, 219–22.

4 Huebert, Introduction, p. 10. Proclamations commanding the gentry to return to the country had a long history, stretching back to the reign of Elizabeth. There were seventeen of them between 1596 and 1640; their sheer number suggests their futility. See D.M. Palliser, *The Age of Elizabeth: England under the Later Tudors 1547–1603*, 2nd edn, London and New York, 1992, p. 244.

5 Martin Butler, *Theatre and Crisis 1632–1642*, Cambridge, 1984, p. 169.

6 Huebert, commentary, p. 52.

7 *Essays, Mainly Shakespearean*, Cambridge, 1994, p. 344.

8 Huebert, commentary, p. 177, reads the speech differently, assuming that the false glass is Kickshaw's description of her; but that would work against the self-disgust the rest of the speech makes clear.

9 Huebert, Introduction, pp. 12, 16.

10 In Gascoigne's *Supposes*, well within the New Comedy tradition, the heroine is regularly having sex with her lover. Shakespeare suppresses this detail when he adapts the story in the Bianca subplot of *The Taming of the Shrew*.

11 All references to *A Jovial Crew* are to the Regents Renaissance Drama edition, ed. Ann Haaker, Lincoln, 1968.

12 Derek Hirst, *Authority and Conflict: England 1603–1658*, London, 1986, pp. 196–213.

13 *Theatre*, pp. 273–4.

14 *Masterless Men: The Vagrancy Problem in England 1560–1640*, London, 1985, p. 57.

15 David Farley-Hills, *The Comic in Renaissance Comedy*, London and Basingstoke, 1981, pp. 153, 156–8.

16 Beier, *Masterless*, p. xix.

17 Ira Clark, *Professional Playwrights: Massinger, Ford, Shirley, & Brome*, Lexington, 1992, p. 160.

18 R.J. Kaufmann suggests that the final entry into Beggars' Hall could be an image of good fellowship as well as of ruin: *Richard Brome, Caroline Playwright*, New York and London, 1961, pp. 172–3. His own view of the play as the work of a disenchanted writer (pp. 169–70) implies that the emphasis should be on ruin.

10

Conclusion

THE fixed and predictable setting of Roman comedy, the space between houses that contains, and defines, a tightly plotted action on a local, domestic scale, is replaced in English Renaissance comedy by a freedom of movement characteristic of romance. This not only allows journeys in which the setting itself shifts, but entails freedom of other kinds: freedom to deal not just with family issues but with matters of state; freedom to pause and explore the implications of the desires that drive the characters, desires for love, money or power; freedom to question the workings of the society in which the action is set. The journey itself can be a reflection of the world that has been left behind. In the wood outside Athens the lovers of *A Midsummer Night's Dream* confront exaggerated images of the fears and desires they brought with them. Bartholomew Fair is not just a place of licence where the inhibitions of society are relaxed but a mirror of that society, as prostitution and the London marriage market look disconcertingly alike. The beggars of *A Jovial Crew* similarly reflect the society they appear to have escaped: all the estates of England are there, the beggars' ties with the respectable world shadow the latter with guilt, and their beggary is a prophecy of England's impending ruin.

For the Athenian lovers and for some (not all) of the visitors to Prospero's island the journey can be a maturing experience, the beginning of a new life. But those who journey to Bartholomew Fair, to the market-driven London of *Michaelmas Term* or to the fashion-driven London of *The Lady of Pleasure* can find their lives and values, even their identities, broken down. Shakespeare's characters may find themselves by losing themselves, but those of Middleton, Jonson and Shirley simply lose themselves. By the same token sexuality, fulfilling in Shakespeare, wipes out the identities of the new-made prostitutes in *Michaelmas Term* and *Bartholomew Fair*; and Aretina's encounter with Kickshaw takes place in darkness and anonymity. The general instability of identity affects not only characters who have left home territory – tempted women, and dupes like Bartholomew Cokes – but characters who try to shift identities as a means of power. The disguised hero of *The Malcontent* is an unstable mix of Malevole and Altofront and his 'real' identity seems more shadowy than his adopted one. Having gained his will through illusions, Quomodo overreaches, becomes the victim of his own deceptions, and ends by having to make a desperate attempt to prove that he exists at all.

The freedom English comedy takes to deal with matters of state is a departure from the New Comedy expectation of a small-scale action in which the stakes are low. And yet in comedy's questioning of greatness something of the New Comedy perspective may survive. Even Lyly's Cynthia is not quite immune: celebrated as a magic power to be worshipped and obeyed, she is also under scrutiny as a mortal ruler, and there are delicate hints that she might be subject to questions and misgivings. The kind of authority she represents then retreats to the margins, as the monarch becomes an offstage figure glimpsed from a distance in *Friar Bacon and Friar Bungay*, *A Midsummer Night's Dream* and *The Lady of Pleasure*; even King James as the final arbiter of *Bartholomew Fair* takes that role for one performance only. In *A Jovial Crew*, written on the brink of England's first experiment with republicanism, the court is no longer the centre of society but simply one of its estates. When the central authority figure appears in Jacobean comedy it is in the unstable, internally divided figures of Malevole–Altofront and Prospero, who still keep a kind of control but are under a scrutiny more overt than that which affects Cynthia. When Jonson's Overdo tries to play the central authority figure, the scrutiny becomes devastating, and he collapses. No one plays this role with any confidence in Caroline comedy, leaving us to suspect it has become unplayable.

In *The Tempest* the power of Prospero's magic trumps the power of the state: the well-dressed and important people we see in the opening scene are helpless and useless in the face of the storm. As their titles go for nothing at sea, on the island they cannot even use their swords. Yet Prospero surrenders his magic, as Friar Bacon has done before him. Behind the magicians' recognition that their power is greater than a man should have may be not just religious scruple but comedy's insistence on the human scale. Even Lyly's Cynthia is ignorant of her full capacity for magic and tentative about using it. The problem-solving plots of comedy (boy gets girl, lost children get parents) suggest that the business of the genre is to fulfil its characters' desires. Yet these comedies are full of images of renunciation: Endymion gives up all claim on Cynthia other than that of adoring her; Margaret, having tried to renounce the world, renounces Heaven instead; the reformed characters of *The Malcontent* long to retreat from the world; Titania surrenders the Indian boy and Caliban submits to Prospero; the authority figures of *Bartholomew Fair* – Wasp, Busy, Overdo – renounce their authority in the face of comic humiliation; Springlove gives up the beggar life and Aretina, whether or not she will give up London, is prepared to give up its pleasures. Even Helena, having regained Demetrius, renounces total possession of him: he is 'Mine own, and not mine own'. The great renunciations of Bacon and Prospero alert us to smaller renunciations that happen all the time as characters adjust to the human scale, the traditional low-life scale of comedy, in order to live in society and with each other.

These renunciations of power and desire have an urbane quality in more romantic comedies, though the urbanity is tinged with a little regret in the cases of Margaret and Titania as we sense a reduction in the characters. More satiric comedies show power and desire as themselves reductive, implying the wisdom of those who renounce them. Stephano and Trinculo reduce everything to its cash value; so do Antonio and Sebastian. In *Michaelmas Term* and *Bartholomew Fair* desire becomes consumerism as social life is reduced to a marketplace. In Jonson the goods are worthless; in Middleton the people themselves are goods, and they too are worthless. Those who try to gain an edge in such a world are finally reduced themselves. The power-plays of Antonio and Sebastian go nowhere, and the rebellion of Caliban and his cohorts lands them in the horse-pond. Quomodo, having operated a brilliantly successful cheat, makes a desperate attempt to secure his winnings and loses everything. The prize in *The Malcontent* is a dukedom that seems unstable and illusory, just one more role to play. Even the desire for freedom can end in the discovery that freedom is an illusion, as it does for Caliban, for Aretina and for the wandering gentry of *A Jovial Crew*.

These plays, like the Tudor interlude, have something to say. But they do not say it through the pat debates of the interlude, in which each character represents one position and argues it explicitly until a final judgement is given; that tradition, though present, is absorbed almost to the point of invisibility. Instead, Renaissance English comedy develops its eclectic idiom through comic actions that draw initially on New Comedy and romance, and eventually on earlier English comedies as a tradition builds and plays start to feed on their immediate predecessors – *Bartholomew Fair* parodying the romantic journey-and-rival-wooers motifs of *A Midsummer Night's Dream*, Shirley offering a gentrified version of Middleton's mercantile London. Recurring features, like family resemblances, change through the generations. In the onstage devils of *Friar Bacon* magic is acted out in front of us, at once demonic and carnivalesque. The demonic is reduced to a disturbing hint in *The Tempest*, where devils are replaced by enigmantic, shape-shifting spirits; it is absorbed into metaphor in *Michaelmas Term*, where Hell becomes a city much like London, and in *Bartholomew Fair*, where the hell-mouth becomes Ursula's pig-tent.

Strongly centred plays like *The Malcontent* provide concentrated images of society; plays with more dispersed attention, like *Friar Bacon* and *A Jovial Crew*, give a cross-section. Concentration and variety fuse in *The Tempest* and *Bartholomew Fair*, where a wide range of characters are brought together in a tightly defined location. We can see, just faintly, the outline of a Tudor interlude like Heywood's *Play of Love*, where type-characters representing different positions debate on a bare stage. *The Tempest* is set on a remote island, *Bartholomew Fair* an easy walk from the playhouse; yet each location has another, literal identity: the stage itself. Whether a fit-up stage at court, the permanent stage of the Globe or Blackfriars or the removable stage of the Hope – *Bartholomew Fair* today, bear-baiting tomorrow – the stage is a place of experiment, and comedy at this time is an experimental form, re-examining its own procedures and trying different ways of seeing the world. Brome's beggar-actors are in a way a paradigm for the whole theatrical enterprise: on the margins of society, constantly on the move, finally under threat of closure, they offer their spectators a reassuring fantasy tale of loss and reunion and a disconcerting reflection of their own lives.

Barton, Anne, *Ben Jonson, Dramatist*, Cambridge, 1984.

Bradbrook, M.C., *The Growth and Structure of Elizabethan Comedy*, new edn, London, 1973.

Braunmuller, A.R. and Michael Hattaway, eds, *The Cambridge Companion to English Renaissance Drama*, Cambridge, 1990.

Butler, Martin, *Theatre and Crisis 1632–1642*, Cambridge, 1984.

Caputi, Anthony, *John Marston, Satirist*, Ithaca, N.Y., 1961.

Carroll, William C., *The Metamorphoses of Shakespearean Comedy*, Princeton, 1985.

Clark, Ira, *Professional Playwrights: Massinger, Ford, Shirley, & Brome*, Lexington, 1992.

Donaldson, Ian, *The World Upside-down: Comedy from Jonson to Fielding*, Oxford, 1970.

Farley-Hills, David, *The Comic in Renaissance Comedy*, London and Basingstoke, 1981.

Finkelpearl, Philip J., *John Marston of the Middle Temple*, Cambridge, Mass., 1969.

Gibbons, Brian, *Jacobean City Comedy*, 2nd edn, London and New York, 1980.

Haynes, Jonathan, *The Social Relations of Jonson's Theater*, Cambridge, 1992.

Hunter, G.K., *John Lyly: The Humanist as Courtier*, London, 1962.

Leggatt, Alexander, *Shakespeare's Comedy of Love*, London, 1974.

Leinwand, Theodore B., *The City Staged: Jacobean Comedy, 1603–1613*, Madison, Wis., 1986.

Pincombe, Michael, *The Plays of John Lyly: Eros and Eliza*, Manchester and New York, 1996.

Rowe, George E., Jr, *Thomas Middleton and the New Comedy Tradition*, Lincoln and London, 1979.

Saccio, Peter, *The Court Comedies of John Lyly*, Princeton, 1969.

Salingar, Leo, *Shakespeare and the Traditions of Comedy*, Cambridge, 1974.

Scott, Michael, *John Marston's Plays: Theme, Structure and Performance*, London and Basingstoke, 1978.

Shapiro, Michael, *Children of the Revels*, New York, 1977.

Slights, Camille Wells, *Shakespeare's Comic Commonwealths*, Toronto, Buffalo and London, 1993.

Weld, John, *Meaning in Comedy: Studies in Elizabethan Romantic Comedy*, Albany, 1975.

INDEX

Anne of Denmark (Queen) 113
Aretino, Pietro 164
Ariosto, Ludovico
   I Suppositi 4
Aristophanes 3
Assarsson-Rizzi, Kerstin 36
Austen, Jane 2
   Emma 10
   Pride and Prejudice 10
Ayckbourn, Alan 2

Barnes, Peter 139
Barton, Anne 151, 165
Beaumarchais 2, 6
Beaumont, Francis
   The Knight of the Burning Pestle 3, 5,
     60
Beaumont and Fletcher 7, 135
Beckett, Samuel 13–14, 23
Beier, A.L. 170
Berry, Philippa 17
Blackfriars playhouse 8, 70–1, 89, 109, 136,
   182
boy actors 6, 8, 14, 28, 64, 71, 73, 84, 96
   see also Blackfriars; Children of Paul's;
     Children of the Revels
Brome, Richard 136, 156
   A Jovial Crew 9, 156–7, 169–77, 179, 180,
     181, 182
Brook, Peter 109
Buckingham, George Villiers, Duke of
   The Rehearsal 60
Butler, Martin 170

Caroline comedy 7, 156, 180
censorship 69, 70–1, 73
Césare, Aimé
   Une Tempête 124
Chamberlain's–King's company 46, 63, 70–1,
   84, 109, 136, 156
Chapman, George 6–7
   Bussy d'Ambois 89
Chapman, George, Ben Jonson and John
   Marston
   Eastward Ho 94
Charles I 159, 163, 170, 177, 180
Chaucer, Geoffrey
   The Canterbury Tales 63, 165
Children of Paul's 12, 70, 89, 107
Children of the Revels 136
Christian Terence 4
class 32–3, 39, 63–4, 91, 94–5, 104, 105, 106,
   110, 161–2

clothing 10, 90, 94–6, 106, 114, 117, 119, 141,
   144–5, 147, 160–1, 163, 166
clowns 4–5, 27, 32–3
Clyomon and Clamydes 5
Cockpit (playhouse) 156
Colley, John Scott 84–5
Commedia dell'arte 3, 4
Commedia erudita 4
Congreve, William
   Love for Love 10
   The Way of the World 10
court performances 8, 12, 30, 63–4, 152–3
   see also masques
Crupi, Charles W. 41

Dee, John 44
Dekker, Thomas and John Webster
   Northward Ho 89
   Westward Ho 89
disguise 9, 32–3, 76–8, 87, 97–100, 104, 105,
   106, 148–50, 165–6, 180
Donaldson, Ian 137
dream 9–10, 22, 56, 65, 85–6, 125
Dryden, John
   Sir Martin Mar-all 11

Elizabeth I 7, 12–23, 28, 29, 42–3, 53–4, 72,
   83, 113, 153, 180
Empson, William 36
Etherege, Sir George
   The Man of Mode 10
Ettin, Andrew V. 34

Famous Victories of Henry the Fifth, The 32–3
Farquhar, George
   The Beaux' Stratagem 3
fashion *see* clothing
Finkelpearl, Philip J. 70, 77
Foakes, R.A. 85
fools *see* clowns
Forster, E.M.
   A Passage to India 118
friendship 24, 33, 52, 56–7, 146

Gascoigne, George
   Supposes 4, 178
Gilbert and Sullivan 3
Gill, Roma 100–1
Globe playhouse 8, 109, 110, 182
   see also Chamberlain's–King's company
Golding, William
   Lord of the Flies 110
Goldoni, Carlo 6

Goldsmith, Oliver
  She Stoops to Conquer 10
Greene, Robert 6, 147
  Friar Bacon and Friar Bungay 5, 7–8,
    30–45, 46, 47, 48, 49, 51, 52, 53, 57–8,
    60, 62, 67, 72, 73, 79, 90, 93, 99, 100,
    109–10, 120, 130, 142, 157, 166, 180–1,
    182

Hands, Terry 138
Haughton, William
  Englishmen for my Money 7
Haynes, Jonathan 151
Helgerson, Richard 7–8
Henrietta Maria (Queen) 162, 263
Heywood, John 6
  A Play of Love 5, 13, 182
  The Play of the Weather 5
Hieatt, Charles W. 41
Hirst, David 139
Hobbes, Thomas
  Leviathan 177
Holland, Peter 63
Hope playhouse 8, 136, 137, 151, 182
Hunter, G.K. 12, 20

Inns of Court 70
interludes 4–5, 7, 9, 43, 181–2
Ionesco, Eugene 140

James I 8, 72, 73, 94, 113–14, 131, 152–3, 177,
    180
Jones, Inigo 113–14
Jonson, Ben 6–7, 135, 143, 153, 156
  The Alchemist 135
  Bartholomew Fair 8, 9, 135–55, 156, 157,
    163, 164, 165, 166, 168, 175–6, 177,
    179, 180, 181, 182
  The Case is Altered 135
  The Devil is an Ass 107
  Epicoene 3
  Every Man in his Humour 11, 135
  Every Man out of his Humour 135
  The Masque of Blackness 133
  The Masque of Queens 113
  Oberon 114
  Sejanus 135, 151
  The Staple of News 3
  Volpone 3, 135
Joyce, James
  Finnegans Wake 152

Kafka, Franz 150
Kind Hearts and Coronets 11
King's Men *see* Chamberlain's-King's
  company

Kyd, Thomas
  The Spanish Tragedy 71

Lady Elizabeth's Men 136
Ladykillers, The 11
Lamming, George
  Water with Berries 129
Laud, William 170
Levenson, Jill 26
Lyly, John 6, 12–13, 89, 147
  Endymion 7, 8, 9, 10, 12–29, 30, 31, 32,
    33, 34, 42, 43, 46, 47, 48, 52, 53, 54,
    56–7, 61, 67, 70, 72, 73, 75, 90, 109–
    10, 113, 137, 146, 165, 177, 180, 181
  Euphues 12

Marcus, Leah S. 137
Marlowe, Christopher
  Doctor Faustus 37, 38, 64, 120
  Tamburlaine the Great 31
Marston, John 70, 80
  The Malcontent 8, 9–10, 70–88, 89, 90,
    91, 92, 93, 106, 110, 115, 118, 119, 121,
    124, 147, 148, 149, 156, 162, 164, 167,
    168, 180, 181, 182
masques 82–3, 113–15, 118, 128–9, 131–2
Massinger, Philip 156
Medwall, Henry
  Fulgens and Lucrece 4–5
Mencken, H.L. 147
Merry Devil of Edmonton, The 7
Middleton, Thomas 30, 89, 100
  A Mad World, my Masters 89
  Michaelmas Term 8, 9, 10, 86, 89–108,
    110, 112, 114, 119, 129, 141, 143, 144,
    156, 157, 158, 161, 163, 164, 167, 179,
    180, 181, 182
  The Phoenix 72, 148, 149
  A Trick to Catch the Old One 89
  Women Beware Women 129
Middleton, Thomas and Thomas Dekker
  The Roaring Girl 10
Middleton, Thomas and William Rowley
  The Changeling 166
Milton, John 177
  Paradise Lost 98
misogyny 25, 26, 75, 76, 165–6
Molière 6
Montrose, Louis Adrian 49
morality plays 63–4
More, Sir Thomas
  Utopia 110
Mozart, W.A.
  The Magic Flute 136
Mucedorus 5
music 55, 71, 77, 113, 114, 118, 125

New Comedy 2, 3, 4, 5, 8, 9, 34, 168, 175,
        180, 182

Orton, Joe
        What the Butler Saw 2
Ovid
        Metamorphoses 120

Patterson, Annabel 67
Peele, George 6
        The Arraignment of Paris 14–15, 43
        The Old Wives' Tale 5, 35
Pincombe, Michael 25
Plautus
        Menaechmi 6
        see also Roman comedy
play within the play 37, 60–4, 143, 152, 175–6,
        182
Pope, Alexander
        The Rape of the Lock 160–1
Porter, Henry
        The Two Angry Women of Abingdon 7
private playhouses 7
        see also Blackfriars; Children of Paul's;
        Cockpit
prostitution 90, 91–2, 95–7, 140, 141, 144–5,
        146–7, 152, 159, 164–6, 179, 180
public playhouses 7
        see also Globe; Hope; Rose; Theatre

Rabelais, François 150
Raleigh, Sir Walter 120
Restoration comedy 7, 168
romance 5–6, 7, 8, 179, 182
Roman comedy 2, 3–4, 7, 13, 67, 179
Rose playhouse 30
Rowley, William and John Webster
        A Cure for a Cuckold 167–8

Saccio, Peter 13, 25
Salingar, Leo 151
satire 3, 7, 70–1, 72, 79, 80, 106, 169
Shakespeare, William 5, 6, 10, 135, 147
        All's Well that Ends Well 163
        As You Like It 10, 31, 128, 144
        The Comedy of Errors 6
        Cymbeline 109
        Hamlet 75, 113
        Henry IV Parts One and Two 12, 32, 33
        Henry VIII 109
        King Lear 22, 141, 153
        Love's Labour's Lost 60
        Measure for Measure 3, 72, 95, 148
        The Merchant of Venice 10, 31, 52

        A Midsummer Night's Dream 6, 8, 9–10,
        14, 46–69, 72, 79, 83, 86, 90, 91, 93,
        99, 100, 109–10, 111, 116, 119, 127, 129,
        137, 144, 163, 175–6, 179, 180, 181, 182
        Much Ado about Nothing 10
        Pericles 109
        The Taming of the Shrew 4, 178
        The Tempest 8, 10, 47, 99, 104, 109–34,
        135, 136, 137, 138, 142, 144, 147, 148,
        149, 150, 152, 154, 168, 171, 172, 179,
        180–1, 182
        Twelfth Night 3
        The Winter's Tale 109
Shakespeare, William and John Fletcher
        Cardenio 109
        The Two Noble Kinsmen 109, 146
Shapiro, Michael 144
Shaw, Bernard 4
Sheridan, R.B.
        The Critic 3
Shirley, James 156
        The Lady of Pleasure 9, 10, 156–69, 173,
        177, 179, 180, 181, 182
Sidney, Sir Philip
        Apologie for Poetrie 4, 5–6, 7
        Arcadia 146
        The Lady of May 14–15, 153
South Park 11
Spenser, Edmund
        The Faerie Queene 16, 20, 48, 54
Stansbury, Joan 53
Stoppard, Tom
        Jumpers 3
        The Real Inspector Hound 60
Strindberg, August
        Miss Julie 117

Tarlton, Richard 116
Terence *see* Roman comedy
Theatre (playhouse) 46

Voltaire 113
von Rosader, Kurt Tetzeli 36

Waith, Eugene M. 138
Webster, John
        Induction to *The Malcontent* 70–1, 84
Weld, John 41
Wharton, T.F. 74
Wilde, Oscar
        The Importance of Being Earnest 2
Wycherley, William
        The Country Wife 165